FATAL FASCINATION

FATAL
FASCINATION

Where Fact Meets Fiction in Police Work

Phil and Karen McArdle

Houghton Mifflin Company

Boston   1988

For Sean McArdle

For information about permission to
reproduce selections from this book,
write to Permissions, Houghton Mifflin
Company, 2 Park Street, Boston, Mas-
sachusetts 02108.

*Library of Congress
Cataloging-in-Publication Data*
McArdle, Phil.
Fatal fascination: where fact meets
fiction in police work/Phil and Karen
McArdle.
    p. cm.
Bibliography: p.
Includes index.
ISBN 0-395-46789-6
1. Police — United States.
2. Criminal investigation — United
States. I. McArdle, Karen.
II. Title.
HV8141.M296 1988   87-30757
363.2′0973 — dc19   CIP

Printed in the United States of America

V 10 9 8 7 6 5 4 3 2 1

Designed by Jennie Bush, Designworks,
Inc.

The authors are grateful for permission
to quote from the following sources: *The
Never-Ending Wrong* by Katherine Anne
Porter. Copyright © 1977 by Katherine
Anne Porter. By permission of Little,
Brown and Company in association with
the Atlantic Monthly Press. "Walter
Gordon's Beat Survey," reprinted by
permission of the Berkeley Historical So-
ciety. "Six Gold Stars: On the Beat with
Dexter H. Mast, OPD." Copyright ©
1980, Express Publishing Co. *Night
Cover* by Michael Z. Lewin. Reprinted
by permission of Wallace and Sheil
Agency, Inc. Copyright © 1976 by
Michael Z. Lewin.

ACKNOWLEDGMENTS

Special thanks to Richard Curtis and Ruth Hapgood for their confidence in this project. Thanks also to the staff members of the San Francisco, Berkeley, and Oakland public libraries; the Tulare County Free Library (Visalia); the Bancroft Library, University of California; and the California State Library at Sacramento. We are especially in debt to Bill Sturm, of the Oakland Public Library's Oakland History Room, for sharing his knowledge of Oakland; to Vivian Hurley of the Tulare County Free Library; and to the friendly voices at the Berkeley and Albany libraries' "Night Line" services. We are also grateful to the Mystery Writers of America, Northern California Chapter; the British Consulate, San Francisco; Ken Pettitt and Bob Yamada of the Berkeley Historical Society; Melody Ermachild; Sergeants Brad Kearns, Ron Zein, and Frank Lowe; Lieutenant John Sterling (retired) and the Street Narcotic Enforcement Unit, which was created to deal with violence related to the narcotics problem; Chief Virgil Epperson, Seaside Police Department; and Florence Jury. We are indebted to many more people than we have named here — especially the police officers who have shared their knowledge with us.

In some instances, names have been changed at the request of participants in the events described herein.

Many of the stories in this book take place in Oakland and Alameda County. This is due to our experience as residents of the East Bay and to our long association with the Oakland Police Department. Our explanations of police procedures are, however, based on standard police work, except where specifically indicated. This book is not an Oakland Police Department publication. Any errors it contains are our responsibility.

CONTENTS

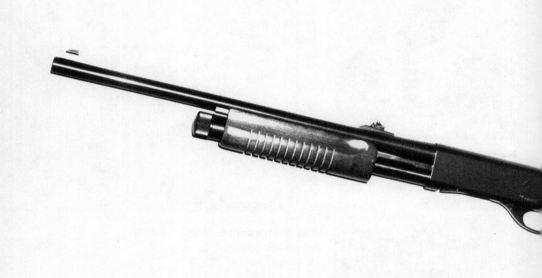

On your morning walk along the seashore you find a body in a clump of tall grass at the top of a sand dune. You go to a pay phone and call the police. A few agonizing minutes later the black and whites roar up, lights ablaze and sirens blasting. Then the officers get out of their cars and appear to mill around aimlessly while their car radios splutter and cackle.

What is going on?

At ten o'clock on a cold, rainy winter night, you are standing at the corner of Fifth and Main. The light changes and you look to your left just before stepping off the curb. You freeze. Speeding toward the crosswalk you almost entered is a police car with its Christmas tree all lit up. Not a sound comes from its siren. You can hear its wheels hiss on the wet pave-

ment. It slows down a little in deference to the stoplight, but it begins to accelerate even before it has passed through the intersection.

What is going on?

You are strolling down Main Street on your way to work at seven o'clock in the morning when a police car pulls up to the curb behind you. The officer quickly exits the vehicle and starts walking toward you. You recognize him and prepare to say good morning when you see that he is not looking at you. He has a fixed, intent expression on his face and a slight pallor. His eyes are cold, and you realize that he is looking straight through you. He strides on by and disappears from view into the alley between two buildings.

What is going on?

If you had wandered into televisionland you would probably know. The cop is Kojak, Starski, Lacey, or T. J. Hooker. The plot is familiar: an old friend from the past is really the villain; the hero's new love will be a murder victim in the penultimate scene; our hero races across the city to warn the guest star not to drive his car and gets there just in time to see it explode; there is a car chase, and a shoot-out on an industrial superstructure, with the bad guy falling three stories to his death.

But these television incidents are fantasy. What is going on here is reality, the greatest mystery of all — real police going about their business, especially the dangerous side of it. They don't have time to stop and talk to you. If you move closer and hang around to watch, they tell you to move along. Keep-

ing your distance, you are frustrated by seeing too little.

This book will give you a closer look. It is about practical police procedures and the way of life of police officers, today and yesterday. It is based on what we have learned on the job and off during our association with East Bay police departments over the past twelve years, and on our historical studies of law enforcement. Oakland and the East Bay are our main points of reference, of course, but we have made a special effort to see that what we say applies to police work in general.

The book is about how the police handle real cases, both the ones they handle well and the ones they mess up. It is also about the criminals, the courts, the lawyers, the crime reporters, and the other characters who make up the police officer's world. Then, for good measure, it's about fictional cops too, and how they measure up against the real thing; about popular fallacies; and about the sometimes clever, sometimes grotesque mirror that movies, television, and the printed page hold up to reality.

Excuse me, sir — ma'am. You saw what happened a few pages back? Stick around. I'd like to talk to you, please.

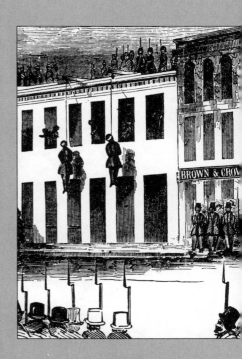

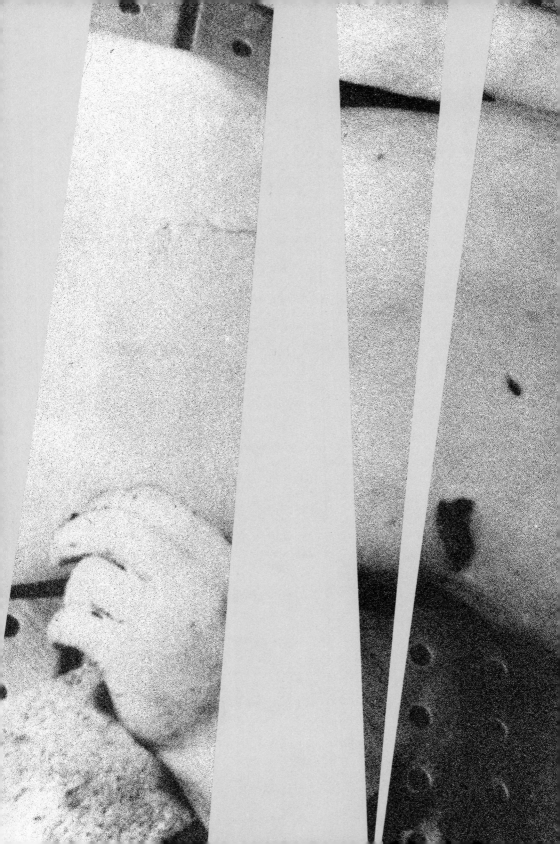

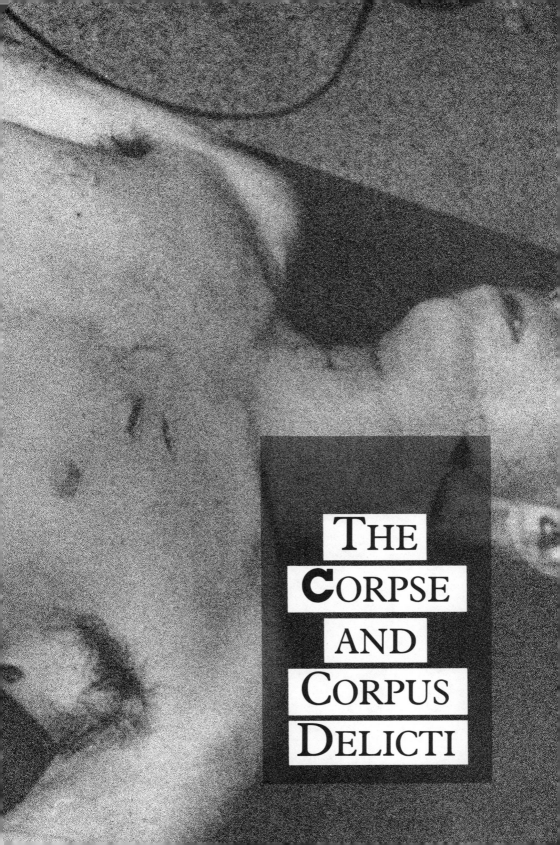

THE CORPSE AND CORPUS DELICTI

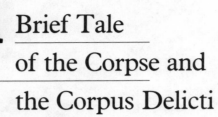

A Brief Tale of the Corpse and the Corpus Delicti

You are walking along and trip over Bill, stone cold, jaw slack, and eyes staring unwinkingly up at the sky. You have found a human body, a corpse.

Has a crime been committed? you wonder.

Turning Bill over, you find a knife plunged to the hilt in his back — a fact or circumstance that makes it evident that a crime has been committed. You have now found the body of the crime, the corpus delicti.

"Help! Murder!" you cry.

(turn to page 4)

IN THE DEAD OF NIGHT

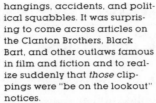

Police work deals with people's hopes, fears, and weaknesses; this gives it a deep consistency from one generation to another. At this primary level, technological changes seem superficial.

Our appreciation of this was renewed by materials we found in quiet corners of Bay Area libraries and by the old inspectors' scrapbooks we found moldering away in the back room of an Oakland Police Department training facility in the hills above that city. Later we found more scrapbooks in the Oakland History Room of the Oakland Public Library.

The scrapbooks were a working file of newspaper clippings pasted in day by day, year after year — a record of long-forgotten robberies, murders, confidence games, trials, hangings, accidents, and political squabbles. It was surprising to come across articles on the Clanton Brothers, Black Bart, and other outlaws famous in film and fiction and to realize suddenly that *those* clippings were "be on the lookout" notices.

Mixed in with the seemingly endless collection of disasters and misfortunes were anecdotes that brilliantly illuminated the permanent qualities of police work. To share these with you, we will dip into the old inspectors' scrapbooks from time to time.

One way in which real police work has always differed from fiction is that assignments frequently end in anticlimax. Part of the difficulty of the job is that if an officer lets uneventful calls make him careless, he may lose his life.

It was a cold, bleak afternoon [said Oakland Officer Tom Downey], the last day of December 1881. The sun had been trying to shine all day, but it had failed ignominiously. There had been a drizzle all day, and everything was wet. Toward night a heavy fog blew up from the bay, and the wind whistled around the old hall in a very depressing manner. We had a roaring fire in the stove, and were waiting for something to turn up. Nothing had come in all day, and the force hadn't earned its salt.

Toward 8 o'clock the foreman of Seymour & Sabin's Threshing Machine Works on First street came in to tell Captain Pumyea a story that pointed very strongly to a possible child murder. There lived in the neighborhood a family with one child. The woman was the child's stepmother, and it was well known that she used to ill treat the poor little thing. For two days nothing had been seen of the child, and the Seymour & Sabin's foreman said that under one of the sheds in an out of the way and unusual corner of the place he had discovered some fresh earth turned up. He had driven a stake at the place, and in several places it had encountered something hard, very much like a coffin.

Captain Pumyea detailed Officer Hewitt and myself to investigate the supposed infanticide. It was a nasty piece of work, and it was pretty near midnight before we got down there with lanterns and shovels. We were all muffled up in great coats, with our stars buried out of sight beneath many mufflers, and to shade our faces we wore slouch hats. We looked very much like brigands, and I'll tell you what, it was very creepy digging for dead babies at midnight on the last day of the year. The lanterns gave out very uncertain light, and the gusts of wind and fog nearly extinguished them several times.

I can't say I'd enjoy digging for dead babies in the daytime, much less at midnight.

We had just thrown a few shovels full of earth off, when Hewitt's shovel struck something hard and metallic with a dull, ringing sound, such as I fancied a full metallic casket would give, when a head appeared over the fence along side of us, and the appearance startled me so I nearly fell over the lantern.

"What are you doing there?" demanded the man, for it was evidently a real flesh and blood man.

"Fixing a water pipe," replied Hewitt, in spite of the fact that people don't usually choose 12 o'clock on a wet, windy night to fix water pipes.

"Well, you needn't bother about fixing that pipe," replied the man, "for I fixed it myself yesterday."

I don't believe that man ever knew we were a couple of officers digging for a murdered baby, because we didn't exactly feel like telling him.

The Brief Tale Continues

Now, suppose *you* are the police officer sent to the scene. There is Bill, stone cold, jaw slack, and eyes staring unwinkingly up at the sky. Clearly, a corpse. Or is he?

Not breathing? Check.
Heart not beating? Check.
Eyes dilated? Check.
Fouled himself as anal and bladder sphincters relaxed? Check.

So Bill is dead. Do you preserve the scene and have the district sergeant call for the standby homicide team and the coroner, as is the rule with any unattended death?

Not yet. So far you have determined that Bill is clinically dead. Very likely he is going to stay that way, but some who are clinically dead can be resuscitated. And as long as there is that chance for Bill, he's going to get it. You are going to have to call for an ambulance — even if it means the paramedics trample a perfectly fine crime scene — unless you can determine that Bill is biologically dead.

Biologically dead? That means Bill's brain has totally and irreversibly stopped functioning. But how are you going to find that out? You can't pull out a handy pocket micro-electroencephalograph.

You have to use your common sense. You decide he is biologi-cally dead if he can't be alive. For instance, if his head is not attached to his neck; if rigor mortis has set in; if his brain, heart, or liver is lying on the ground; if postmortem lividity has developed; if he spent last week at the bottom of the swamp; if he has been incinerated; if ants or other insects or animals have begun to feed or nest on him; if putrefaction has set in — then Bill is biologically dead.

You push up on the jaw and find it is not really slack but rigidly open. Bill's whole head moves. Rigor is setting in. Bill is biologically dead. You call for the homicide detail and the coroner. While waiting for the specialists, you try to estimate when Bill bought it. What do you look for?

As a breeze comes up, the day is cooling off, and so is Bill. That's something to notice. All his life, in warm or cold weather, fur-clad or jay-naked, Bill stayed approximately 98 degrees Fahrenheit. Now he is becoming or has become the temperature of the ground, the stones, the trees, and the air.

His size, fat deposits, clothing, and the heat and humidity of the environment all affect how quickly his internal temperature will change, but that stuff is for the specialists. You simply slide your hand under his jacket between his arm and chest. The slight warmth tells you he was still alive not too long ago. If he had felt cold and clammy in this warm weather, you would have concluded that he had been dead at least eighteen to twenty-four hours.

Now you look at Bill's coloration and where the colors are. You're checking his postmortem lividity.

When Bill was alive, the contractions of his heart pushed the blood through his body. When his heart stopped, the pressure stopped. Gravity took over, pulling the blood downward into the parts of his body nearest the ground. Those parts have turned a purple bruise color. That is lividity. It would have happened no matter what position his body was in. If Bill had died upright, the lividity would be in his legs and, to a lesser extent, in his arms and hands. If he had died standing on his head — well, you get the point. Lividity begins to show an hour or two after death. After that, because the blood coagulates, turning Bill's body won't change the pattern of discoloration.

You note the waxy yellow of Bill's bloodless face and the purple of the visible parts of him nearest the ground. So Bill died at least an hour ago as he is now, on his back. Only the purple on the upper surface of his right arm — seemingly flung over his head — shows it to have been moved an hour or more after death.

Next, how stiff is Bill? You check the progress of rigor mortis. You already know his face and jaw are affected. That is where the stiffening of muscles starts, beginning eight to twelve hours after death. So you can make a working assumption that Bill has been dead at least that long. The rigor will then slowly extend downward, reaching Bill's feet about eighteen hours later. At that point his whole body will be rigid and, if turned, will move all of a piece, like a board or a statue. That stage usually lasts twelve to twenty-four hours. Then rigor will leave his body in the order it arrived — face and jaw first, feet last — taking another eight or ten hours to pass off. Sometimes it can take a good deal longer, up to three or four days. But Bill's neck is just beginning to stiffen; his shoulders and arms (as well as the rest of his body) are limp.

There are a lot of things that can affect when rigor mortis begins and ends. If Bill had some strong emotion (like fear of death) or strenuous exercise (like running from his murderer) just before he died, he would stiffen up more quickly. If he was very athletic, the process would slow down. Put him on ice, and it would slow down some more. Warm him up . . . and who knows? The experts argue about the whole business anyway.

Rope off the area (if you can find a rope), and press a couple of reliable-looking civilians into service to keep the gathering crowd back. Pull out your notebook and ballpoint.

What to write? For your own information, record your estimate that it would take Bill at least eight hours to stiffen as he has. Body temperature and extent of the rigor mortis imply that Bill was alive at least sixteen hours ago. Finding out when and how Bill's arm was moved may narrow that down a little.

In a few minutes the specialists will be here with the cameras, calipers, and plastic bags, variously measuring and recording everything in sight. So what else goes into your patrolman's notebook?

The rule is: note all your actions and everything you have observed up to this point. And never touch, move, or alter anything in any way until it has been identified, recorded, measured, and photographed.

Write down first the things you might easily forget or become confused about. What was it that the two men on the edge of the crowd had said that seemed so peculiar? Something about the third time being the charm with Bill . . . better make a note of it. Then

write down things that have changed already or that will be different by the time the specialists arrive.

Better get the names and addresses of people who might be connected with the incident. Once they disappear, they may be gone forever. Look! That woman who said she might have seen something — that one there, holding the crying baby — she's sidling away. And the dusty footprints of the gigantic hound that are blowing away in the wind! Don't let anyone near them. Measure and sketch them. They may be an important clue. That wad of gum over there, looking freshly spat out on the ground — and so easily trod into it.

It looks as if Bill will wait. But actually his condition is changing rapidly. His staring eyes have already lost their luster through evaporation.

It is important to know when Bill expired, both in discovering his murderer and in making a case against him or her. Also, insurance on his life or who inherits his estate may revolve around the time of his death. The sooner after death Bill is examined, the more definitely the time of death can be fixed. The medical examiners should be here in anywhere from three minutes to half an hour, but they may be longer. So hold on tightly to your ballpoint, your notebook, and your breakfast and take a good look.

Tell those people to stand back, please. Stand back.

Oh my God, there's the Channel 5 mobile news unit.

What's keeping those slugs from homicide?

A HANDY GUIDE TO WHO DONE IT IN MYSTERY FICTION

WHO DID IT FOR SURE?

In romance mysteries:

The one left over after all the right couples pair off.

The man who is handsome and charming, but whose eyes are a little too close together.

In TV series:

The detective's old friend, newly back in town and asking his help. Listed in the credits as "guest star."

The detective's old flame, newly back in town and asking his help. Listed in the credits as "guest star."

The detective's new flame.

The detective's valet's old flame.

The detective's valet's new flame.

The detective's maid's ex-husband.

Always:

The suspect with a cast-iron alibi.

WHO ELSE IS INVOLVED IN THE CRIME?

The good old boy.

Either the richest man, the sheriff/police chief, or both in any small, rural, or Southern town.

If the good guy is from the big city, the whole town is hiding a guilty secret.

Any gorgeous, sexy woman who comes on strong to the hero — unless he is amazed, gratified, suspicious, self-deprecating, and not in a series, in which case it may be love.

The heroine's husband, who swept her off her feet in a whirl-wind romance and about whom she knows nothing, except that he is rich and power-ful or rich and mysterious. He often simplifies matters by being killed in the first chapter or while the titles roll.

WHO DIDN'T DO IT?

The butler.

The only black.

The detective if she is a woman.

Any woman who has a young child dependent on her.

The police sergeant's wife and mother of his children.

The young man whom the heroine meets by chance at the beginning of the story, instantly dislikes, and is remarkably rude to.

Della Street.

A WORD OF CAUTION

The slender man in the dark three-piece suit is a hit man.

THE
POLICE

C.O.P.s

They were standing on the steps.
. . . The sun was dying in a blaze
of red and gold. "You think of
everything," said Vicky. "You
ought to be a detective. I mean,"
she added hurriedly, "a policeman."

"Perhaps I shall be," Bland
said, "one day."
— Detective-Inspector-to-be Bland, in
Bland Beginning by Julian Symons

In some criminal justice courses it
is said that the word "cop" had its
origin in an abbreviation used by
the English police on reports in
the nineteenth century: "C.O.P.,"
standing for "constable on patrol." Others say the word came
from the slang for one who "cops"
or captures. It is not hard to see
that there might be some connection between these two definitions.
The slang origin has also been
traced to the old French "*caper*,"
to capture or seize.

The word "police," as a desig-
nation for public safety officers,
became current in 1829 when Sir
Robert Peel used it in the legisla-
tion that created the London municipal police. "Police," in this
usage, is fittingly traced to the
Greek word for city, "*polis*." Most
modern police officers are urban
men and women.

In 1879, when Oakland Mayor
Washburne Andrus reported to
the city council on the condition of
the police department, he made
some astute remarks about its role
in the life of the city and about
the ideal character of the police
officer:

The reputation of a Police Department has a great effect upon
the order and quietness of any city.
It is cheaper and easier to prevent
crime than to detect it. The knowledge that policemen are vigilant
and intelligent, and are present in
the places where required, exerts a
powerful influence in preventing
the commission of crime.

Temperate habits, cool and deliberate judgment, tact and shrewd-
ness, combined with firmness and
decision of character, are among
the requirements of a police officer.
Gentlemanly deportment, coupled
with the ability to cope with unruly
characters, are required. The number of arrests is not a test of efficiency, for that must, to a great
extent, depend upon the respect-
ability of the neighborhood in
which an officer is stationed for
duty.

Not everyone sees the police
this way. In *Cross-Examination*,
which appeared in the late 1920s,
A. L. Cornelius gave the following
description of police officers:

Policemen as a class are usually
not well educated, skilled mechani-
cally, or industrially. They are men
above average in physical strength
and appearance who have lacked
sufficient persistence to acquire an
education or learn a trade. Their
contacts with the criminal element
tend to make them suspicious of
human nature. They are daily engaged in the prosecution of others
and, of course, in defending their
own acts. Their entire attention is
focused upon the derelictions of
mankind. Therefore, it naturally
follows that when a person is
charged with a crime, the officer is

Oakland Police Dept.

naturally predisposed toward belief in his guilt. . . . A policeman's duty also tends to make him officious, dictatorial, and arbitrary toward individuals. Policemen as a class are inclined to be vain and somewhat egotistical. They do not, however, lack courage as their numerous encounters with the criminal element bear abundant witness.

This view probably has comforted many a defense attorney.

Nowadays, the average police officer is usually better educated than the person he arrests and often as well educated as the defense lawyer. Many officers have passed bar exams. This change in the attributes of American police officers is due to the professionalization of police work pioneered by two California police chiefs, August Vollmer of Berkeley and William Parker of Los Angeles.

Chief Parker was responsible for the crisp style of policing

shown in Jack Webb's *Dragnet* series. Gene Roddenberry, the creator of *Star Trek*, worked for Parker at one time, and based the hyperlogical character of Mr. Spock on him. When you stop and think about it, Joe Friday and Mr. Spock would have understood each other.

Egon Bittner, a distinguished student of police work, has suggested that what is unique about the police is that they are the only civil officers of government authorized to use force to resolve conflicts between citizens. How they use this power is a constant issue in our society, one that is defined by the legislatures and the courts and redefined again and again. One reason for this is that out there on the streets, where they are all by themselves, where judges and senators are rarely seen, police officers must employ "discretion" in doing their job — that is, they must decide whether to act and

Rookie pig. Officers held a contest to caption this photograph. The winning entry read, "Gee, Sarge, do you mean I passed probation?"

how to act. Then, if they write a traffic ticket or shoot it out with a murderer, they quote the law as the authority for their decision. The trouble is, any officer who abuses his power also cites the law as justification.

As it is with the use of force, so it is with many other aspects of police work. Beyond a certain point, very little can be done by the courts or by police management to limit the discretionary power of the officers. There are times when the officer must decide what to do and how to do it, whether to invoke the law or to use force. No matter how many orders the chief issues or how dense the case law on a subject becomes, external authorities cannot control those moments.

We all know that there are many times when officers decide not to issue traffic tickets. There are also incidents, dreadfully serious and much less widely known, when officers choose not to confront murderers. Whether the decision is tactically justified or due to a momentary loss of nerve, these are the moments when, concerned as we are about limiting the use of force, we have to face the fact again that there are times when force must still be used. These considerations underline the necessity of choosing decent people to be police officers.

In a subtle and really remarkable essay, "The Development of Policemen," William K. Muir juxtaposed the well-known aphorism, "Power tends to corrupt and absolute power corrupts absolutely," against the observation that "if power corrupts, it also sometimes ennobles." He considers that four possible responses are open to a person who steadily exercises power over others — responses he names corruption, reciprocity, avoidance, and ennoblement. He describes corruption as the subjective and irresponsible use of power; reciprocity as the transformation of power relationships into "exchange relationships" (power brokering, influence peddling); avoidance as a refusal to exercise power (under-enforcing or not enforcing the law); and ennoblement as what happens when "the office makes the man."

Muir shares the opinion of other students of the police that "avoidance of power" is the most common failing among law enforcement personnel. He notes that "if we have been successful in our efforts to civilize some of the barbarian out of man, then the avoidance of power ought to be a desirable response, for under civilized conditions the hurting of another is the doing of a distasteful thing."

Granted the benefits of avoidance, then, what does it cost? Muir answers: "When the opportunity to exercise power is spurned, the chance 'to make the lives of other men better' is missed. The policeman who ignores a call to assist in calming a marital dispute, the President who fails to invoke the power of the Justice Department to stem inflation, . . . the general who will not shape up his army, . . . these are individuals with lost opportunities, missed because they fear the . . . responsibility of bearing the consequences of their power. [They waste] their potential for equalizing one man's condition relative to that of others, of evening up the opportunities of wife relative to husband, of old relative to young, of the insecure relative to the secure, of the civilized relative to the uncivilized."

When Joseph Wambaugh's *The New Centurions* appeared, police officers suddenly found themselves being represented in fiction by a gifted and morally alert writer who knew their work from the inside as no previous novelist had. Wambaugh's novels are one of the most surprising results of the professionalization of American police work. Education makes people articulate, and the cops will be able to speak and write for themselves pretty well from now on.

This does not mean that there will be no more unflattering pictures of the police. The authority they wield will always be looked at ambivalently. In *Murder in the Fifth Position* by Edgar Box (a pseudonym of Gore Vidal), the novel's hero, an amateur investigator, says, "I have a dislike of policemen which must be the real thing since I'd never had anything to do with them . . . outside of the traffic courts. There is something about the state putting the power to bully into the hands of a group of subnormal, sadistic apes that makes my blood boil. Of course, the good citizens would say that it takes an ape to keep the other apes in line but then again it is piteous indeed to listen to the yowls of those same good citizens when they come afoul of the law and are beaten up in prisons and generally manhandled for suspected or for real crimes; at such moments they probably wish they had done something about the guardians of law and order when they were free . . ." Cops would be surprised if this attitude disappeared.

In the sixties, when "pig" succeeded "cossack" and " bull" as a term of abuse, a small cottage industry grew up selling souvenirs with pig designs to the police: coffee cups, pencil holders, stuffed animal mascots. Even today, the Oakland Police Department's football team calls itself the Thunderhogs. In spite of their critics, the police persist in thinking well of themselves. A veteran sergeant we know considers police officers, as a group, the people in our society best able to deal with emergencies.

After you have known a number of police officers over a period of time, you begin to realize that the thing they all have in common — no matter what their size, shape, sex, race, religion, or lack of religion — is that somewhere along the line, each of them made a decision to be one of the good guys.

Robert Stinnett

*P*olice Ranks

Speaking in the broadest terms, there are two types of employees in a police department — those who are officers and those who aren't. Police officers formally take an oath to become members of the department. They have the generally recognized powers of law enforcement officers and are referred to as sworn personnel. The non-sworn employees are just that — not sworn in or trained as peace officers. They are called civilians.

In Oakland the chain of command for sworn personnel is as follows: chief, deputy chief, captain, lieutenant, sergeant, police officer. This hierarchy changes from time to time, and in the past has included inspectors, detectives, and corporals. Ranks that are inactive are kept on the books, reserved for possible future use. It does not seem likely that any of them will be reinstated, but government agencies rarely abolish classifications. They like to save these things for rainy days.

Two parallel ranks do seem to be gone forever, patrolman and police woman, now succeeded by the sexually nonspecific rank of police officer.

The names of the ranks reveal the military model for police organizations. Historically, when the first modern police departments were formed in England, the best organizational model available was the British army, and so its structure was followed. But even though many police officers are veterans of military service, a police department is not an army, and police officers are not soldiers. The sworn personnel are really civilians too.

A list of ranks is only one way of describing the distribution of authority in a police agency. Another is through its actual operations. The operating (or functional) chain of command proceeds through unit heads: from the chief down to the bureau chief, to the watch commander, to the sergeant at the head of a squad or to the officers supervising independent units.

"Civilianization" of jobs not directly involved in the use of force or in making arrests has long been heralded as a new direction in police administration. It costs a lot less. It also frees trained officers for street duty. Non-sworn personnel doing jobs formerly filled only by police officers include criminalists, dispatchers, animal control officers, technical writers, computer programmers, clerks, and typists. This trend reached a new level in Oakland when a civilian was assigned as head of the Planning Section.

However, each time a police function is "civilianized," there is one less spot available for a police officer off the street. Officers need to come indoors from time to time for relief from the stress of the job and, sometimes, while they recover from injuries. Even when they don't need to come in, many want to. The inside jobs are often the key to advancement and can be desirable political plums. It was a sad day for some officer back in the 1920s when the chief first hired a civilian typist.

Oakland Police Dept.

Night scene: On the dogwatch.

Not Meant to Be a Cop

In Oakland, as elsewhere, not enough qualified people walk into city hall and fill out application forms to meet the city's need for new officers, so the police department sends recruiters around to places where more potential new members may be found — colleges, job fairs, and so forth. Once a large enough number of applications have come in, a regular series of tests is set up. Each applicant must pass a written examination, a physical agility test, a psychological examination, an oral interview, and a background investigation (credit, neighbors, criminal record, etc.) before being accepted for the police academy. An important aspect of the recruit selection process is recognizing and eliminating people who have personality disorders, who are wanted felons, or who simply are not the right type for the job.

It is surprising how many wanted men apply for work as police officers. When one is identified during the background investigation, he is invited to the office on the pretext of discussing his credit history or some other aspect of his background.

People come in who have warrants on them all the time, a veteran background investigator told us. "Mostly for minor things like parking. Nowadays, a lot of agencies are not issuing warrants for misdemeanor parking tickets and instead are putting holds on the vehicle registrations. So in addition to checking the computer systems for warrants, we also check with DMV for holds.

"Felony warrants turn up too," the investigator said, "though I haven't had any for a while. In one case, a year or so ago, I had an applicant with two kidnap and two robbery warrants from Monterey. When I found the warrants, I invited the applicant to come in for a discrepancy interview and invited two investigators from Monterey County to come up for the session. They popped him right in the office.

"Mental problems? I had an applicant who had two warrants for child molesting. When we got to talking about it, he said that it was because of mental stress he had suffered after losing his job. But it turned out that he lost his job as a supermarket checker because he kept making passes at little girls who came into the store."

This is the cover of a recruitment folder from the days when we had policemen and policewomen instead of police officers.

" The professional police officer ... with dedication and integrity he serves that men may know justice, equality and freedom under the law."

are you man enough?

Oakland Police Dept.

Training

Recruit training takes place in the academy and in the probationary field training program. After the officer has completed them both and has been on the street for a year, he or she then begins taking the refresher courses known collectively as in-service training.

In the academy the new recruits learn the things necessary to the job — self-defense tactics, shooting pistols and shotguns, police driving techniques, first aid, the penal code, the local ordinances, report writing, types of crimes and how to recognize them, the socioeconomic and racial makeup of the city, and much, much more. It is a very demanding program. The training is given in classroom lectures, at the firing range, in the gymnasium, and in role-playing exercises held outside the classroom.

When the recruits graduate from the academy, they enter the field training program. Each new trainee is paired with an experienced officer, known as the field training officer or FTO. The FTO supervises the trainee's work, helps in the development of skills not fully mastered in the academy, and teaches lessons about patrol work based on his or her own experience.

Police officers often have an ambivalent attitude toward training. Joseph Wambaugh, who was himself an instructor in the Los Angeles Police Academy, has shown this in his novels. He is formidably knowledgeable about all aspects of police work. He knows *all* the ivory tower stuff. At the same time, he has a wholehearted appreciation of the anti-intellectual skepticism of many street cops — the gut feeling that nobody knows as much about the job as they do. ("Where do they think I came from?" a frustrated captain in the training division once said to us. "Do they think I was hatched behind this desk?")

There are instructors who use their classes as an opportunity to tell war stories. We have heard some chatter about how to get around the regulations and even hints about how to break the law with impunity. We have also sat in on classes that were brilliantly taught—on high-risk felony car stops, symptoms of drug abuse, and crowd control.

Cynical field training officers sometimes set out to undermine what is taught in the academy on the theory that "now we will show you what it's *really* like." But what is taught in the academy is usually more up to date and technically correct than the practices followed by street vets of this type. They are usually intellectually lazy and do not keep up with changes in the profession. Too many FTOs from this bunch and the chief's policies will not be followed — especially those addressing new social issues.

The administrative remedy in Oakland is to make FTO spots voluntary. Burned-out veterans don't volunteer; ambitious officers do. Being an FTO helps in the race for promotion to sergeant. At a certain point, the ambitious street officer has got to cross a conceptual line and begin to think like a manager: he must identify with the chief's agenda and begin to feel that it is right to support it when training recruits.

Uniforms

In the early days of American police work, many departments adopted policies requiring all officers to work in plain clothes. They reasoned that uniforms would make officers too visible to the criminal element. It is true the plainclothes officer could often approach a crime in progress more easily than a uniformed officer, but this advantage had certain limitations. Sometimes people couldn't distinguish the officer from the felon. For this and other reasons, it gradually became clear that uniforms were desirable. The most important advantage of high visibility was that it reassured law-abiding people that an area was safe and warned possible law-breakers to behave. The uniformed officer's presence deterred a large number of small crimes. In a situation where a serious felony was going down, uniforms prevented confusion as to who was who.

There were advantages and disadvantages on each side of the question. So, instead of picking one or the other, the police departments collectively decided to use both and to exploit the particular advantages of each.

There is ancient lore associated with uniforms. The badge is universally worn on the left side, supposedly following the practice of ancient soldiers, who carried shields on their left arm, keeping their right hand free to carry weapons. The service stripes worn on uniform sleeves go back to the Roman custom of awarding soldiers copper bands worn around the wrist as a sign of loyal service during a campaign.

Over the years a pattern has developed in the wearing of uniforms. Patrol officers almost always work in them. Detectives and administrators generally work in plain clothes. They reserve their uniforms for formal or ceremonial occasions.

There are still odd little situations revolving around whether to wear a uniform or not. Some, but not all, officers are reluctant to wear their uniforms when coming to work on public transit. They do not want to be recognized or called on for assistance before their shift starts. On the other hand, officers working in plain clothes at headquarters will make a pinch when they are out on the street running an errand — and come back to the building extremely pleased with themselves.

Uniforms definitely set a person off from the general public. Until you get used to it, you feel incredibly conspicuous wearing one. The same is true of driving a marked car.

> "*The Case of the Missing Can Opener* by John James Mack had three errors of procedure in the first two pages, and had at least provided Grant with a pleasant five minutes while he composed an imaginary letter by its author."   Josephine Tey, in *Daughter of Time*

Sectors, Districts, and Beats

Since the birth of modern police work in England, the basic aim of police departments has been to control crime and other dangers to public safety within their jurisdictions. To do this, a territorial strategy based on patrol has been universally adopted. From time to time someone tries to think up an alternative, but thus far no one has found anything equally effective.

The territorial strategy determines the shape of police departments everywhere and gives them a hierarchical structure. The beats are at the bottom of the hierarchy, and the office of the chief is at the top. The purpose of the various intermediate levels of command is, as directed by the chief, to assist officers on their beats. On the whole, that is what they do, even though the beat officers sometimes feel neglected.

Over the years the Oakland Police Department has been organized in a number of different ways, some more effective than others. Currently, it has three major bureaus: Field Operations, Investigations, and Services. The backbone of the Bureau of Field Operations is the Patrol Division, which is deployed as follows:

The city's eight square miles are divided into two geographical sectors, each commanded by a lieutenant. The sectors are divided into five districts — three in one sector, two in the other — usually supervised by sergeants. The districts are divided into beats, and each beat is usually staffed by one patrol officer. In all, there are thirty-five beats. Within the area to which he or she is assigned, the patrol officer is responsible for public safety. To patrol the city twenty-four hours a day, 365 days a year, the Patrol Division operates three watches: the dogwatch, the day watch, and the swing shift. Each watch is supervised by a captain known, naturally, as the watch commander.

Within this general structure there is room for many variations. If, for example, an unusual number of burglaries are being reported from one area of the city, special units can be sent there to reinforce the regular patrol operation. Similar reinforcements can also be used to saturate areas suffering from outbreaks of street-walking and dope dealing. So, what is it like down in the trenches, on the beat where one officer is responsible for the safety of hundreds of people? In *Policing a City's Central District*, Albert Reiss analyzed one of the walking beats in downtown Oakland. He found that during a three-week period the beat officer was dispatched sixteen times as the primary officer to handle a call for assistance, and that he was dispatched as a cover or backup officer three times. The beat officer "covered in" on his own initiative twenty-seven times. He made three felony arrests, thirty-one misdemeanor arrests, issued sixty-three traffic citations, and handled one traffic collision — all during this period. He also prepared twenty reports and spent fifty-two hours on preventive patrol.

Batons

Uniformed police officers carry batons. Though sometimes called a stick, a baton is never called a billy club or nightstick. In the hands of someone who knows how to use it, the baton is a fearsome thing.

Department-issued batons come in two sizes, short and long. The short baton is a foot long, the long baton about two feet. They are made of hardwoods — ironwood, hickory, or oak. Officers have the option of buying their own, but privately owned batons must meet departmental specifications.

The baton is used when nonlethal force is required in self-defense or when needed to take a person into custody. Misuse of the baton is a serious matter; it is a criminal assault to strike a prisoner with a baton to punish him for having resisted arrest. As one command officer told us, "Anyone who misuses a baton should be promptly attended to and discharged or severely disciplined."

For the officer, striking with a baton is preferable to punching with a fist because there is less chance of injury; you can hurt yourself hitting someone. The human hand, bare and unprotected, is a fragile instrument. But the fistfight is so ingrained in American lore that the impulse to punch somebody can be hard to

resist. Consequently, it is not unusual to see young officers walking around with hand injuries. But they learn. You hardly ever see a veteran officer with such an injury.

The baton is also superior to the fist because is it more certain to finish the encounter quickly. Punches can be inefficient, since their strength and impact vary so much. Some people can take a really good punch almost without noticing it. But a properly placed blow from a baton is usually enough to stop an arrestee's resistance. It will "get his mind right," as the officers say.

The proper technique in using a baton is to step back from the opponent, not to close in on him. This minimizes the opponent's opportunity to seize the officer's pistol — the most crucial safety issue for the officer — and provides the officer with a better chance to control the encounter. And when the suspect sees the baton drawn, it gives him one last chance to give up.

The officer must be certain his opponent does not have a knife or some other deadly weapon. The officer also needs to be able to choose the area he will strike. The allowable spots are the shoulder blade, the solar plexus, the ribs, the outer bicep and inner elbow, the hand, the thigh, knee cap, calf, shin, and ankle. Forbidden targets for the baton are the head, the side of the neck, the throat, the armpit, or the kidney. Blows to any of these areas can cause a serious — even fatal — injury.

Controlling a fight and ending it quickly are ideals, but circumstances don't always cooperate. In mixing it up with an opponent who has the initiative, proper fighting is not always the best policy. An officer who loses a fight

may also lose his life.

Most officers would rather use the baton than Chemical Mace because the baton is easier to control. If the wind is wrong or the space

WALTER GORDON'S BEAT SURVEY

Most departments conduct beat surveys from time to time. They require the officers to write up their beats, so that when changes in personnel occur, at least some of the information acquired by the officer who has been patrolling the beat can be passed on to his successor.

One of the notable members of the Berkeley Police Department in the 1920s was Walter Gordon, the first black on the force. He earned a degree in law while working as a police officer and became a successful attorney. Gordon was appointed to high offices in California by Governor Earl Warren, and President Eisenhower appointed him governor of the Virgin Islands in 1955.

But in the 1920s he was a patrolman, doing the chores that generations of police officers have done as they work to keep a clean beat. For a view of what life was like on the street in those days, here are some extracts from Walter Gordon's survey of Berkeley's beat 20 in 1929.

Upon going on duty at midnight, one should cover the entire district, hurriedly but carefully with particular attention to the dark streets which are without houses. The streets around San Pablo Park and the ends of the streets west of San Pablo Avenue have afforded good places for thieves to drop and strip cars. If these localities are covered it is quite easy to ascertain the approximate time when cars are dropped. If they are left in large numbers, a special detail would have an easy job catching the culprits. . . .

A large number of spooners will be found parking in these same areas, whose credentials, with reference to operators licenses and registration certificates, should be scrutinized very carefully. If there is no question as to the ownership of the car . . . [and] the occupants . . . are of age, it is not out of place to allow them to remain. Couples will be found who are not as discrete as they should be. . . . If they are of age, it has been a policy to reprimand them and order them to move on. Sometimes this procedure is advisable when they are under age, because one might do a girl more harm than good by taking her to the police station, and subjecting her to the humiliation of many knowing her predicament. . . .

Having covered these outlying districts the officer should begin trying the front and rear doors of the district. He should not begin trying them at the same time every night. . . .

The West Berkeley beat is over two miles long and one mile wide. . . . The officer will have to keep moving during the course of his tour of duty in order to cover this district effectively. He will travel 50 to 60 miles per night. . . .

. . . He must be ever alert to detect fires. His duty is to protect property against fires as well as thieves. . . .

The Standard Oil and Pullman Shops in Richmond cause a large stream of traffic along San Pablo

Avenue between 6 and 8 A.M. There is traffic congestion at San Pablo and University which is augmented by the fact that it is a street car transfer point. Likewise the Golden Gate Ferry has caused an increase in traffic. A traffic signal has been installed at the intersection, which has aided wonderfully in the solution of the congested condition. . . .

The officer will find it advisable at least once a week to stand on the corner (of San Pablo and University avenues) and watch traffic. Let the motorist see you and he will hesitate to violate the law. It is advisable to vary the days that you stand there so they will never know when you are likely to whistle them down. An arrest is not always necessary. . . .

Many motorists run out of gas on San Pablo Avenue in the early morning. The gas stations are closed, with the result that the cars are left, which is a violation of the parking ordinance. It does not seem quite fair to tag a car when it is out of gas or out of commission, because the owner was not careless or malicious in his violation. A careful examination of the car will reveal the reason for it being left. Always check up on stolen cars. The officer is not wrong in the judgment of the writer when he fails to tag such cars. . . .

. . . Many foreigners reside in the district and often times their homes are quarantined because of contagious diseases, but they do not realize the significance of quarantine. They will allow their children to leave their homes and play in the streets. The officer must note this during the daylight and take whatever action is necessary.

Reprinted by permission of the Berkeley Historical Society

too confined, Mace can blow back and disable the officer as well as the suspect. Furthermore, any use of Mace gets it on the officer's clothing. Driving around in a patrol car while reeking of Mace is really impossible.

Certain people with severe mental disorders, as well as people under the influence of PCP, are not bothered by Mace. The baton is effective against these people, but much more force is required than in ordinary situations.

*H*andcuffs

Handcuffs are a temporary restraining device, nothing more. Used correctly, they help protect the officer from the prisoner and help prevent the prisoner from escaping. They *assist* in achieving these two purposes; they don't do them by themselves. A police officer can get in trouble quickly if he thinks that, having handcuffed a prisoner, he has subdued him.

Recently an officer of the Immigration and Naturalization Service picked up two men in Oakland who were suspected of being illegal aliens. Neither resisted arrest, and the officer took them into custody in a casual low-key style. He handcuffed one man's right hand to the other's left hand, in order to secure them without inconveniencing them too much. Then he popped them into the back seat of his car, a plain, unmarked vehicle. He confiscated a backpack belonging to one of the men and stowed it on the front seat without bothering to search it. Everything in order, he started to

drive to the INS office in San Francisco.

Then the arrest went bad. When he stopped at a red light, one of the prisoners reached with his free hand into the backpack on the front seat and pulled out a pistol. He pointed it at the officer and demanded his gun. The officer leaped out of the car. The prisoner jumped into the driver's seat and stepped on the gas. The officer drew his gun and got off one shot as his car roared away.

Later the car was found near the waterfront. The prisoners (presumably still handcuffed to each other), the backpack, and the pistol were all missing. The car was undamaged except for the back window, which the officer's shot had frosted.

The prisoners are still missing. The officer is lucky to be alive.

The key to this incident appears to have been the officer's overconfidence. He had probably made the same type of arrest many times, but this time he misread the arrestees. He should have searched the backpack or put it in the trunk or, at least, on the floor of the front seat. If he had searched the backpack and found the pistol, his approach to the arrest would have been less casual. He should have remembered that his car did not have a cage (a wire mesh separating the front and

(text continues on page 28)

UNION MACHINE WORKS

PUTTING THE BRACELETS ON

FBI Agent Ben Tisa developed an excellent handcuffing technique and instructed Oakland officers in how to apply it. The following pictures, in which Officer Dan Endaya puts the bracelets on Officer Jimmy Martines, are from a detailed sequence of photographs we took to illustrate Tisa's method.

"Put 'em up! Higher!"

"Spread those feet."

Get the cuffs ready,

and move in carefully.

Brace him while you seize his left hand.

Apply the first handcuff.

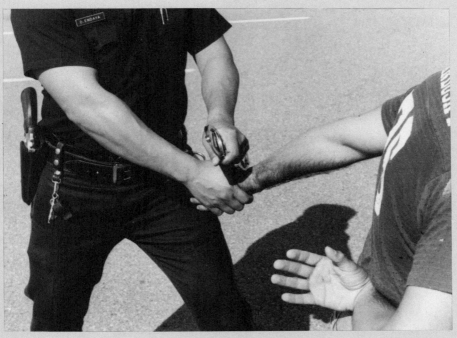

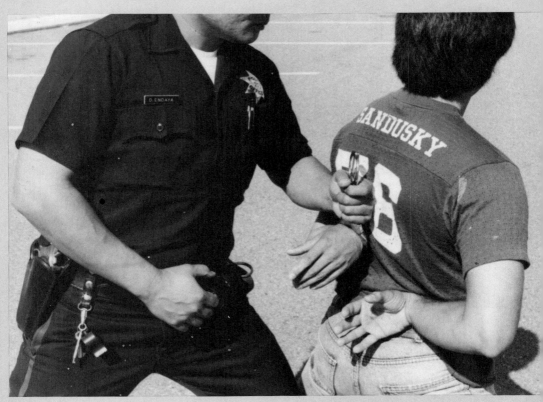

Keep control of him.

Apply the second
handcuff.

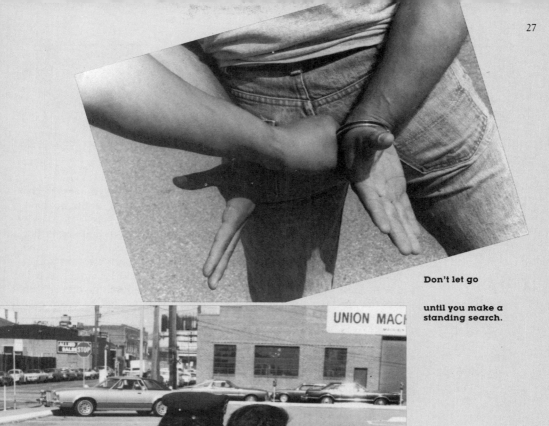

Don't let go

until you make a standing search.

back seats). If he had only one pair of handcuffs, he should have handcuffed the prisoners right hand to right hand, to limit their freedom of movement. He also had the option of calling for assistance from the municipal police. Any of these measures might have kept the prisoners from getting out of control.

An Oakland officer once told us about an arrest it gave him the shivers to remember. He had received a report that a woman on his beat had shot and killed her husband and then walked away from her house. He went looking for her. When he found her walking along the sidewalk, he pulled up beside her and said, without looking at her, "O.K., lady, get in the back. They want to talk to you downtown." She did, and he delivered her to the jail, unsearched and unhandcuffed.

When the jailers searched the woman, they found that she had the murder weapon, a .45 automatic, in the pocket of her apron. "The only thing that saved me," the officer said, "was that once she had shot her old man, she had done all the shooting she wanted to. I think she hardly even noticed me."

It does not seem worthwhile to list the technical errors in this arrest. Some successful arrests seem to be based on instinctive perceptions that override the ordinary rules of technique. In this instance, for example, the officer read the psychology of the situation perfectly just from seeing how the woman walked along the street. He probably could not have said just what it was he saw, but he acted on it. Not looking at her seems to have been precisely the right move. This was not something that could be taught, and it was not something the officer who made the pinch felt he could ever do again.

The usefulness of technique is that it can be repeated and can prevent the hideous situations that develop when instinct is wrong. Proper handcuffing procedure is based on the recognition that they are only a temporary restraint. Too much must not be expected of them.

It is an elementary safety precaution to pin the prisoner's hands behind him or her. Even then, a prisoner is not necessarily harmless: he may be able to slip his arms under his feet and bring his hands up in front of him. Most prisoners do not try this, but it requires only a certain amount of agility. A prisoner who does it and gets away with it is quite dangerous. With his hands in front of him, he may be able to remove a hidden handcuff key from his clothing or use one built into the tongue of his belt buckle. Or he may be able to choke the officer from behind, disarm him, and escape.

These things have all happened, and consideration of them defines the limitations of handcuffs but does not undermine their value. Handcuffs will do what they are supposed to when they are used correctly.

BROKEN HANDCUFFS

While preparing some material on the officer-safety aspects of dealing with PCP abusers, we found a photograph of handcuffs broken by a suspect who was in the custody of the Pasadena police. When Oakland officers saw this, some were shocked and some laughed nervously. Some thought it was a mistake, that it had to be impossible for anyone to break handcuffs that way.

The photograph and its explanation seemed correct to us, but, considering how myths and legends begin and then pick up momentum, we decided to find out whether anyone in Oakland had had a similar experience. Our search led us to Officer Tim Sanchez. He came up to the office with a broken pair of handcuffs, and this is the story he told:

"The suspect was a white working man, five feet nine, one hundred and sixty pounds. His mother put in a call saying he was acting strangely. We found him in the back yard of her house, screaming, glassy-eyed, and with no shirt on.

"I managed to talk him into coming out front," Sanchez said. "We handcuffed him and put him in the back of the car. He began to kick out the windows, so we pulled him out and put him face down over the trunk of the car. While I tried to tie his feet together with a piece of rope, one officer held each of his arms. He spread his legs apart and broke the rope, and then he spread his arms apart and broke the handcuffs. So they handcuffed him again, and I green-sheeted him."

"Green-sheeted" means that, instead of arresting the man for a criminal violation, Sanchez decided to send him to the county's emergency psychiatric ward. The term comes from the color of the form used to commit people for observation who are "a danger to themselves or others."

Sanchez met the man on the street several weeks later. "He was as nice a person as you could want to meet anywhere," Sanchez said. "He told me, 'I'm not going to take any of that PCP stuff anymore. It's too strong.' I asked him about his wrists, and he said, 'Oh, they were sore for a couple of days.' "

Tim Sanchez

Firearms

The basic firearms used by police officers are pistols and shotguns. In recent years the .357 Magnum has increasingly become the sidearm of choice among patrol officers all across the country. The .357 fires a round that is larger, travels faster, and hits harder than the .38 caliber service revolvers that were the unchallenged standard for many years. However, plainclothes detectives and command officers not wearing uniforms still favor small, lightweight .38 revolvers. The shotgun is the preferred firearm for most high-risk situations. At the distance shown below, which is correct for a felony car stop, it is much more effective than a pistol. The sound of a shotgun being cocked is unmistakable and menacing.

A .357 Magnum being drawn from a clamshell holster.

Top right: This .38 has attended many luncheons and civic affairs.

Bottom right: Officer Fred Peoples gets the drop on "Captain Bob" Middleton, a notorious oyster pirate.

Oakland Police Dept.

Oakland Police Dept.

Oakland Police Dept.

*P*olice Jargon

As a group, police officers are exceptionally skilled when it comes to adjusting their diction to the audience they are addressing. They consciously enjoy this, and many are virtuosos at improvising alternate versions of the same dialogue directed to different people, giving the first rendition in perfect official English, followed by others that are bawdy, profane, or surrealistically farcical.

Most police officers speak standard English in ordinary conversation — if calling crazy people "5150s" and criminals "perpetrators" can be called standard. But they learn to speak several other languages during their careers: psychology, business, public administration, law, and street talk, in addition to the jargon of their trade.

At the turn of the century, when newspapers spoke of strong-arm robbers as "footpads," house burglars were called "porch climbers" in Oakland, and burglars who specialized in stealing from hotel rooms were called "hotel thieves" (there were enough of them to make this a regular category). When an officer used the call box to report his whereabouts to the station, he called in for a "mark." To make a raid on a gambling den was "to pull a joint." An advertising hand-bill or political leaflet was a "dodger"; this word does not seem to have a modern equivalent.

Today, "they walked him" means a jury found a guilty defendant innocent. To "pop" someone means to make an arrest or issue a citation. "The joint" means state prison, but "the bucket" means city jail. A "maggot" is a contemptible petty criminal, and a "slug" is a person who is physically or socially undesirable. ("Once you've said 'slug,' you've said it all.") A "wobbler" is an offense that may be charged by the district attorney as either a felony or a misdemeanor. A "rap sheet" is an arrest record.

Sometimes phrases are varied for the sake of novelty. An officer assigned to a desk at headquarters ("downtown") is a "building rat," but might also be called a "house mouse." A rookie will be described as a "new kid"; a veteran, an "old-timer," a "dinosaur," or a "fossil."

When it is time to go to work, it is time to "hit the bricks." This is a current phrase, but because most officers today patrol in cars, it must be a holdover from the days of foot patrol, when bricks were actually used to pave the streets.

A "swoop" occurs when officers converge on a location simultaneously and unexpectedly to make arrests (for example, to clear an intersection of dope dealers). "Trolling" means sending plainclothes officers into an area frequented by prostitutes and their customers; an arrest is made when a male officer is solicited by a hooker, or a female by a john. A body that's been lying there for a while may be de-

WORDS TO LIVE BY

"When I first got my gun, I could not wait to take it out of the holster and spin it, like a cowboy. My feeling was one of playfulness. But after the training course this quickly changed to a deep, powerful respect. I learned that holding a gun is like holding a bomb in your hand. When a gun fires, it has no friends. A shot is never reversible. Once you make the decision to pull that trigger, and it doesn't take much pressure to pull it, there's no way of stopping the bullet that has been set in motion. You cannot take a gun for granted no matter how long you've had it."

From *Psychologist with a Gun* by Harvey Schlossberg and Lucy Freeman.

scribed as a "stinker" or a "bloater." If it has been in the bay, it's a "floater."

In official reports and when talking among themselves, officers use the numbers in the penal code or the municipal code to indicate a person's status or identify an offense. These numbers vary from state to state; the examples here are from California. A "5150" is a person who is "a danger to himself or others," and a "647b" (sometimes it's shortened to "b") is a prostitute. A "314" is indecent exposure, and a "314x" means indecent exposure, female. ("A 314x will draw cars from all over the city," an old-timer said. "I rolled on one once at a supermarket, and by the time I got there the parking lot looked like a dealership for used police cars.") A "10851" is a stolen car, a "415" is "disturbing the peace," and a "187" is a murder. (These are pronounced ten-eight-fifty-one, four-fifteen, and one-eighty-seven.)

The radio revolutionized patrol procedures and led to the development of a whole new type of jargon — the numbers and letters of the police radio code. The code reduces the amount of time required to transmit and receive messages, and it covers things not enumerated in the penal code. Every department has its own radio code. In Oakland, to be "out of service" for a meal is to be "908-A" (nine-oh-eight-A), and to go off duty is to go "908-D." "924" means "go to your station — that is, meet someone (usually a supervisor) at a predesignated location. A "code 3" is a hot call, an emergency assignment the officer must go to with "all practical haste" (red lights and siren optional)." The call nobody wants to hear is "940-B," which means, "officer needs immediate help." It used to mean an officer had been shot. It still can, but now it usually means, "Send cover. I've got a situation that's getting out of hand."

"I suppose there is not a man in the world who, when he becomes a knave for the sake of a thousand dollars, would not rather have remained an honest man for half the money."

Georg C. Lichtenberg

*D*aily

Bulletins

One of the principal devices police departments use to inform patrol officers about wanted criminals (known or suspected) is the old-fashioned daily bulletin. Every day a list of wanted people is compiled by the watch commander from chits sent to him by detectives. The detective writes a brief paragraph with the following information: the crime, by penal code section number; where it occurred; the name of the suspect, if known; the description given by the victim; whether the detective wants the patrol officers to arrest or merely locate ("field contact") the suspect; and any other pertinent information. This is printed in the daily bulletin for three, five, or seven days, depending on the seriousness of the offense. If the suspect is arrested while the crime is still being listed, the detective will write a notice to cancel it. The daily bulletin, or DB, is such a useful, practical tool, it is hard to see how it could be improved. It is more commonly used than the all points bulletin but is rarely mentioned in fiction. Here is a hypothetical but typical DB item:

No. 6 (10 Mar) ATTN ALL UNITS: Wanted for 187 PC: SIKES, William, AKA Bill or Billy Boy. DOB 12-14-51, MW 5-11, 160#, brn SF, wrnt #218560, bail $100,000. Subj has previous Oakland address of 455 7th St. Info received by SFPD is that subj has been observed hanging around the Oakland Greyhound depot in the night hours and is sleeping in a vacant lot at 24th and Market. Beware susp's dog. Weapon used in the 187 was a knife. Photo at CAS. Sgt. C. Dickens, CID.

When the jargon is peeled away, you will find that this item is very straightforward and tells you a lot about the suspect. The offense in this case, 187 PC, is murder. Others frequently found in the daily bulletin are 211 (robbery), 261 (rape), and 245 (assault with a deadly weapon). "AKA" means "also known as." The DOB tells us when he was born. "MW" means "male white." (Designations by sex and race includes FN, MN, FW, MM, FM. Asians turn up rarely in daily bulletins, so their race is usually spelled out.)

The presence of a warrant number and amount of bail tells us that the investigation has proceeded quite far and that the detectives have convinced a judge that they have strong reasons to arrest Sikes. It does not mean that he has jumped bail; only that once he is arrested, it will take a lot of money to get him out.

The additional information is that the crime occurred in San Francisco and that the suspect is a former Oakland resident trying to hide out on his old turf. A police officer would infer that unless this suspect is picked up quickly, he will commit additional crimes in order to put some money in his pocket. By mentioning the weapon, the detective is warning the beat officers that Sikes is armed and dangerous. "CAS" is the Crime Analysis Section. "CID" is the Criminal Investigation Division. (Different police departments have different names for these units.)

The details giving the known whereabouts of the suspect are important for officers working the downtown district. The former address alerts officers in the east end that the suspect may still have friends or relatives there to whom he may turn for help. But the bulletin is addressed to all units because the suspect is hot and the Homicide Section had decided to wind up the investigation quickly.

When Bill Sikes is apprehended, the detective will write a cancellation notice along these lines: "No. 10 (12 Mar) ATTN ALL UNITS: Cancel want on 187 susp Bill Sikes. Subj apprehended and in custody." If the detective feels that the arrest involved particularly good police work, he may add a special thanks to the arresting officers or to the patrol division in general ("Thanks to all for outstanding response") or even allow himself a rhetorical flight: "Susp surrendered to F.B.I. due to uncomfortable social environment caused by O.P.D. Thanks to all — Sgt. C. Dickens, CID."

*T*he Police
Blotter

Prisoners must not be held incommunicado. Every police department is required to maintain a register of the people it is holding in jail, and the information on the register must be available to the public. This register, or arrest log, used to be called the police blotter. Today's police blotter is computerized. Where the register is kept varies from one department to another, based partly on the public's need. In Oakland, copies are kept at the jail office and at the Warrants Section.

Actually, the jail maintains two lists of people in custody. There is the arrest log at the back of the jail (the "receiving section"), where the prisoners arrive, and also a file in the front office, which lists people who have been booked and put in cells. (Computer terminals will soon be installed to merge the two lists, so that when a prisoner arrives and his name is typed into the computer at the receiving section, it will be immediately available in the front office.)

The receiving section's arrest log is a temporary list, which records primarily the fact that Johnny has arrived at the jail. Documenting the formal transfer of custody from the arresting officer to the jailers, it is the first step in the booking process. For the moment, it is the only written evidence showing that Johnny is in custody at the jail.

If Johnny's arrest is an ordinary one, it will take about four hours

(text continues on page 38)

JACK LONDON GETS ARRESTED

When prisoners were booked in the nineteenth century, the pertinent information was written in arrest logs, massive books that were typically one and a half feet wide (three feet wide when open), three feet high, and six inches thick. The entries were made in columns, as in an account ledger. The clerks wrote with pen and ink, and because standards of penmanship were wonderful then, the names of the common drunks, burglars, and other miscreants were written in flowing copperplate script. The books were designed as an ongoing record, but they do contain lots of corrections, stains, and blots; inevitably, they became known as police blotters.

In 1912, Oakland police regulations said that "Captains shall keep a police blotter at their respective stations, in which shall be entered the full name of every person detained, the time, place and cause of such detention, the offense charged, the name of the arresting officer and a list of the property or a statement of the matter to be introduced in evidence." This was a policy of many years' standing.

On February 10, 1897, Jack London was arrested by the Oakland Police Department. The events that led up to the arrest were novel at the time. London was twenty-one, a dropout from the University of California at Berkeley, and an active member of the Socialist Labor Party. The Oakland chapter of the party decided to mark Lincoln's birthday by challenging the city ordinance that made it "unlawful for any person to conduct or take part in any public meeting held on any public street . . . unless permission to hold such a public meeting has been first obtained in writing from the Mayor." Volunteers were requested, and London stepped forward. At the appointed time,

he mounted a soapbox, opened his mouth to declaim, and was arrested.

London considered he was striking a blow for free speech; to Officer Henderson he was committing a misdemeanor.

In those days, the jail was in the basement of city hall, about four blocks from where London was to speak. Within a few minutes, he was in the clink and being booked. Here is the information the clerk carefully wrote, column by column, in the police blotter, the "Arrest Book for the Month of February 1897":

1. Date: Wednesday 10
2. Time: 8:10 pm
3. Name of Officer: Henderson
4. Party Arrested: John London
5. Place of Arrest: 10th & Broadway
6. Nativity: U.S.
7. Age: 21
8. Feet: 5
9. Inches: 7
10. Complexion: Dark
11. Read and Write: Yes
12. Weight: 150
13. Occupation: Student
14. Offense Charged: Violating Ordinance — Speaking on Street
15. Result: Bail, $5
16. Property: (left blank)
17. Residence: Oakland

London posted the $5 bail and was released, which is why item number 16 was left blank. When his case came up before the police court judge, London demanded and received a jury trial. He spoke so convincingly in his own defense that the jury came in at 11 to 1 for acquittal, and the city dropped the charges. When this was reported to the police department, the word "Dismissed" was stamped under item number 15.

The ordinance remained in the municipal code and in a modified form is still there today.

Jack London when he was known in Oakland as "the boy socialist."

to book him. Part of this time he will be kept in a holding cell while the jailers deal with other prisoners, and part of it he will spend on the telephone, calling an attorney or members of his family. Johnny has to be fingerprinted and thoroughly searched. His property must be inventoried and a receipt prepared, so that he can reclaim it later when he gets out. As they separate Johnny from his property, the jailers look for weapons, contraband (usually drugs), and evidence. Then he is screened for medical problems and may be given tests for drugs or alcohol.

Booking follows a standard procedure, and the jailer records each step on departmental forms that are filled out in triplicate. At the end of the process one copy is routed to the front office and placed in an alphabetical file; the others go to the court and to investigators. Then Johnny emerges from the limbo of booking and is officially identified and certified as a prisoner. This is record keeping, of course. A good while before the paper reaches the desk up front, Johnny has been locked in a cell. Nevertheless, if anyone telephones the jail or actually goes there to check on Johnny's whereabouts,

the staff consult the forms filed in the front office. The vast majority of telephone calls to a prisoner are from members of the family. Arrest is a nasty experience for the prisoner, even if he is a repeat offender. It never loses its impact on the family.

At the Warrants Section, the police blotter is a pile of bound computer printouts. This jumble is properly termed the Arrest and Offense Log. Informally, it is the alpha log. As now constituted, the alpha log is a monthly miscellany, a list of the names of suspects, complainants, arresting officers, and case numbers. The case numbers are the key to retrieving the officers' written reports from the files.

Although originally intended to prevent abuse of the police's power to arrest, today the alpha log is rarely referred to by lawyers. It is used most frequently by victims who want copies of crime reports so that they can file insurance claims.

Lonnie Daniels, a *San Francisco Examiner* reporter, told us that when he wants to find out who is in jail, he telephones the front office. He is generally able to interview prisoners immediately in San Francisco, but it takes forty-eight hours to set up an interview in Oakland. "I hate to do jail interviews," he says. "If the person is rich, he will have seen a lawyer before talking to the reporter. If he's poor, the reporter is likely to be the first person he sees, and he's likely to spill his guts, saying things he shouldn't. If he's innocent, you hate to see him in there. If he's guilty, you want to keep a distance between you and him. It's better for the prisoner to have the forty-eight-hour delay in Oakland, but it's worse for the newsmen; in forty-eight hours, the paper will have lost interest in the suspect unless it's a big case."

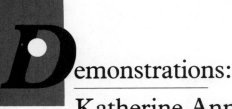emonstrations: Katherine Anne Porter's Policeman

Katherine Anne Porter, the author of *Ship of Fools,* was one of the demonstrators against the execution of Sacco and Vanzetti in Boston in 1927. It was an unpopular cause, and the pickets risked attack by people who believed that the two anarchists were guilty. A large number of Boston policemen were detailed to the scene of the demonstrations to keep the lid on.

Before long a routine had been worked out. The pickets would march around the State House until arrested. When arrested, they submitted quietly, went to jail, and were bailed out and allowed to return to the State House the next day. The protests were carried out peacefully, ceremoniously, almost ritually. They resembled many demonstrations conducted today. Here's how Porter described the marches in her book *The Never-Ending Wrong:*

Each morning I left the hotel, walked into the blazing August sun, and dropped into the picket line before the State House; the police would allow us to march around once or twice, then close in and make the arrests we invited; indeed, what else were we there for? My elbow was always taken quietly by the same mild little blond officer, day after day; he was very Irish, very patient, very damned bored with the whole incomprehensible show. We always greeted each other politely. It was generally understood that the Pink Tea Squad . . . had been assigned to this job, well instructed that in no circumstance were they to forget themselves and whack a lady with their truncheons. . . .

The first time I was arrested, my policeman and I walked along stealing perplexed, questioning glances at each other; the gulf between us was fixed, but not impassible. . . .

Here are some notes of my conversations with my policeman during our several journeys under the August sun, down the rocky road to the Joy Street Station:

He: "What good do you think you're doing?"

I: "I hope a little. . . . I don't believe they had a fair trial. That is all I want for them, a fair trial."

He: "This is no way to go about getting it. You ought to know you'll never get anywhere with this stuff."

I: "Why not?"

He: "It makes people mad. They take you for a lot of tramps."

I: "We did everything else we could think of first, for years and years, and nothing worked."

He: "I don't believe in showing contempt for the courts this way."

Katherine Anne Porter
(fourth from left) and
"her" policeman
marching off to jail.

I: "Neither do I, in principle. But this time the court is wrong."

He: "I trust the courts of the land more than I do all these sapheads making public riot."

I: "We aren't rioting. Look at us, how calm we are."

He (still mildly): "What I think is, you all ought to be put in jail and kept there till it's over."

I: "They don't want us in jail. There isn't enough room there."

Second day:

He (taking my elbow and drawing me out of the line; I go like a lamb): "Well, what have you been doing since yesterday?"

I: "Mostly copying Sacco's and Vanzetti's letters. I wish you could read them. You'd believe in them if you could read the letters."

He: "Well, I don't have much time for reading."

Third day:

The picket line was crowded, anxious, and slow-moving. I reached the rounding point before I saw my policeman taking his place. I moved out and reached for his arm before we spoke. "You're late," I said, not in the least meaning to be funny. He astonished me by nearly smiling. "What have we got to hurry for?" he inquired, and my scalp shuddered — we moved on in silence.

This was the 23rd of August, the day set for the execution, and the crowds of onlookers that had gathered every morning were becoming rather noisy and abusive. My officer and I ran into a light shower of stones, a sprinkling of flowers, confetti, and a flurry of boos, catcalls, and cheers as we rounded the corner into Joy Street. We ducked our heads and I looked back and saw

other prisoners and other policemen put up their hands and turn away their faces.

I: "Can you make out which is for which of us? I can't."

He: "No, I can't, and I don't care."

Silence.

He: "How many times have you been down this street today?"

I: "Only once. I was only sent out once today. How many times for you?"

It was now late afternoon, and as it turned out, this was the last picket line to form. The battle was lost and all of us knew it by then.

He (in mortal weariness): "God alone knows."

As we stood waiting in line at the desk, I said, "I expect this will be the last time you'll have to arrest me. You've been very kind and patient and I thank you."

I remember the blinded exhaustion of his face, its gray pallor with greenish shadows in it. He said, "Thank *you*," and stood beside me at the desk while my name was written into the record once more. We did not speak or look at each other again, but as I followed the matron to a cell I saw him working his way slowly outward through the crowd."

Though it happened so long ago, all this has a familiar sound. Katherine Anne Porter's policeman showed what would now be called "a reasonable concern for the arrestee as an individual." Although such demonstrations were new in those days, he did his share to help keep the situation civil.

An officer we know inspects all the signs being carried in a demonstration and makes a point of telling the person whose sign shows the most artistic care and attention to detail that he or she has won the police award for the best placard of the day.

THE POLICE
CALL IT STRESS

Oakland Officer Pete Pruitt (left) listens to Sergeant Leroy Sargent. Unarmed, riding his motorcycle to work, Sargent heard shots fired in front of police headquarters. He saw one woman with a pistol standing over the prostrate body of another and shooting at her. He jumped off his motorcycle and leaped on the woman from behind, disarming her and suffering a gash on the forehead in the struggle. The woman had attempted to murder her rival for a man.

Bill Knowland, Oakland Tribune

San Francisco Officer Miguel Granados kneels in prayer beside the body of his partner, Officer Donoso Cortes, who died in a motorcycle accident.

Jim Mahoney, *Boston Herald*

Boston Police Officer
Alan Keith (left) is led
away from his horse,
Tivoli, after they were
struck by a hit-and-run
driver. Keith sustained
minor injuries, but Ti-
voli, his mount for
three years, suffered a
broken leg and had to
be destroyed.

nne Fitzmaurice, San Francisco Examiner

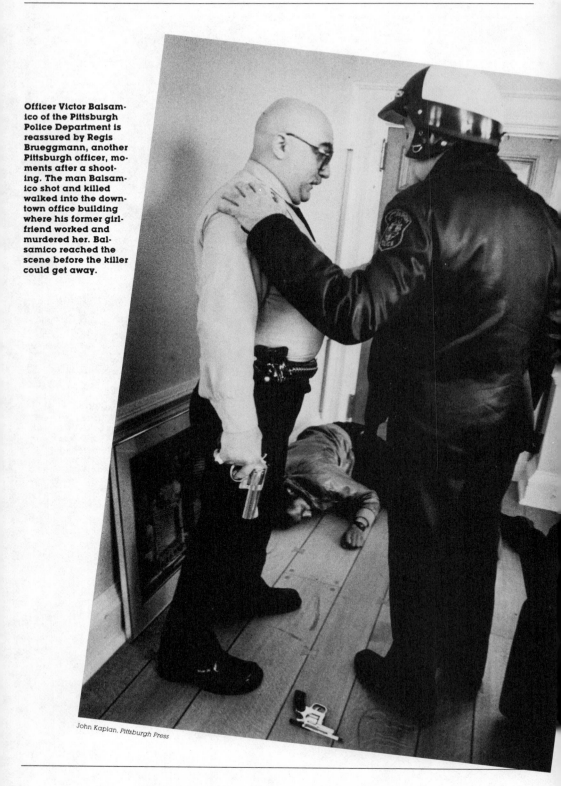

Officer Victor Balsamico of the Pittsburgh Police Department is reassured by Regis Brueggmann, another Pittsburgh officer, moments after a shooting. The man Balsamico shot and killed walked into the downtown office building where his former girlfriend worked and murdered her. Balsamico reached the scene before the killer could get away.

John Kaplan. *Pittsburgh Press*

Vollmer, the Professional

August Vollmer, Berkeley's chief of police from 1905 to 1932, was a leading figure in the professionalization of American police work. He believed, and instilled the belief in many others, that police officers should be skillful crime fighters: highly trained, eager to apply the latest scientific and technological developments to their work, and deeply concerned about the welfare of their communities. Although these ideals have not been universally accepted — much less achieved — his influence as a police chief was immense. Vollmer was a good investigator and based much of what he accomplished as an administrator on his personal experience.

Six feet tall, lean, physically tough, Vollmer had a commanding presence. His colleague and biographer, Alfred E. Parker, wrote, "His face was sun-bronzed; his gray-blue eyes direct, at times stern . . . ; his dark hair was parted on the left side; and his wide mouth, firm and set in determination, was capable of laughter. He had the face of a professor, of a scholar; he could have passed for an executive at the head of a big business organization. His manner, when he walked about visiting the various offices in his department, was forceful, dynamic, displaying an enthusiasm that made it obvious he was in love with his work."

Vollmer was born in 1876. As a young man he enlisted in the army and distinguished himself as a brave soldier during the Spanish-American War. He saw action at the siege of Manila and in the suppression of Aguinaldo's guerrillas. After the war he returned to Berkeley. Certain only that he did not want to work indoors in an office, he got a job as a mailman. Late one afternoon as he made his rounds, he saw a runaway flatcar rolling downhill. It was headed straight toward the depot where a commuter train was unloading passengers. He chased down the flatcar, jumped aboard, and turned the brake, stopping the car short of the depot. This brave deed brought him to the attention of Friend Richardson, the editor of the *Berkeley Daily Gazette* and a political power in the city. Richardson had been looking for a good candidate for the office of town marshal, and he persuaded Vollmer to run. Vollmer was elected, and he took office on April 15, 1905. He soon found his vocation in law enforcement.

At that time the marshal's office had three deputies. Vollmer's first official act was that of a born administrator: he requested the appointment of nine more. While waiting for the city council to approve the request, he commenced to enforce the law by raiding a notorious downtown opium and gambling den.

Vollmer and his deputies, armed with pistols and sixteen-pound sledgehammers, made their way through dark streets toward the gambling den. The noise they made awakened its watchdog. Several alert gamblers succeeded in fleeing the scene, but the new marshal and his men broke down the doors and arrested fourteen Chinese who had been too absorbed in their pleasures to heed the barking dog. They also seized a considerable quantity of opium, opium pipes, slot machines, fantan cards, lottery tickets, and a .42 caliber pistol. Vollmer and his deputies felt they had done a good night's work.

The gamblers — mostly cooks for well-to-do families — were bailed out by their employers and provided with a good defense attorney. When the lawyer realized that Vollmer had failed to diagram the layout of the place, he grilled him on it. He even had him draw a map of it in the courtroom. "I did so," Vollmer recalled years later, "putting windows where there were really doors, and doors where there were only solid walls. The next day, at that lawyer's request, the jury was taken to the place and found it entirely different than my chart showed." The lawmen were unable to testify that they actually saw the opium pipes in use at the time of the arrests. "As a climax," Vollmer recalled, the lawyer "mixed the defendants in a crowd of Chinese men, and demanded that I identify each suspect individually. I couldn't tell them apart. The jury was out just thirty minutes before it returned with its not-guilty verdict in all cases."

Vollmer was generally good-humored, but he had a temper. The debriefing that followed this fiasco must have been something. Afterward, he set about learning the rules of evidence. The next raid he led, directed at Berkeley's most prosperous gambling den, was a complete success. The pro-prietors were convicted, their white and Chinese patrons were fined, and the equipment was destroyed. Vollmer had the satisfaction of padlocking the place.

The Berkeley police became exceptionally proficient raiders. Earl Warren, when he was the crusading district attorney of Alameda County during the 1920s, preferred to use them rather than the local police in other cities where he was closing down gambling dens, brothels, and distilleries.

Vollmer's first raid and its aftermath illustrate one of his principal characteristics. When he suffered a setback, he found a solution to the problem that caused it and then improved on the solution, sometimes elaborating on it for years.

Vollmer did not like to lose cases or to leave them with loose ends. On one occasion, a deputy was called to the scene where a dead man had been found with a bottle of potassium cyanide powder clutched in his hand. The Alameda County grand jury conducted a hearing on the death and brought in a finding of suicide. But Vollmer was not satisfied with this, because, on the basis of the little that he had learned about the man, there seemed to be no reason for him to kill himself.

Some days later an informant showed up at Vollmer's office with the tale of a lovers' triangle that the dead man had been involved in. Vollmer then sought out Professor Jacques Loeb, a biologist at the University of California, and discussed the case with him. He learned that potassium cyanide kills instantly and causes the muscles to relax immediately. If the man had taken cyanide, he would in all probability have dropped the bottle at the moment of death instead of holding on to it. Vollmer concluded that the bottle was a "plant" and that the death was a murder.

He had the case brought back to the grand jury for a rehearing. But the jurors decided that without photographic proof, the deputy's testimony that the bottle was in the victim's hand was hearsay. They reaffirmed the original finding. Still convinced that a murder had occurred and the murderer had gotten off scot-free, Vollmer realized that his lack of photographs and insufficient knowledge of toxicology cost him the case.

He responded by equipping his department with cameras and, as new cases turned up, having detailed photographs taken of crime scenes. The study of toxicology he took up himself. Some years later, in 1916, he hired an expert chemist away from the university and, working closely with him, created the first scientific crime laboratory in the United States.

Vollmer was Chief Petersen's guest in Oakland in 1915. From left: Chief Petersen, Commissioner Anderson, Chief Vollmer, Officer Eddie Hughes, and Captain Bock. "Petersen was a good chief," one old-timer said. "He couldn't be frightened."

Oakland History Room. Oakland Public Library

A class in microscopy at the Berkeley Police Department in 1915. Vollmer is seated at left, and Dr. Albert Schindler is standing. Note the enlargements of fingerprints on the wall, the mug shots above the door, and the pinups behind the telephone.

This approach to solving problems made Vollmer famous as an innovative police chief. A problem was an opportunity to improve the efficiency of his department. No matter where the idea for the solution came from, he followed it from one development to the next, as far as it would go.

Vollmer was quick to use new technology and to extend its applications. To increase the mobility of his patrol force, he put his officers on bicycles. Other departments had used bicycles in emergencies, but Berkeley was the first

American department to use them full time for regular patrol duties. Later, he had his officers patrol on motorcycles. When the automobile became available, he took full advantage of it, and was the first to use radios to broadcast to patrol cars.

"One of Vollmer's great attributes," said an officer who served under him, "was his extraordinary ability to encourage other people to develop ideas and to develop [new] practices. . . . He had faith in people." This can be seen in his sponsorship of the work done by

John Larson and Leonarde Keeler in creating the first practical polygraphs. Vollmer had contempt for the third degree, and embraced the polygraph as a tool that would make it obsolete.

In 1908, Vollmer began a revolution in police training with the famous Berkeley police school. This was the first formal in-service training program set up by an American police department. It began as an in-house project designed to meet the needs of his officers, and it led — in California and many other states — to recruit schools, regular in-service classes for veteran officers, university courses in criminology, and the requirement that officers have at least some collegiate schooling.

The first program Vollmer put together for the school reflected his interest in a mixture of theoretical and practical learning. Vollmer himself, along with Oakland's captain of detectives, Walter Petersen, taught police methods. Professor A. M. Kidd, of the University of California Law School, gave a series of lectures on difficult points in the law, and Walter Helms, a U.C. professor of parasitology, taught the principles of sanitation.

Sanitation laws were included because there was bubonic plague in Berkeley at the time, and the patrol officers needed instruction in how to deal with it. This helped establish the practice of making the curriculum of police academies flexible. In addition to the permanent parts of the curriculum, classes were almost always being offered that dealt with some pressing current problem.

Many of the practices Vollmer established in Berkeley, and many of his innovations, such as the crime laboratory and the police academy, have become standard elements of American policing. There are numerous students of law enforcement who believe that the Berkeley Police Department under Vollmer was the most effective and creative municipal police department ever developed in the United States.

"It has been observed, with some truth, that everyone loves a good murder."

F. Tennyson Jesse

"We love to overlook the boundaries which we do not wish to pass."

Dr. Samuel Johnson

SCENE
OF
THE
CRIME

Detectives

Denny Holland was a first-rate Oakland police detective in the 1880s whose memory for faces earned him the nickname of "the camera eye." One day a reporter asked him what it takes to become a detective.

"Well," Denny answered, "there are several requirements, my boy. The same question was asked me some time ago by an old gentleman who said he had a son bent on becoming a detective. I told him to let the boy go ahead and not think of stopping or discouraging him in any way. To become a detective, I said, he must be a good feeder, must eat plenty. Then he must be a good sleeper, and last but not least, he must be a good church member; go to church not less than three times a week. The father wanted to know if his boy couldn't be apprenticed to the detective business before he became a full-fledged thief catcher. I told the old man that he might send the boy over to Harry Morse's in San Francisco, where I understand they employ boys shadowing people. But in the case of such a boy as the old man described his son to be, I advised that he be placed under the tuition of the Pinkertons, nothing lower would be suitable for his genius. The parent left the office, saying he would think the matter over."

After dispensing this beguiling cloud of mystification, Denny went off "to witness the boat race on the creek, where he thought some suspicious characters might also be in attendance."

Jean Belin, a detective well-known in the first half of the century, entered the French police service as a constable and even-

tually became comissioner of the Sûreté. He gave a different account of the requirements for detective work. Initially, he wrote in his memoir, "I failed to fulfill the qualifications for a detective as laid down by the celebrated Monsieur Lepine, the prefect of police of Paris.

"Lepine was a remarkable char-

William J. Burns at work late in his career.

acter: a man of undoubted if unpredictable ability, with idiosyncrasies and prejudices no one could overcome. He had ruled that no man more than five feet seven could be admitted to the detective force. At the same time, no uniformed constable was allowed on the streets unless he was five feet nine. And I came in between. Lepine contended that an ordinary uniformed cop ought to be impressive by reason of his height and physical fitness. On the other hand, a detective should be unobtrusive in appearance. In these respects he was inflexible. He went even further. He insisted on personally inspecting every recruit. If any applicant for the plain-clothes branch had red hair, or a pot belly, or any other marked distinguishing feature, he had no chance. A mole on the face or a scar on the hand was sufficient disqualification no matter how able the man might be. I have often thought about Lepine's strange foible in this matter but, although I was angry at the time, I have come to the conclusion that in the long run he was probably right."

Belin came to believe that "In real life a man with the distinctive appearance of a Sherlock Holmes or the moustache of a Hercule Poirot would never get near his quarry. The clever and successful detective must look exactly what he is not — a commonplace member of the community, going about his business like a million others."

William J. Burns, whose career lasted from 1888 into the mid-1920s, was thought by some experts to have been America's greatest detective. The founder of the Burns International Detective Agency fit only one of Lepine's specifications. According to Gene Caesar, his biographer, Burns was "a short, stocky fellow" but he had "flame red hair and a matching moustache. . . . Florid in speech as well as in complexion, the man was far more suggestive of a successful salesman or even a theatrical personality than a highly skilled detective." Burns usually spoke of his triumphs of deduction as "just common sense," his own way of saying, "Elementary, my dear Watson."

In fiction, Inspector Queen and Sergeant Velie certainly conform to the physical pattern demanded by Lepine and endorsed by Belin. In *The Perfect Crime*, to take a typical description of them, we encounter, "Inspector Queen, a wiry little man with a gray moustache, Sergeant Velie towering at his side." Although Velie is a plain-clothes officer, his commanding height shows that he came up through the uniformed ranks.

It is possible, though, that Belin underestimated Sherlock Holmes and Hercule Poirot. A Belgian, Poirot is short, only five feet four. Like many private detectives in real life, he is a retired police officer. His cases do not normally involve members of the underworld, who might have had occasion to deal with him in his official capacity. As an unofficial investigator working cases where the suspects are not professional criminals, he has no need to conceal his identity, and his mustache, while it is a trademark, is not a handicap. We'd like to think that, if it would have made the difference in solving a case, Poirot would have chopped it off — with regret, but without hesitation.

Sir Arthur Conan Doyle tells us that Holmes was a master of disguise, and this trait has been joyfully — and successfully — exploited by the actors who played him. Basil Rathbone's most stunning Holmes disguise was a simple change of clothing, from tweeds to white ducks and a straw boater, in which he did a delightful vaudeville turn.

The real police detectives most likely to use disguises are those assigned to vice units. The persistence of counterculture styles makes the assumption of a disguise easier than it might be otherwise. As soon as a plainclothes officer doffs his suit and tie and puts on a Grateful Dead T-shirt and blue jeans, he is almost ready to go out and work drug cases. If his hair, beard, and mustache grow scraggly and he has a genuine Marine Corps tattoo on his arm, he is really set. On his looks, he couldn't possibly belong to the establishment. He doesn't look as if he would ever burn anybody.

The qualities needed by a good investigator are today what they were in Denny Holland's time: knowledge of human nature, the ability to observe precisely, persistence, and the capacity to assemble isolated pieces of information in a meaningful way. A difference between now and then is that detectives are given formal training in professional classes to enhance their native abilities.

In Oakland, as elsewhere, the current practice is to assign officers to different areas of the department throughout their careers — to make them generalists rather than specialists. Consequently, almost every sergeant is assigned to the Criminal Investigation Division and spends some time as a detective (or, to use the departmental term, an investigator). How long depends on a number of factors. There are police officers who do not enjoy detective work, and there are good officers whose talents do not lie in that area. Other officers like the work and are good at it, but find it too disruptive of their family lives.

The volume of work can be crushing. When Chips Stewart was running Oakland's CID, he was interested in "caseload management." He prepared a report showing that in one year, "there were 41,000 reported felony crimes investigated by 59 investigators. This is a caseload of 695 per investigator or approximately 3.5 cases a day to investigate. . . . These cases are not of equal complexity. Some cases can be processed and cleared within two hours, but others may require a team of investigators to work a month to complete."

AN APRIL FOOL'S STORY

Frontier humor could be rough and ready. Here is a tale from the inspector's scrapbooks, told by Oakland Police Clerk Tom Downey in the late 1880s while sitting around the station swapping war stories with other coppers and a reporter.

The only time I ever was fooled on April 1st was in 1882, I think. Some one reported that there had been a stabbing affray in Dan Hart's saloon on the corner of Second Street and Broadway, in which a man had been killed.

The report was serious and Denny Holland and I started down to the saloon. Everything was in confusion and there was a well defined trail of blood running from the saloon and into the street and around the corner. We forgot that it was April 1st when we discovered the drops of blood on the sidewalk. We followed the trail, which was only too plain, around two blocks until it entered an old, deserted house, just the place to hide a body. The trail of blood led down cellar and as we entered we saw laying on the floor the body of a man. Detective Holland dropped on his knees beside the body.

"Is he dead?" I asked.

"Dead — drunk," replied Holland.

The blood was that of a turkey, and the whole affair was a put up job.

DOMESTIC LIFE

In this scene from Michael Z. Lewin's novel *Night Cover*, Lieutenant Powder of the Cincinnati Police Department intervenes compassionately in the life of a subordinate.

Salimbean's problems were more suited to the Canteen than they would have been to the open-plan Night Room. He was fraying and didn't have the perspective on himself to admit it. He'd been in detective division for two and a half years. The vastly increased responsibilities which detective sergeants carry were straining him on the job and the job was straining him at home. Powder knew Salimbean's situation cold.

"You ever think of going into some other kind of work, Harold?" Powder asked. No point in beating around the bush.

"What?" said Salimbean, his worst fears seemingly coming true. All he needed now was to be chucked out. Or demoted. His wife called him "the big hot-shot detective." His middle child's grades had taken a sharp dip since he came into detective division. "The big hot-shot detective. Hot shit!"

"Sugar?" Powder asked.

"Thanks." Salimbean stirred in two.

"You're a pretty good detective, Harold," said Powder. "Pretty good cop."

Quizzical frown, but, "Thanks."

"But you're having troubles at home, aren't you?"

"Well . . ." he began, feeling that loyalty required him to deny the obvious. "I think my wife would have preferred me to take Traffic," he said. That wasn't disloyal, was it? Preferred wasn't the word. "Got to be a big hot-shit detective!" over and over, night after night.

"Can't think of a sensible wife who wouldn't," said Powder, though he could think of some wives who weren't sensible.

"I didn't want to write tickets all day."

"I can see that," Powder mused. "But your problems at home have been showing here, Harold."

"They have?"

"Late a lot. Tired. The edge is off. What is it, she just beginning to realize that things don't get better for cops' wives?"

"I don't honestly know what she thinks anymore," said Salimbean, and he knew that more than the hem of the slip was showing.

"What are you going to do about it, Harold?"

Silence for a few moments. "I'll just have to try harder, I guess."

Powder shook his head. "You can't try harder. You don't have much try left in you. You're a responsible cop, you're giving it what you've got."

Salimbean nodded. It was true.

"I'm making you an appointment with Lieutenant Gaulden. When's your next day off?"

"What the hell will Lieutenant Gaulden be able to do? What can anybody do? It's my problem, Lieutenant Powder, I'll just have to work it out."

"Look," said Powder gently, "it's just not worth ruining your home life about. I know. I've seen it. I've been through it. I've got a wife I don't talk to except the kid's home from college. It's not worth it. Makes you cranky. You don't want to end up like me, son, believe it. Gaulden has seen it, too; he's in charge of personnel. I want you to talk to him, see what we can find you in the force. If not, my advice would be to consider looking around outside. I'm not talking about becoming a night watchman. Something to use your training. When's your next days, Harold?"

"Sunday and Monday." He knows, Salimbean thought. We're on the same shift.

"All right, I'll get you an appointment on Monday. It's off the record, by the way. You're not so far over the edge that I have to put it on paper, don't think that."

"I didn't."

"I'd just hate to see you get stuck in a groove because you thought there was no way out. Only difference between a groove and a grave is the depth. That's why I'm sending you to Gaulden on your off day. Let you know the time."

"OK," said Salimbean, who was thoroughly dispirited. He was getting used to a cloud over his world at home, but he hadn't thought the sunshine had ended at work. God, what a life!

Oakland Police Dept.

Leave him to get used to it, thought Powder. "I gotta go back upstairs now," he said, rising. "Take your time." Powder walked to the stairwell. Now, an intelligent guy like Salimbean in the statistics department, he thought, and we'd get decent organized rosters out of them.

She'll kill me, Salimbean was thinking. Having to come in on an off day.

Detectives in a homicide investigation class in 1944 or 1945 examine a mannikin. William Powell clearly had the better role; Louise Brooks was no dummy.

How Homicide Investigations Go Wrong

Homicide scenes are messy, confusing, and crowded. How well the officers handle the scene before the detectives arrive can make or break an investigation. For writers working on murder mysteries, here are some procedural errors that make detectives cringe.

To begin with, it is not always easy to tell when a person is dead. When an officer thinks a victim may still be alive, he must call for an ambulance. (You would not want it any other way.) So it happens sometimes that a dead person is sent to a hospital. But any time the corpse is taken away before the technicians and detectives arrive, reconstruction of the crime becomes much more difficult.

Even an experienced officer can misjudge the seriousness of a victim's injuries. When an officer delays in taking a statement from someone who has been mortally wounded in order to call for medical help, he may miss the opportunity to obtain a dying declaration.

As soon as news of a killing goes out over the radio, officers from all over converge on the scene. Even off-duty officers turn up. Without proper supervision from the district sergeant, crowds of sightseeing officers get in the way, duplicate one another's work, and contaminate the evidence.

Murder weapons possess a curious fascination even for the police, and at a poorly supervised scene, one of the officers will inevitably pick up the weapon—and damage its value as evidence.

It is a different problem when a suspect is identified and too many officers take off in hot pursuit. This leaves the scene inadequately controlled, so that evidence is lost and witnesses are not interviewed. Under these circumstances, murder weapons disappear and witnesses are not identified or wander off or get together to compare stories.

Poorly written homicide reports cause two kinds of problems. If a negative statement by a witness ("I didn't see a thing") is not recorded, the witness may turn up at the trial with a story chock full of unexpected details. Similarly, when houses in a neighborhood are canvassed and no record is kept of the addresses where no one was at home, adverse witnesses can also turn up unexpectedly in the courtroom.

Facing page: Two kinds of role playing. William Powell, as Philo Vance, inspects the body of a dancer, played by Louise Brooks, in the 1929 movie *The Canary Murder Case*.

"There is something about a closet that makes a skeleton terribly restless."

Wilson Mizner

THE GOLDEN RULE
OF THE INVESTIGATION OF DEATH

Never touch, move, change, or alter anything
in any way until it has been identified,
recorded, measured, and photographed.

Dying Declarations

Ellery Queen and other mystery writers employ dying declarations (as well as dying clues) in their stories. Critics occasionally attack this device on the grounds of improbability, but in fact if a detective is lucky enough to obtain a dying declaration, the case usually turns on it.

Definitions of the dying declaration and the rules governing its admissibility as evidence vary somewhat from state to state. Colorado's definition is clear and may be taken as representative: "A dying declaration is a statement concerning the cause of death, made by the victim of a homicide who, at the time of the statement, knew he was dying and felt death was immediate and inescapable."

In court, a dying declaration has the same strength as a statement by a living witness. But like any other statement or piece of evidence, its meaning has to be established. A defense attorney would want answers to some of the following questions: Was the victim a competent witness or delirious? Did he have a reason to mislead the officer? Would he have blamed an innocent person? Did he want to protect someone? Was he misunderstood? Does other evidence support the declaration? Was the declaration a statement of a fact or only the victim's opinion? (The victim's opinions cannot be admitted in court, although they may help the detective's investigation.)

Dying declarations are rare, because most murder victims die before the police arrive. Even so, dying declarations have figured in many cases where death was not instantaneous. In one bizarre old case, a man was shot in the heart, lived to make a dying declaration, and was even able to go horseback riding two weeks later.

It happened near Porterville, California, on January 28, 1908. Two ranchers, former friends, argued about some cattle that had wandered from one ranch to the other through a hole in the fence separating them. William Cord found the hole, which was close to John Pawley's house, and began to mend it. Pawley came out of his house, and the quarrel began. Without warning, Cord pulled out a pistol and shot Pawley at point-blank range. Pawley fell to the ground and called out to his wife. While she helped him into their house, Cord mounted his horse and rode away. He went to Porterville and gave himself up.

Pawley's wife sent for a doctor, and the Porterville police called Visalia for the sheriff, the district attorney, and a shorthand reporter. The doctor expected Pawley to die at any moment and did what he could to make him comfortable. The sheriff and the district attorney took a dying statement from Pawley.

But Pawley did not die. Instead, he began to rally, so he was moved to a hospital, where his condition continued to improve. He was weak from loss of blood but, even so, managed to walk to Porterville several times. The doctors were unable to find a bullet in him, and they decided he was recovering. At his request, he was released from the hospital and sent home.

On the sixteenth of February, Pawley rode into town. While there, he had a shave and a haircut. Later, before returning home, he ate a heavy supper. About ten o'clock he complained of a pain in his right side, which grew steadily worse. A doctor was called, and shortly afterward Pawley died. The autopsy showed that Cord's .38 slug had lodged in Pawley's heart, where it had been held in place by the surrounding tissue and a blood clot. For some reason or other, the bullet slipped loose, blocked his heart, and killed him.

William Cord was tried for murder. The jury was out for twenty-one hours and took twelve ballots before finding him guilty of man-slaughter. Cord appealed. One of the arguments he advanced was that Pawley's statement to the district attorney was not truly a dying declaration and should not have been used in evidence, because Pawley lived for two weeks after making it.

In affirming Cord's conviction, Justice Shaw wrote: "It was not necessary that the person should be at the time in the throes of death, or that he should die immediately, or within any specified time . . . in order to give the declaration probative force. . . . In the present case the evidence shows that this wound was necessarily fatal and that his dissolution therefrom was in progress continuously from the beginning to the close. The remarkable thing is that he lived so long in such a condition. He was never on the road to recovery, as appellant contends, but was constantly on the brink of death from a recurrence of hemorrhage."

HOW GOOD A COP ARE YOU? #1

It is Sunday afternoon. You are in uniform and patrolling your beat in a marked car when a call comes over the radio. A person working overtime at the waterfront has reported a heavyset man in a gray windbreaker and a red and white ski hat suspiciously prowling around a neighboring warehouse. You get the address and start over to see what is going on. While you are en route, you receive another report: shots have been fired at cars passing the warehouse, and cover officers are being dispatched.

As you arrive you hear a shot, and then you see a man in a red and white ski hat running toward the rear of the warehouse. You don't see a weapon in his hand, but you draw your service revolver and follow. "Freeze! Police!" you shout. Ignoring you, he disappears around the side of the building.

You turn the corner and begin to move along the side of the building. Then from behind a dumpster the man steps out and points his gun at you. Quick! What do you do?

1. Give him his *Miranda* rights.
2. Shoot the gun out of his hand.
3. Shoot to kill.
4. Announce loudly that your partner is behind the man and has him covered.
5. Dive for cover.

Answer to How Good a Cop Are You? #1

3. If you didn't shoot to kill you are probably dead. The subject is out to kill you, and your chances of reaching adequate cover in time or of shooting the gun out of his hand are practically nil.

Sir Arthur Solves a Case

Sir Arthur Conan Doyle as a young man.

When Sherlock Holmes solved a case, Watson and Lestrade were mystified until the master revealed the iron chain of reasoning that led to the villain's undoing. Baffled too were the original readers of Sir Arthur Conan Doyle's stories.

Nowadays, we are so familiar with Holmes and his methods that we are not held in such suspense until the dénouement, even when reading one of the stories for the first time. We so enjoy the by-play between Holmes, Watson, and Lestrade that it is easy to underestimate how barren of information the road to the solution of Holmes's puzzles once seemed. To his first readers, the solutions were not inevitable.

Although he credited one of his professors in medical school, Dr. Joseph Bell, as the inspiration for Sherlock Holmes, Conan Doyle himself was an excellent amateur detective. Once Holmes became famous, many people sought out his creator for assistance. In his biography of Conan Doyle, John Dickson Carr shows us how the writer solved several cases step by step. Notable is "The Great Wyr-

Bettmann Archive

ley Mystery," in which he cleared the name of a man falsely imprisoned for maiming horses and cattle, and identified the actual criminal. His investigation was truly Holmesian. But there are other cases Conan Doyle solved that Carr did not unravel for us. In them we can renew the mystification that familiarity with the Holmes stories has dulled over the years.

On September 21, 1907, the *Oakland Tribune* carried a piece datelined Long Beach, California, and headed CONAN DOYLE TRACES HEIR. Here is the story, with its subheads:

Locates Former Oakland Resident Who Will Come Into Fortune

Through the efforts of Sir A. Conan Doyle, creator of Sherlock Holmes, Frank Sharp, formerly of Oakland, but now living in Santa Ana, and working for a small salary on the Pacific Electric Railway, will come into a great fortune. Sharp left Wales, his native land, many years ago, and when he came to America ceased to communicate with his British relatives, some of whom were very wealthy, and they lost track of him. Finally death claimed one who had not forgotten the young man, and who appears to have bequeathed his entire estate to Sharp.

Doyle Takes Case

All efforts to locate him proved futile and finally Doyle was prevailed on to take the case. He traced Sharp to this section, and yesterday City Marshal Young was surprised when he received a neat letter bearing the detective-doctor's crest and signature, asking him to get Sharp's exact address. He succeeded in doing so during the day and the information is already in the mail. It would be interesting to know by what process he followed the movements of Sharp to this section.

It certainly would be.

This little news article calls up the whole romance of Baker Street — the client appearing out of nowhere with an apparently insoluble problem and the solution materializing inexplicably in due time. Conan Doyle may have made inquiries in Oakland, but we have not been able to find traces of them.

IT'S A FALLACY

● **The hair and nails on a human body grow after death.**

This only appears to be true. The skin around the nail bed and hair follicles shrinks as the body loses moisture. But no actual growth takes place.

A Body in the Water

Let us suppose that you are a mystery novelist, and the necessities of your story compel you to drown a character named Fred or to chuck his dead body into a river. What will become of Fred?

There are people who believe that if Fred is dead before being put in the water he will float, but if he dies in the water he will sink. We're not sure where this misconception comes from (it sounds like a superstition), but once dead, Fred will sink.

If he is wearing clothing that gives him buoyancy, Fred may sink slowly. However, the usual effect of clothing is to sink the body faster. Either way, how quickly Fred goes down does not depend on how or where he died.

As to how far down Fred will go: he will go to the bottom, however deep that may be, unless he encounters an obstruction or an extraordinarily strong upward current. (Such currents can be found near nuclear power plants.) The deeper Fred goes into the water, the less buoyant he will be. Water pressure increases at the lower depths and compresses residual gases in the stomach and chest cavity.

Once on the bottom, Fred will have truly reached his nadir. Then, as he begins to decompose, the new gases formed in his body will inflate his tissues, and he will begin to rise. Unless he meets an obstruction, he will reach the surface again.

If Fred is thrown into the water during the summer, he will reappear within two or three days. If your story requires his death during the winter, he should not come back up for two or three weeks, depending on how long the cold water retards his decay. (You may choose the length of time.)

Once decomposition starts, the tendency of bodies to float is strong; it's hard to keep a normal body down.

A common error in searches for bodies in the water is to begin looking too far downstream. The surface current of a river is usually much faster than the deeper currents; a body sinks rapidly, usually reaching bottom near where it was last seen. On the riverbed itself there is practically no current at all, so a body there does not move downstream. It follows, then, that Fred should reappear very near where he sank.

If there is no one around when Fred reaches the surface, he will, of course, begin to drift with the current. How far it carries him before he is discovered is a matter of luck — or of plotting.

Going from the larger cities out into the remote rural communities one finds a steadily decreasing percentage of crimes that have to do with money and a proportionate increase in the frequency of sex as a criminal motive.
          Dashiell Hammett, "Memoirs of a Private Detective"

THE CASE OF THE MISSING DOG

In her column in the old *Liberty* magazine, Princess Alexandra Kropotkin gave us this story about the mystery writer S. S. Van Dine.

S. S. Van Dine and Scotty

Mr. Van Dine had a blue-ribbon terrier named Scotty. Scotty ate breakfast with Mr. Van Dine every morning. One morning he didn't show up. Mr. Van Dine went to look for him, and found a man's footprints in the yard. "That man snatched my dog," said Mr. Van Dine.

He measured the footprints to a thousandth of an inch. Took plaster casts of them. Swore he'd catch the thief if it kept him sleuthing until doomsday! Late that afternoon Mr. Van Dine heard a howling and a yowling under his tool shed. Discovered his dog wedged in there hunting a rat.

What about the mysterious footprints in the yard? Mr. Van Dine, by painstaking comparative measurements, determined that they were his own.

IT'S A FALLACY

● A murder victim's last expression — fear, anger, etc. — will be fixed on the face of the corpse.

Death generally produces a relaxation of all muscles. Sometimes a cadaveric spasm may cause something to be tightly clasped in the hand, but facial muscles never spasm at death. The face assumes a completely relaxed appearance.

Melody Ermachild, P.I.

Melody Ermachild is a private investigator.* A slim, attractive, competent, and tough-minded woman, she is a partner in the Oakland firm of Ermachild and Simon. She is one of a new breed of investigators who have

* This material is based on a presentation Melody Ermachild gave to the Northern California chapter of the Mystery Writers of America on December 7, 1985.

never been police officers, having trained first as paralegals and then moved into investigatory work.

The real life of a P.I. is different from mystery novels, movies, and television, Ermachild says. One of the misconceptions mystery writers foster is that private investigators are crime fighters working with the police.

Ermachild has found a very strict dividing line between the police and private investigators who work for the defense. "Cops do not give or share information with P.I.s," she says. "This is a one-way street. The private investigators do provide the police with information, but it is not reciprocated."

A THOROUGHLY FICTIONAL COP

Masao Masuto, E. V. Cunningham's Japanese-American detective, is head of homicide on the Beverly Hills police force. He is presented to us as a cop more sensitive than most, but he is amazingly free from the stress that real police feel. When, upon leaving headquarters one night, a sniper's bullet grazes his cheek, he goes back in, gives a few orders, and gets a bandage. Then he trots right back out into the dark yard without a twitch of fear that the sniper might still be there.

As you'll read in the following paragraphs, having shot a suspect in self-defense does not cause an emotional crisis in his life. But, unlike most fictional cops, he does worry for a couple of hours.

Masuto went into the sun parlor, which he liked to think of as his meditation room. It was cold here, but that was good. It would help him to stay awake. He sat down cross-legged and tried to make his mind empty and calm. But he could not erase Wainwright's words from his mind. They had no evidence to convict Crombie of the murders. . . . In the fraction of the second when Crombie was shooting at him, had he come to a decision to be both judge and jury? Could he have wounded Crombie and

taken him alive? His shoulder was a better target than his head.

But as much as he asked himself the question, he was unable to come up with an answer. The gray light of dawn was in the sky before his mind stilled itself and he stopped asking the question and was finally able to meditate.

It is a good thing that it didn't occur to Masuto during that fraction of a second that, taken alive, Crombie could have been, at minimum, put away for the attempted murder of the detective. The shoulder may be a better target than the head, but a bullet hole in it doesn't necessarily stop someone from pulling that little trigger and blowing an officer away.

From *The Case of the Poisoned Eclairs* by E. V. Cunningham.

Ermachild is definitely not a police-oriented person; she prefers working for defense attorneys. She has been part of the defense teams for John deLorean, the auto maker; Stephen Bingham, the radical lawyer; Felix Mitchell, the Oakland drug dealer; and People's Temple member Larry Layton.

At the time of John deLorean's drug trial, she was employed by Palladino and Sutherland, a San Francisco investigatory firm. With other members of the agency she worked to develop information to impeach an important prosecution witness. DeLorean was found innocent. In the Stephen Bingham murder case, she represented her own agency. Bingham also was found innocent.*

The defense teams that Ermachild is on do not always win. Larry Layton was tried for conspiring to kill Representative Leo Ryan. Ryan was shot to death at the airport in Guyana on the same day that Jim Jones led his congregation in mass suicide and murder. Layton was convicted.†

In the case of Felix Mitchell, her job was to dig up information to show that the prosecution's witnesses were unreliable characters. There was plenty to dig up: many of them were former members of Mitchell's gang who had committed serious crimes, including murder. The prosecution gave them immunity to testify against him. "They [the prosecution] took the

wind out of our sails," Ermachild recalls, by revealing all this information when they put the witnesses on the stand. This effectively prevented the defense from destroying their credibility. She described Mitchell as "arrogant but intelligent, sophisticated, and suave."

She is sometimes asked, "How can you defend all these people?" "I have ethical and moral problems all the time," she says. But her job is not to judge the client, or even to clear him. It is to let the lawyer know the facts of the case, so he or she will know how to plead. She believes in the constitutional right to a fair trial, and that her work protects it by ensuring a good defense for the accused. In addition, she says, "I like to be in the middle of some of the major issues of the day." She has sympathy for the underdog. "I am a bleeding heart underneath," she admits.

In one of her less celebrated cases, a thirteen-year-old girl was accused of murder. Investigating for the defense, Ermachild showed that, for reasons that never became clear, the child was intent on convicting herself. A gifted pathological liar, she had milked details of the crime from the sheriff's deputies who interrogated her and fed the information back to them. Ermachild's evidence cleared the girl.

She is interested in "abuse of force" cases — that is, cases in which people may have suffered wrongful death at the hands of the police. Working on them, she investigates the backgrounds of the accused officers.

She is also interested in resolving what she considers a "new type of crime — the harassment of women." In these cases, where a man's compulsive pursuit of a woman is often dangerous, the legal system cannot provide as

---

* Bingham was accused of murder in the death of convict-author George Jackson. It was alleged that he provided Jackson with a pistol for an attempted escape from San Quentin. Jackson, two other prisoners, and two guards died in a hail of gunfire. Bingham fled the same afternoon. He was brought to trial thirteen years later.

† Layton's first trial ended in a hung jury, his second with a conviction and sentence of life imprisonment. He is seeking a third trial on the grounds that his defense as presented by his lawyers was inadequate and that he is innocent by reason of insanity.

much protection for the victim as is needed. Her own firm has helped a number of women change their identities, so that they have been able to escape harassers and start secure new lives.

Like other private investigators, she does missing-person cases and works for corporations who need low-profile investigations of such crimes as embezzlement. Large companies often find it expedient to track down embezzlers and other thieves without exposing themselves to the publicity that can result from an official police investigation. In such cases, the object is to find the embezzler, stop the crime, and arrange for reimbursement of the company. "The embezzlers are fired, of course."

Is her work dangerous? Yes and no. When people in the ghetto or the underworld find out that she works for defendants, they accept her presence and answer her questions. "I get a lot of information from men who don't take me seriously — that is, I make sexism work for me." But she has also found that people who have information are often quite willing to give it to someone who shows an interest in them and the thing they know about.

In fiction, private investigators handle one case at a time. Ermachild wishes she had that luxury. A lot of the stress in her work comes from juggling as many as thirty cases — and their attendant court dates, motions, hearings, and emergencies.

As an employer herself, she knows what qualities to look for when hiring a private investigator. First, the applicant must be a good writer. Investigators write reports to lawyers, often describing a witness the lawyer won't see until the trial begins. Second, the applicant must have a good, varied background so that he or she can deal successfully with the different types of people encountered on the job. In addition, the applicant must have stamina and curiosity "to the point of voyeurism."

Ermachild's rates are $450 a day, or $50 an hour. For state-financed cases — those in which the state is required to provide investigators for the defendant — she gets a lower rate, except for death penalty cases.

Where will all this lead? "When I grow old," she says, "Miss Marple is my idea of what I would like to be."

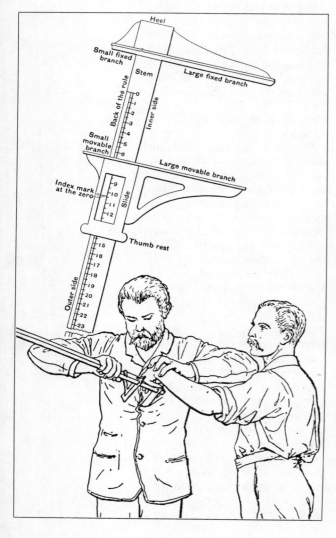

Heel

Small fixed branch

Stem

Large fixed branch

Back of the rule

Inner side

0
1
2
3
4
Small movable branch
5
6

Large movable branch

Index mark at the zero
9
10
11
12

Slide

Thumb rest

15
16
17
18
19
20
21
22
23

Outer side

CANNON FIRE AND LOAVES OF BREAD

There was a long silence, profound and unbroken; then a deep, sullen boom came floating down out of the distance.

"What is it!" exclaimed Joe, under his breath.

"I wonder," said Tom in a whisper.

"'Tain't thunder," said Huckleberry, in an awed tone, "becuz thunder — "

"Hark!" said Tom. "Listen — don't talk."

They waited a time that seemed an age, and then the same muffled boom troubled the solemn hush.

"Let's go and see."

They sprang to their feet and hurried to the shore toward the town. They parted the bushes on the bank and peered out over the water. The little steam ferryboat was about a mile below the village, drifting with the current. Her broad deck seemed crowded with people. There were a great many skiffs rowing about or floating with the stream in the neighborhood of the ferryboat, but the boys could not determine what the men in them were doing. Presently a great jet of white smoke burst from the ferryboat's side, and as it expanded and rose in a lazy cloud, that same dull throb of sound was borne to the listeners again.

"I know now!" exclaimed Tom; "somebody's drownded!"

"That's it!" said Huck; "they done that last summer when Bill Turner got drownded; they shoot a cannon over the water, and that makes him come up to the top. Yes, and they take loaves of bread and put quicksilver in 'em and set 'em afloat, and wherever there's anybody that's drownded, they'll float right there and stop."

"Yes, I've heard about that," said Joe, "I wonder what makes the bread do that."

"Oh, it ain't the bread so much," said Tom; "I reckon it's mostly what they *say* over it before they start it out."

"But they don't say anything over it," said Huck. "I've seen 'em and they don't."

"Well, that's funny," said Tom. "But maybe they say it to themselves. Of *course* they do. Anybody might know that."

The other boys agreed that there was reason in what Tom said, because an ignorant lump of bread, uninstructed by an incantation, could not be expected to act very intelligently when sent upon an errand of such gravity.

"By jings, I wish I was over there, now," said Joe.

"I do too," said Huck. "I'd give heaps to know who it is."

The boys still listened and watched. Presently a revealing thought flashed through Tom's mind, and he exclaimed:

"Boys, I know who's drownded — it's us!"

From *The Adventures of Tom Sawyer* by Mark Twain

PRIVATE DETECTIVES — SNEAKS AND SPIES

Private detectives have not always been universally admired. Even before the Pinkertons and outfits like "Black Jack" Jerome's agency became deeply involved in antiunion work, the private eyes had their critics. This short editorial appeared in the *Oakland Tribune* in 1888 and found its way into one of the old police scrapbooks.

A private detective was arrested in Los Angeles for receiving stolen goods and now lies in jail. It would be a good thing if others of his kind were put behind bars.

The private detective has assumed too great proportions and the times are ripe for him to be pruned and clipped into shape. Not all private detectives are scoundrels, but freed from the strict accountability exacted from the detectives attached to the regular police service they run a great risk of becoming law breakers instead of detectors of law breaking.

Complaint is general all over the country of their practices. In one guise they form an armed body of mercenaries at the command of whomsoever will pay them, and under this cloak they have time and again committed murders.

They are used for digging up evidence in divorce cases and in such matters it is usually expected that they will stop short of subornation of perjury. They are always ready to effect a composition of a felony and they constantly defeat the ends of justice. If detectives are really so greatly needed as would appear from the number of these private agencies the only safe thing to do is to appoint capable men of known good character upon the police force, where they may be amenable to discipline. This having been done it should be declared a felony for a man to poke his nose into other people's business on the plea that he is a private detective, which means in plain English, spy and sneak.

hen a Police Officer Shoots

For a police officer, shooting a criminal is not as simple and clear-cut as in the movies. The movie cop shows he is a sensitive guy by the twitch in his lower eyelid as he presses the trigger. Then he goes about his business. In life, it does not happen that way. Here is the story of one police shooting and its consequences.

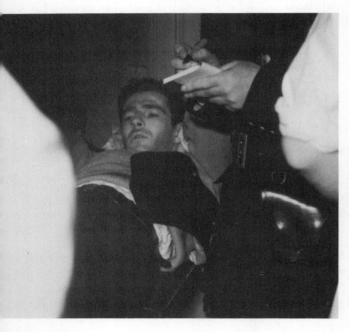

Frank, the officer involved, is a ten-year veteran. A man of good character, he is widely popular with sworn and non-sworn personnel. One night Frank and another officer had parked their patrol cars near a freeway on ramp when a car came speeding by. A girl leaned out the passenger window and screamed for help. The car skidded to a stop, and the driver pushed her out the door. She landed in the gravel at the side of the road, her face bloodied, her clothes torn off. Frank's partner rushed to take care of the victim while Frank set out after the car. The race was on.

After a high-speed chase and pursuit on foot, Frank trapped the man in a cul-de-sac. The man turned toward Frank, with one hand going to his belt as though he were reaching for a gun. So Frank shot him, wounding him. He took him into custody, called an ambulance, and put him in it.

Then Frank threw up.

Police departments recognize the trauma that comes with having shot someone. Officers involved in a shooting have a choice: they can take three days of administrative leave or come back to work the next day. Frank chose to return the next day. "I didn't want to sit around home thinking about it."

It took him a full workday to recover from the nervous shock. "After that, I second-guessed myself thousands of times. I had nightmares and daydreams about it. For months afterward, I had no rest from it."

But that is not the whole story. The arrest led to four years of civil litigation and continuing mental stress and strain for Frank.

Willie, the arrestee, was charged with kidnapping and assault with intent to commit rape. Then Willie's attorney notified the city that he intended to sue the city

NOT SHOOTING

Harvey Schlossberg, an officer in the New York City Police Department, and his partner respond to a potentially nasty call.

From the radio there came word that a man was standing in the middle of East Fourth Street in Brooklyn with a shotgun, refusing to let traffic go through. We parked the car on the corner, seeing a man with a shotgun standing in the middle of the street next to a car.

Tom said, "I'll go down one side of the street, and you go down the other. I'll make a lot of noise to attract his attention. You creep up on him."

Tom distracted the man, who then turned his back on me. I got within six feet of him without his observing me. Then I stepped out, gun drawn, and barked,

"Drop your gun or I'll blow your brains out."

The man turned around, gun still in hand. At that moment, if I had been a really good cop, I probably would have shot him, believing he intended to shoot me. But I didn't shoot. I think perhaps intuitively, I knew he was not a criminal by the expression on his face and the way he held the gun.

He didn't fire either. All he said, to my surprise, was: "I won't drop the gun."

I heard the words come out of my mouth, "Well, then lay it down."

"He stooped and gently laid the gun on the ground. I walked over and picked it up. It was an unloaded shotgun. He could have been shot, perhaps killed, merely for holding an unloaded gun, I thought.

"What are you trying to do?" I asked him.

"I'm glad you finally arrived," he said.

My mouth fell open in surprise. "See that guy?" he said.

He pointed to a second man, one I had not seen, who was cowering nearby. "He sideswiped my new car. I was holding the son of a bitch until the police came."

It had been dangerous for this enraged driver of a sideswiped car to turn on me with a gun in hand, the signal for me to shoot. He was lucky I was such a bad cop.

From *Psychologist with a Gun* by Harvey Schlossberg and Lucy Freeman.

---

and Frank for the injuries done to his client during the arrest. The city offered to settle out of court for $15,000. Willie refused and filed suit for $1 million from the city and $365,000 from Frank.

The city increased its offer to $100,000. Willie turned it down, and the case went to trial in civil court.

Frank felt morally betrayed by the city's policy of trying to buy off the criminal. When he protested the settlement offered to Willie, a city attorney said to him, "Look, it's not your money."

But that was not how Frank saw the issue. He told us, "Although everybody on the department knows you are clean, a settlement offered to a bad guy makes it look to the public as though you had done something wrong. You feel your reputation is hurt."

All criminal circumstances are eliminated from consideration in a civil suit unless the plaintiff or his attorney "opens the door" by referring to some of the plaintiff's criminal behavior or record. Willie's attorney did "open the door" a little bit, but not enough in the judge's opinion. Frank's attorney could not introduce evidence or even mention the fact that while the civil case was proceeding, Willie was simultaneously being tried for kidnapping and attempted rape.

After four weeks of hearings, the jury awarded Willie $102,000 from the city, but nothing from Frank. "When the news of the award hit the front pages, I wanted to go and hide." Frank became disillusioned: the judgment convinced him that the judicial system was not designed for the innocent but was set up for the criminals. "Too many judges are ex–defense lawyers," he said. "The city officials act to lessen their own burden. They don't care about you.

"But you never get beyond the

HOW GOOD A COP ARE YOU? #2

You are patrolling your beat just after sunrise when you see a 1982 Honda parked in a grove of trees just off Frontage Road. You decide to investigate.

As you near the car, you notice what looks like two bullet holes in the door window on the driver's side. Through the window, you see a man in a bathing suit sitting upright behind the wheel. There is dried blood on the left front side of his head, extending down that side of his body and forming a damp pool of blood on the seat.

You examine his body and find that rigor mortis has completely set in. There is a purplish discoloration the full length of the right side of his body. His right hand clutches a gun tightly.

Questions

1. What special police units would you ask the radio dispatcher to send to the scene?
2. Would you search the area for clues or a suspect? If so, what should you look for?
3. Did the man die instantly? Is it possible to tell?
4. Was the gun placed in his hand before or after death? Is it possible to tell?
5. How long has the man been dead?
6. Was the body moved any time after death?

Answers to How Good a Cop Are You? #2

1. A homicide investigator and a criminalist. The coroner will come too, when contacted by the homicide investigator.
2. If you go looking around, you may destroy footprints, tire marks, and other evidence. At the scene of this kind of crime, your main objective is to "freeze" the scene and protect the evidence.
3. The great deal of bleeding you saw indicates that the man lived for some time after having received the wound.
4. A gun cannot be put in a dead man's hand so that it will be clutched tightly.
5. The extensive rigor mortis, which has not begun to pass off, shows that the man has been dead approximately twenty-six to thirty hours.
6. Yes. The purplish discoloration down his right side is postmortem lividity, caused by the settling of blood within the corpse. It indicates that the man had been lying on his right side when he died and had been moved to the sitting position sometime afterward.

incident," Frank said. "It crops up in all sorts of ways. For example, I went to make a loan application, and there it was: 'Have you ever been sued? What was the result?' Also, if you're ever in litigation again, the past will be brought up. The lawyers will look for 'indications that you have a propensity for this violent behavior.'"

The support he got from his fellow officers was another problem. "People were well meaning, and I was kind of a hero — 'Hey, you shot that asshole.' They were supportive because it was a clean shooting. I appreciated their confidence in me, but nobody asked me how I felt.

"Subconsciously, it's always with you," Frank explained. "Your peers don't let you forget about it. They send you clippings on the guy's current activities. You get phone calls at home about Willie whenever he's arrested. You can't tell them to leave it alone, because this is a form of well-meaning peer support. Even district attorneys give me information about him, or call up asking for information about him."

Frank has learned to hide his feelings about the episode so as not to be unfair to the people who supported him. "It is very difficult to deal with the results of your actions, even when you're right. It changes your life. You don't see things the same way you did before."

Willie beat the rap on the kidnap and attempted rape. Frank says, "He lives a charmed life."

**THE
LINEUP**

Alias

"Alias" is the Latin word for "other." As used, it means a name assumed for the sake of deceiving the authorities or potential victims about one's true identity.

Before modern methods of identification became widespread, an alias was much more useful to a criminal confronting the police than it is now. Criminals went to great lengths to keep their real names a secret. One good reason for this was to escape the harsher sentences given to repeat offenders. In 1908, for example, Ernest Reese was arrested and convicted for robbery in Oakland. His rap sheet shows that he used two aliases — one a minor modification of his given name, "Edward Reese" rather than Ernest, and the other completely different, "Edward Johnson." It is interesting that he used "Edward" in both, though. He had already done two terms in San Quentin, one under his own name and the other as "Edward Johnson." Whether it was the Bertillon system or his fingerprints that gave him away or whether he copped out under interrogation is not noted on his arrest record. In any event, the poor devil went back to San Quentin under his own name. The judge gave him ten years.

Confidence operators, prostitutes, and other small-time criminals still find it helpful to use a "street name" in dealing with marks and tricks. The alias may delay pursuit long enough for them to make a clean getaway. If a suspect is stopped by the police, the alias may help him avoid arrest on an outstanding warrant for an earlier crime or obtain lower bail than he would otherwise be entitled to.

Not every assumption of a false name is necessarily for bad purposes. For example, by adopting an incognito, a well-known person may conceal his or her real identity under an unobtrusive name to ensure privacy. Perhaps incognitos were used more often in the days before photographs were spread far and wide by mass communications, when a simple change of name could let a king pass as a mere duke. Nowadays it would be difficult for Elizabeth Taylor to pass as "Betsy Smith" without a disguise of some sort.

Whether the pen names of mystery writers are aliases or incognitos is a tough question. Some prolific writers adopt pseudonyms in order not to glut the market with stories under their own names or in order to write something other than what their genre audience expects. Others do it to protect their positions in the literary world as "serious" writers.

John Dickson Carr followed a common procedure for an alias when he chose his pen name inverting his real name and coming up with "Carter Dickson." Not many writers do this, however. Agatha Christie was also "Mary Westmacott"; Erle Stanley Gardiner, "A. A. Fair"; Gore Vidal, "Edgar Box"; C. Day Lewis,

"Nicholas Blake"; and David Cornwall is "John le Carré."

Branko Bokun, the Yugoslavian writer, was a connoisseur of aliases. During World War II he was in Rome as an official representative of the Yugoslavian Red Cross. Unofficially he was an agent of the London-based Yugoslavian government in exile. He ran a small spy ring that, among other useful activities, helped to smuggle Allied soldiers and other hunted people out of Italy. In his memoir, *Spy in the Vatican*, he published this extract from his journal, dated September 26, 1943:

Doling out false documents to the escaped prisoners-of-war was a daring experience to begin with, but after a while it became everyday routine. Illegal actions, like swear words, lose their impact through repetition. We were amused watching the prisoners choosing their Italian names, professions and birthdates.

The English used to Italianize their own name. John Russell, for instance, became Giovanni Rosselli, and Patrick Brown, Bruno Patrizi.

The American prisoners would choose the great names of the Mafia and the most popular Christian name among them was Angelo.

The Russians and Yugoslavs usually decided on the name of an Italian they knew personally, many even taking the name of the head of their ex–prison camp.

Most of the French prisoners wanted to call themselves Garibaldi, others d'Annunzio, Pirandello or Dante, and a few da Vinci.

The Jews used to translate their names literally into Italian. If this was not possible, they would pick either a name from the Roman aristocracy, or the name of a famous person such as Gigli, Caruso, or Valentino. One wanted to call himself Pacelli, and two even suggested

Mussolini! It had proved very difficult to dissuade them.

Even more fascinating was hearing the prisoners stating their age and choosing their new professions. Men up to the age of forty-five would stick to their genuine date of birth. After that, the older they were, the more years they broke off. The woman, before answering, would all say: "Let's see," then after a pause, suggest an age adding coquettishly: "All right?" Oddly enough no one ever changed their actual birthday. It was the one thing that every prisoner wanted to cling to.

In the choice of profession, apart from the English who mostly stuck to their own, the rest would ponder intently before deciding. The Americans usually chose either a university student or a business man, according to their age. The French wanted to be authors or journalists. The Yugoslavs generally decided on school teachers, the Russians, actors, and the Jews mainly plumped for the profession of a musician or an antique dealer.

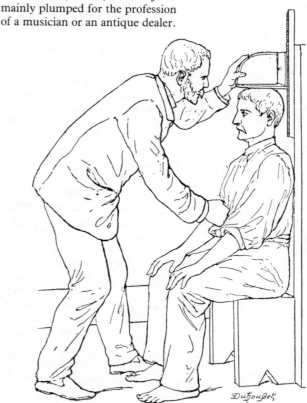

Criminal Argot

Our dictionary defines "argot" as "a secret language or conventional slang particular to groups of thieves, tramps, or vagabonds." Today this type of slang is called street talk. It changes rapidly because it is a set of passwords by means of which small-time crooks identify themselves to each other. Sometimes a phrase will make its way from the street into the general vocabulary; for example, "dough" originally meant stolen money. But the vast majority of these coinages have their day and disappear without a trace. Ben Jonson's wonderful *Bartholomew Fair* is a feast of Elizabethan thieves' argot, but scholars still do not know the meanings of some of the terms used by the play's cutpurses and pickpockets.

The terms come and go, but the need for a "private" language persists. In 1893, an *Oakland Tribune* reporter wrote, "All old policemen know of these expressions, more or less, and many of them have unconsciously fallen into the habit of using them when dealing with the lower stratum, where their duties most frequently lie."

What was true then is true now. Street talk is used by the streetwise, those who think of themselves as in on something hidden from the squares. There is, ultimately, something sad about even the most vivacious street talk: when you have learned it, you still don't know very much. The streetwise are mostly losers.

Detective Tom Downey made an interesting collection of thieves' argot in the 1890s. A few of the words in his collection have passed into general use, but most are quaintly obsolete.

Synonyms for a police officer included "spot," "shadow," and "fox." Thieves were "knucks," "guns," and "hoisters." A forger was a "scratcher," a jewelry thief as "pennyweighter," and a safe cracker an "iron worker." Pickpockets are still occasionally called "dips," but why a pickpocket who specialized in robbing women would have been called a "male buzzer" is a mystery.

Watching for a victim was "piping off." Feeling a victim's pockets from the outside was "fanning," but when the victim was searched for money, he was "whisked." A good haul was a "century" (obviously, one hundred dollars). Stealing a watch was "forking a super."

Before going on a job, a robber might stop at "a lushing tub" (a saloon) for some "nerve tonic" (whiskey). Robbing a bank was described as "touching a jug," and the stolen money was "sugar" or "swag." When the loot (or "whack") was hidden, it was "planted," and so going back for it was "springing a plant."

When the hoister had to flee the scene quietly, this was "padding the hoof." But if his getaway

THE STORY OF A GOLD BRICK

"Gold brick" used to mean a brick or bar of gold, sold by a swindler to a victim, to whom was delivered a spurious brick or some substitute for the real one; from there it went on to mean "anything purchased as valuable which proves to be almost or quite valueless." This meaning of the term has largely passed out of use, and nowadays "goldbrick" is used only descriptively of a malingering worker.

One reason the meaning changed is that stagecoaches no longer carry shipments of gold down from the mines in the western mountains, and we don't see gold bars anymore.

Here is a classic confidence game, pulled off in San Francisco in the late 1880s and reported in the *San Francisco Examiner* — a gold brick scam in which the psychological preparation of the mark was carried out brilliantly.

J. B. Miller, alias W. B. Shaw, an elderly man of respectable appearance, was arrested this after-noon by Detective John Coffey and booked at the City Prison on a charge of grand larceny. Miller is a gold brick swindler, and on July 20 last he swindled J. V. Hull, a carpenter at 837 Geary Street, out of $250. Miller had been hanging around the carpenter shop for several weeks, and to Hull he told a story of having served a term in the Nevada Penitentiary for killing a man. He claimed to have acted in self-defense, but a brother of the victim had vowed to kill him. For that reason he was not content, as he expected to be shot at any moment, as his nemesis was on his track.

Miller said that while he was in the penitentiary a dying convict told him where a gold brick stolen in an express robbery was buried. Miller said that he had dug the brick up and was anx-ious to find a purchaser for it. Hull did not want to make an investment in the brick, but he extended to Miller his earnest sympathy. Miller was a frequent visitor at the shop, and on the morning of the 20th of last July he rushed in and informed Hull that he had to flee from the city as the brother of the dead man was on his track. He had no money, but he felt certain that Hull would advance him $250 until he could redeem the brick. Hull fell into the trap, parted with his coin and received in return a solid brass brick.

Miller fled from here that night and did not return until yesterday, when he registered at a downtown hotel as J. B. Miller of Boston. When he was here before he was known to the police under the name of Shaw. The prisoner was accompanied by a rather pretty woman who says she is his wife. She claims to have married him recently in New York.

The prisoner is well known to the police here, and twenty years ago was at the head of an organized gang of sure thing gamblers and confidence men.

was unsuccessful, he found himself "pinched" (still used today), "jugged" (ditto), "pulled," or "tumbled."

When the robber was taken off to jail, he was brought to the "cooler," a word that is still used sometimes. He would appear before a judge or, in an odd holdover from the eighteenth century, "beak." The prosecutor was "the mouthpiece," which, in an interesting reversal, now refers to the defendant's attorney. If he could afford a lawyer, he might get "out on hocus-pocus" (released on a writ of habeas corpus). But eventually he would be tried and "get the black gown" (be sentenced).

Sometimes old terms make a comeback. In recent years Oakland drug dealers have taken to calling addicts "dope fiends." Whereas this phrase originally expressed the fear and revulsion ordinary people felt for addicts, the dealers use it to show their contempt for their customers.

For a police officer, it is important to be aware of street language because of what it may tell about the person who uses it — for instance, it can help an officer distinguish a real hoodlum from an inexperienced youngster who is into something over his head. For obvious reasons, it can be critically important for undercover officers not to make mistakes with the argot.

Because being streetwise is a professional qualification for communicating with drug dealers (judges expect officers to know the terms), we put a list of slang in a piece we did on narcotics for the Oakland police — with the warning that much of it would soon be obsolete. After it was published, one of the vice officers told me they had a good laugh over it.

Modus Operandi

"M.O." is an abbreviation for "modus operandi" or "method of operation." The phrase refers to a pattern of repetitious behavior in the commission of crimes. If, for example, in ten burglaries in the same neighborhood, the houses were always entered through the kitchen window at about three o'clock in the morning while the occupants were out of town, and television sets and VCRs were the only objects taken, the burglaries would have the same M.O. The police would have reason to think the same person had committed all ten crimes.

If such a series of burglaries were committed in a city patrolled by a department that keeps an M.O. file, and there were no suspects, any efficient detective would look through the file. If it contained any record of a burglar whose method fitted this pattern, that burglar would become the prime suspect in the case. He would be watched very carefully.

When it is practical to do so, police departments keep M.O. files. They have found over the years that criminals stick with an M.O. even after it has tripped them up more than once. Departments that do not keep written files rely on the knowledge beat officers and detectives acquire about who the bad guys are on their turf. In a manner of speaking, they carry informal M.O. files in their memories.

In Oakland, burglary is extremely common but rarely marked by a distinctively personal touch. It would be poor practice for the burglary detail to maintain a written M.O. file because of the vast time it would take to prepare the records. Most of the material would soon be obsolete and knowledge of it useless. This is due to the nature of the crime. Most burglars there are so poor they rarely get out of their own neighborhoods. A lot of them are kids who can't drive yet. Consequently, a burglary is often a "neighborhood crime," and a lot of people think they know who did it. (They frequently do.) At any rate, a burglar who operates in one sector of the city rarely crosses over into another.

But there are places where burglary is sufficiently uncommon that it makes good sense to keep

M.O. files and to convene burglary investigators from neighboring departments from time to time to share information on current offenders.

M.O.s persist because committing a real crime for the first time is a major formative experience for the neophyte criminal. After he overcomes his conscience and his fears, does the deed, and gets away safely, he is elated. He has hit upon a smart way of committing the crime, whatever it may be — burglary, robbery, rape. From then on, he commits the crime over and over again in exactly the same way until his method becomes a unique signature. The working criminal always feels fear and anxiety, but a good M.O. holds those feelings at bay. When it is reinforced by success, the M.O. seems to take the risk out of the crime. This is important, because, far from seeking adventure, what the criminal wants is safety, ease, reliability, and profit.

After he has been arrested, the criminal will frequently talk a blue streak about his crimes and how cleverly he carried them out. When Black Bart told Harry Morse in copious detail about how he robbed Wells Fargo, he was simply conforming to this pattern. It is partly a way of obtaining relief from pent-up anxiety and partly a way of letting the coppers know that, even though they caught him, he is still a pretty smart guy.

As an interrogation proceeds, detectives often strike up a friendly relationship with the suspect. When the confession is complete, it seems natural to the suspect to continue talking. And so he tells the attentive detectives all he knows about how to commit his particular type of crime. Law enforcement agencies sometimes make videotapes of these arias and use them as training material. The suspects are usually flattered to be asked to participate in making the film. These outpourings in the aftermath of arrest are very similar to the closing chapters of mystery novels where the murderer explains what he did and why.

IT'S A FALLACY

● **Expert burglars open combination safes by the feel of the dial and by listening for the tumblers to fall.**

This is the type of thing that people believe because someone they've heard of — usually a friend of their brother-in-law's ex-wife — actually knew of a case of this kind of safecracking. But for practical purposes, burglars open safes in the following ways:

By finding a safe improperly closed — as when the dial is given only a half turn, to make for easier opening in the morning. The burglar has only to turn the dial until the door will open.

By finding the combination in a handy place, such as pasted inside an account book or a desk drawer.

By knocking off the dial and pushing the lock inside with a punch.

By pulling the lock out with a device like an automotive wheel puller.

By drilling the door to expose the tumblers and manually align them.

By peeling the plates off the door and prising the locking bolts back.

By ripping through the top, bottom, or sides of the safe with an ax, chisel, or metal cutter.

By burning through the safe with an oxyacetylene torch or a thermal burning bar.

By blowing the safe up with nitroglycerine or another explosive.

*T*WO

Searches

Search and seizure is one of the most complex and changeable areas of modern criminal law. Mistakes here get cases thrown out on constitutional grounds. When the courts are really active, the rules change quickly — almost, it seems, from week to week. However, the following search has always been illegal, a violation of the Fourth Amendment. The participants in this implausible episode, from Bartholomew Gill's *McGarr on the Cliffs of Moher*, are Chief Inspector McGarr of the Garda Soichana, the Irish police, and Captain Simonds of the NYPD:

At the door to May Quirk's apartment Simonds asked, "Can you pick it?"

There were few locks McGarr couldn't. "Think so."

"Good. I'm going to walk up the hall and around the corner so when I return I'll find the door open. Paddy, you're my witness." Mc-

SEARCH AND SEIZURE IN THE OLD DAYS

This short article from the *Oakland Tribune* of May 11, 1888, was posted in the inspectors' scrapbook for the time.

A bright Oakland sun was sending its direct rays down on the City Hall plaza and on the white City Hall itself, standing by the side of the grassy park. The white glare outside of the hall threw the iron barred entrance of the city prison into blackness. It was little use to try to penetrate with the eye the iron gateway.

Inside there is nothing so dreadful. There are no clanking chains, nor whipping posts. There is a little desk on which rests the register of the prison. Behind the desk is a table, at which sat Police Clerk Downey and Prison Keeper Rand, looking out of the windows at the park watching the pretty nurse girls wheel their infantile charges around under the old oak trees. It was a dull afternoon on police. It was too early for the reporters for the morning papers to be around and too late for the reporters on the evening papers, and the register showed nothing but a succession of wretched drunks.

"Perhaps you may think that the police are infallible," said Tom Downey as he lit a cigarette and strolled to the door to take a look outside, "but we sometimes get very badly left.

"It's well I remember one Sunday morning in 1881. It was July 1st, and the sun was bright and warm. Captain Pumyea was Captain of Police in those days, too, and Holland and I were doing detective duty. The church bells were ringing out their last call to church, and we were all standing around watching the people in their 'Sunday-go-to-meeting' clothes, when a man without a hat and with his hair disheveled came rushing up Washington street.

"He wanted Captain Pumyea, and told him a tale of woe. He had spent the night in the Buswell House, and when he retired the night before, he had $80 in gold in his pocket. In the morning he hadn't a cent, and he suspected some young ladies who had a room next to his. Bortree, Clerk of the Police Court, was just going to church, and we got him to swear out a search warrant, and Holland and I went down and turned the poor girls out while we searched the room, but no $80 was found.

"Suddenly the loser of the money, who had been sitting in a corner bewailing his sad fate, grew almost black in the face, and putting his hand into the watch pocket of his trousers drew forth $80 in gold, just where he had put it and just where he had forgotten to look. We tore up the warrants, apologized to the girls, and missed church that morning."

Garr watched Simonds saunter up the hall. The way he put his feet down, he probably never wore out a shoe.

The apartment wasn't empty.

An old woman, her gray hair braided and piled on top of her head, stood in front of them. A Mauser automatic no different from those McGarr had recently dealt with in Ireland was pointed at his chest. "Come in and shut the door."

Oops! They really should have gone to get a warrant.

And here is a comment from the squad room, in Hillary Waugh's *"30" Manhattan East*:

"Watch the TV, Frank. You can find out what police work is all about."

"Yeah," Ecklin agreed. "See how they win for a change."

Sessions snorted. "The last television mystery I saw had this private detective breaking into the bad guy's apartment to get evidence. He gets caught in the act, shoots it out with the bad guy and kills him. That's a first-degree homicide rap, right? But does our private detective go to the chair? Like hell. In the last scene he's drinking it up with a cop pal of his down in a Greenwich Village dive. Case solved." He laughed. "Television? Jesus."

Assault and Battery

Suppose I didn't like your face. Suppose I picked up my handy tennis racket, and, saying "You old so-and-so, I'm going to rearrange the relationship of your nose to your mouth," I raised the racket over my head and took a swipe at you.

Suppose I missed.

I would be guilty of assault. I was guilty as soon as I raised the weapon, even if I never got as far as a swipe. It is the threatening movement or the initiation of an attack that is the assault.

Suppose I didn't miss, funny face.

I would be guilty of assault *and*

battery. Battery begins when the blow lands. Since I can't actually strike you without initiating the attack, every battery includes an assault.

Suppose I had something more in mind then redoing your face. Suppose I raised that racket to rob you, rape you, murder you, or entertain myself in some other illegal way.

I would be guilty of aggravated assault. My intention to commit a further crime is the aggravating part. It would also be an aggravated assault if I assaulted you with a deadly weapon, such as a gun, an ax, or a '57 Pontiac, even if all I wanted to do was scare you a bit.

Guilty I may be, but not in the eyes of the law until I have been tried and found guilty. You've got two chances at me. You can take me to civil court to sue me for injury. And the D.A. can prosecute in criminal court for the injury done to the public.

Combat Rules

Professions are, from one angle, shared bodies of knowledge. Looked at this way, they are characterized by systematic research and the publication of the results, so that all the members of the profession benefit from increases in knowledge. By these standards, crime doesn't really qualify as a profession. Its practitioners rarely write down what they know. When we speak of a "professional" criminal, we are using the word rather loosely.

In the 1960s in California, an atypical crook was captured after a gunfight with police. When the officers searched him, they found a small spiral-bound notebook in his pocket in which he had written his own methods for committing successful crimes. A practical document, it is not quite what one would expect from Simon Templar.

The following are the "combat rules" this robber had written down for his own guidance and apparently had followed successfully on some occasions (though not at the time of his capture).

A. Taking concealment forces an opponent to seek, thus making him subject to ambush or surprise action.

B. Use cover for protection and also to confuse the opponent as to the next point from which attack will come.

C. A post provides cover but no safe route of departure.

D. In occupied rooms consider using people as a deterrent to the opponent's gunfire.

E. A gunman can draw and fire at a moving target while a man moves 15 feet from a standstill.

F. Before entering a building, know all possible exits and the concealment and cover adjacent to each.

G. If pursued in car, make right turn and stop on left side of street. Get out quick and use door or parked car for cover.

H. On a divided highway pull over to the right as far as possible and near a spot with cover close by. Stop and get out the right door.

I. On other highways, pull over to the left, unlatching door before stopping.

J. Remember that a shot to wound is less danger to him than to you.

K. Police are trained to take less than natural regard for their personal safety when in pursuit of a suspect.

L. Don't grab a hostage, persuade him.

M. Combat means to escape under the possibility of exchange of gunfire; therefore:

1. If indoors, get outdoors.
2. Can the building be effectively surrounded?
3. Commandeer a car for getaway (filling station, stop signal, market parking lot).
4. The only effective defense against radio is to move fast, in an unpredictable course, and use only those areas where support is scarce, or access is hindered.
5. The only safe area is one that cannot effectively be surrounded by the police available.

Gunfire —
at
Automobiles

In life as in fiction, police officers often try to stop a fleeing suspect by shooting at the getaway car. To measure the effectiveness of such gunfire, the Sheriff's Department of Janesville, Wisconsin, conducted some tests in 1963 with rifles, pistols, and shotguns. The results of their work are still valid. They may be interesting to keep in mind as you watch television police shooting at cars to bring them to a halt.

We will give the results of their tests for a .38 caliber revolver loaded with regular ammunition,

since police officers and private detectives often carry this weapon. The target was a 1950 sedan. All shots were fired parallel to the ground.

Test 1. Shot fired at the front door from a distance of ten yards. The bullet penetrated only the exterior metal. It did not enter the interior of the car because of obstructions inside the door (braces, window, door-operating mechanism, armrest, and interior upholstery).

Test 2. Shot fired at the trunk from a distance of twenty-five yards. The bullet passed through the trunk, struck the back of the rear seat backrest, and was stopped by a brace.

Test 3. Shot fired at a tire from a distance of twenty-five yards. The bullet made a hole the size of a tenpenny nail and caused the tire to deflate in about two minutes.

Test 4. Two shots fired at the

"Highway Patrol officers check patrol car windows after gunman wounded 4 people with glass fragments." The gunman used a high-powered rifle.

Chris Hardy, *San Francisco Examiner*

rear window from a distance of twenty-five yards, with the window being mounted at a 45-degree angle to the ground. Neither shot penetrated the window. Each ricocheted upward, struck the molding, and then ricocheted again, up and away. The shots frosted the window with fine fracture lines so that no one could see through it.

If you find yourself disappointed by these results, you have had exactly the same reaction as the Janesville Sheriff's Department. The officers who conducted the test were "alarmed at the lack of authority of the .38 caliber revolver." They found that the .38 was ineffective against an automobile and that the ricochets from the gunfire would create more risk to bystanders than the original flight paths of the bullets would to the felons fleeing in the car. (The danger presented by a ricochet is insufficiently recognized by writers as a reason for *not* shooting and as a cause of injuries not intended by the shooter.) The officers concluded that if the purpose of the shooting is to stop the car, then the driver should be the target. In such instances, "there must be justification for killing the driver, along with any other person in the vehicle at the time."

If the Janesville tests were repeated today, the results would be essentially the same. It is even possible that with "controlled expansion" ammunition, the .38 and .357 pistols would show even less penetrating power, since the energy of the new rounds dissipates so quickly on impact.

How to Search for Bombs

In real life, if Joe knows there is a bomb hidden in someone's house, the best thing he can do is get the person off the premises as quickly as possible. Then he should call the police from a pay phone a safe distance away. But if you're writing a story, you may want Joe to search for the bomb himself. This is how he should go about it.

First, Joe should search alone. If he makes a mistake, he has no justification for blowing up some one else with him. This remains true even if he has a companion who is willing to help. But if they're both going to search, they should do so separately, in different parts of the building.

As he searches, Joe must move with extreme caution. Nitroglycerine is very unstable and can easily be set off by knocking something over. Before entering a room, Joe must pause at the door and listen for noise from a time bomb. Once inside, he must move about as little as possible and make a visual search. He should repeat the same pattern of observation in each room. First, he should look from floor level to the height of his waist; then from hip to eye level and from eye level to the ceiling; finally, the ceiling itself and its fixtures — lights, false ceilings, heating outlets.

HIGH PROTECTION BOMBTHREAT SUIT

Benefits: Offers extended high level protection against fragments for all vital organs in survivable blast environments. Allows maximum mobility. Allows quick donning and doffing by one man.

Technical Data: Material: composite glass, reinforced plastic, laminate and ballistic nylon. Weight: approximately 40 pounds. May be worn in full or partial configuration to suit tactical situations.

Application: Bomb disposal. Gun battles. Barricaded suspects. Sniper situations.

Price — PA800 High protection Bomb Suit $615.00
Price — PA810 High Mobility Bomb Suit
    (includes PA-752 Face Shield) 710.00

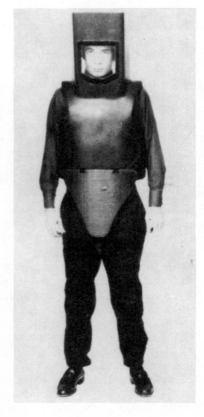

As Joe moves his eyes over the various surfaces, he should watch for different types of hiding places in which bombs can be placed. Drawers, chairs, sofas, beds, loose or raised boards, and stairwell steps can conceal bombs that will explode when an item is moved, sat on, or stepped on. All windows, cupboard doors, and doorknobs must be examined carefully for trip wires before being opened.

Unopened mail should also be looked at. A package bomb is usually about the size of a shoe box. A letter bomb is heavier and bulkier than an ordinary letter. It will weigh from two to five ounces and be rigid at the center, where the pressure-release mechanism that triggers it is located.

Of course, Joe's problems really begin when he finds the bomb.

Two Drug Dealers

This is the story of two Oakland drug dealers, Frank Ragusa and Felix Mitchell. So far as we know they never met, but they both made a lot of money and both were murdered. Frank was twenty-nine at the time of his death, and Felix only two years older. Frank Ragusa was white, a lone wolf, an international operator. He sold LSD and marijuana to the very rich as well as to the merely prosperous. Felix Mitchell was black, and he sold heroin to all comers, but especially to poor people in the ghetto.

Ragusa grew up in New York and came to California in the early 1970s to study at the University of California in Berkeley. Within a year or two he left school and began to make serious money dealing LSD. He soon became a multimillionaire and, with Jennifer, his young wife, moved out of Berkeley's student district into a secluded, high-security hillside home in Oakland's exclusive Montclair District.

To cover his drug dealing and the traveling it required, Ragusa had two fronts, an oriental rug business and a rare book business. He posed as a patron of the arts — this made his case notable at the beginning — funding "little magazines" and other low-profit artistic enterprises. Apparently he en-joyed having writers, artists, and musicians as friends and customers. Not all of his friends were obscure. One of the Rolling Stones gave him a gold record and autographed it for him. Ragusa hung it on the wall in his living room, like a painting.

At the height of his success Ragusa invited Larry Reilly, a boyhood friend from New York, to join him in California. He and Reilly were the same age and had been very close in high school. Ragusa still thought of him as someone special. Normally very suspicious of people, Ragusa trusted Reilly, gave him gifts, and welcomed him into his home.

But Reilly did not prosper in California. He had difficulty holding jobs in construction work. Reilly began to feel his life was not working out. He became depressed and intensely jealous of Frank's success. Instead of selling drugs, Reilly began to use them — heavily. By late 1977, he had begun to show signs of the paranoia that a heavy habit can induce. He went around telling people that Frank Ragusa wanted to kill him.

On January 25, 1978, Frank Ragusa, his wife Jennifer, and his sister Mariane were found murdered in an orgy of berserk violence. Frank had been stabbed twenty-seven times, Jennifer eighteen times, and Mariane six times. (Mariane, an innocent bystander, was only twenty-one and just visiting her brother.) Near Frank's body there was an open, empty safe.

The police conducted a careful search for evidence. The discovery of a bloodstained envelope by Rick Ehle, an evidence technician, was

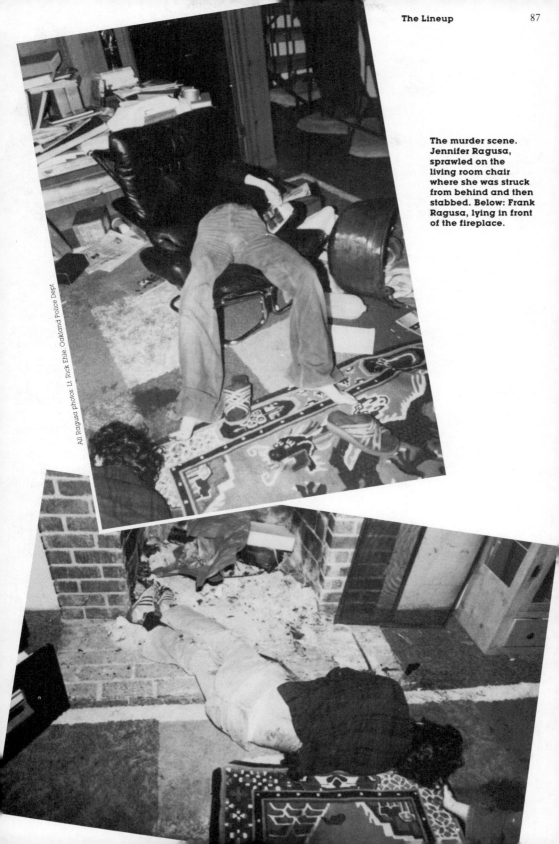

The murder scene. Jennifer Ragusa, sprawled on the living room chair where she was struck from behind and then stabbed. Below: Frank Ragusa, lying in front of the fireplace.

All Ragusa photos: Lt. Rick Ehle, Oakland Police Dept.

The evidence that led to Reilly's undoing: he left a fingerprint in the blood on this envelope.

the clue that broke the case. On one of the stains there was a clear fingerprint. The blood matched Frank Ragusa's, and the fingerprint had been made by Larry Reilly.

When the criminologists applied a sophisticated method of analysis to the bloodstains in the house, they found, in addition to the blood shed by the Ragusas, a few small drops of blood that matched Reilly's. Luck was with them. The genetic markers in Reilly's blood are found in only 1.2 percent of the population.

Of Ragusa's real business there was a superabundance of evidence. The investigators found a box containing 192,000 LSD tabs. Jennifer Ragusa's Oldsmobile was missing, and when patrol officers found it in East Oakland, where it had been abandoned, there were 150 pounds of top-quality marijuana in the trunk. An informer told them that the empty safe usually contained at least $50,000.

The investigators got a search warrant for Larry Reilly's cottage. There they found bloodstained clothing and some of Ragusa's stolen money. It was easy to conclude that Reilly and one or more

accomplices had killed all three Ragusas. Although convicted of the killings, Reilly has never confessed, so there are some loose ends to the case. His alleged accomplices still remain free, and whether robbery was the motive has never been established.

Frank Ragusa was a very discreet dealer. He did not hang around with known criminals. He had never come to the attention of the police. Unraveling his activities led Oakland detectives into joint investigations with Scotland Yard, the West German police, and Interpol.

If Ragusa was a man who wanted wealth and anonymity, Felix Mitchell enjoyed being a high-profile dealer.

Mitchell grew up in San Antonio Village, an East Oakland housing project. He dropped out of high school and by the time he was twenty earned a record as a petty criminal. Despite such an unpromising beginning, he became the first big-time dope dealer to emerge from Oakland's black community. He achieved a level of notoriety some mistook for celebrity.

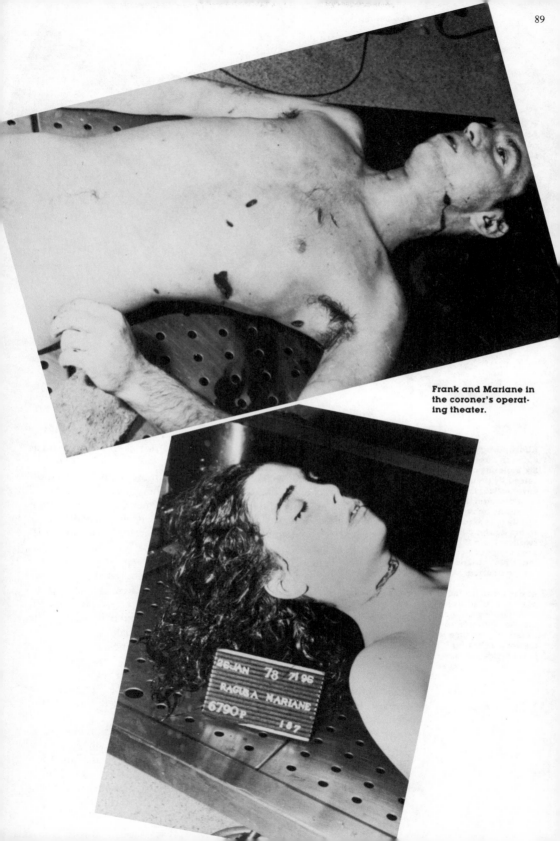

Frank and Mariane in the coroner's operating theater.

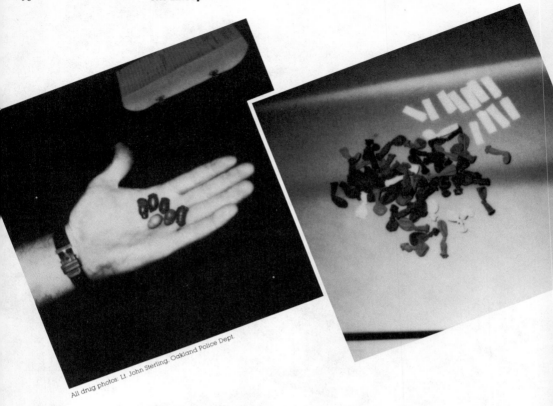

All drug photos: Lt. John Sterling, Oakland Police Dept.

Above: Drugs confiscated in East Oakland: Six balloons of heroin seized by an undercover officer in a buy-bust program. Heroin is usually packaged in tightly rolled balloons, so the dealer can swallow them if he sees the police coming. Note evidence envelope at upper right.

Above right: Balloons of heroin, bindles of cocaine. The balloons are flat, rather than rolled up, because the dealer was hiding them inside his shoes.

In the early 1970s, he and two buddies organized the 69th Avenue Mob and set about changing the narcotics racket in Oakland. The Mob was something different. Felix Mitchell's world was one of constant killings, beatings, and drive-by shootings. Murder and intimidation were his sources of power; fear was a protection for him and his gang. The Mob's shooters carried military carbines, setting a new, high standard for firepower among drug dealers. (Once started, this snowballed. Nowadays, Oakland dealers often carry Uzis, Israeli army submachine guns. They do a lot of shooting and kill a lot of innocent bystanders. They don't care.)

An especially repulsive aspect of Mitchell's operation was its exploitation of children. He hired ten- and twelve-year-olds as spotters to warn of approaching police officers. For this they were paid as much as $400 a week. This was infinitely more than McDonald's or any other honest work would pay them when they became teenagers, and it was usually more than their parents could earn at legitimate jobs. When the Mob was really humming, it provided the kids with careers in crime.

Just as Dickens's Fagin cultivated the lost children of London, Mitchell presented himself to the children of Oakland's housing projects as a benefactor. He gave them rides in his cars, took them on trips, and provided free ice cream during the summer. No wonder they were glad to see him coming.

As part of its merchandising, the Mob occupied housing projects. They began with San Antonio Village and then moved on to others. The projects were con-

verted into secure spaces for dealing drugs. The residents were left in no doubt as to what was expected of them if they wanted to remain healthy. So, in addition to corrupting the children, Mitchell made the adults live in fear.

The strategy was to sell dope as though it were fast food and to prevent law enforcement from interfering. Spotters on the streets and on the rooftops of the projects made sure there were no police around to see the sales; when they did turn up, the dealing stopped. This prevented raids and on-view arrests. Once the addict got inside the right building, an "inspector," a gang member not holding dope, made him show his needle tracks; this kept undercover officers out. Then the addict moved on to the "collector," who took his money, and the "spitter" or dealer, who passed him the drug. Often the

heroin, tightly wrapped in a balloon, would be dropped to him from a third-floor window through a length of garden hose. The addict would never actually see the person who gave him the dope.

Felix Mitchell's heyday was from 1976 to 1983, about eight years. At its peak, his gang comprised about two hundred people. It supplied addicts from the entire East Bay region — East and West Oakland, Berkeley, Richmond, Castro Valley — and for a time even sold drugs ninety miles away, in Sacramento. Nobody knows how much dope Mitchell and the Mob sold. But they made a *lot* of money. One reasonable estimate placed their share of Oakland's "retail drug business" at a quarter of a billion dollars a year.

The ubiquity of the dealers, their violence, their crimes, and the atmosphere of fear they cre-

Above left: A suitcase of marijuana. The large bags sold for $150, the smaller ones for $5. The pistol is a .32 caliber, and beside the suitcase is a balloon of heroin and a bindle of cocaine.

Above: Forty-eight balloons of heroin with cash.

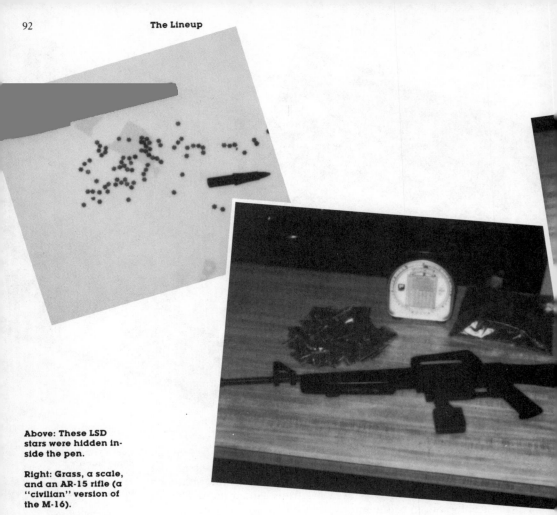

Above: These LSD stars were hidden inside the pen.

Right: Grass, a scale, and an AR-15 rifle (a "civilian" version of the M-16).

DEALER TALK

Here, for what it's worth, is some of the language currently in use among narcotics users and dealers on the street in Oakland. Some are standard terms and have been with us for five or six years. Some are fading. Others are new, with who knows what life expectancy? They may outlast any number of dealers and addicts.

Bag — the amount of a drug packed in a balloon or a bindle; a nickel bag ($5), a dime bag ($10), a quarter bag ($25)

Baskin-Robbins — a quantity of heroin measured out in a small plastic spoon from an ice cream store

Boy — heroin

China White — white heroin from Asia or, recently, a synthetic heroin of the same color

Cook up — prepare heroin for injection by heating and melting it in water

Cut — dilute a drug to a desired strength

Do up — inject drugs

Donkey — someone who transports drugs for a dealer

Girl — cocaine

Hit — to inject a drug; to murder someone

Hype — an addict

Jones — a severe (heavy) habit

Rollers — patrol cars driven by uniformed officers

Rabbit — the person who samples drugs for a dealer

Snitch — informer

Tracks — scars from needle use

Wired — under the influence

ated led the people to demand that something be done about Felix and his competitors. Even Oakland politicians realized that they had to go.

It took a combined city, state, and federal operation to bring down Felix Mitchell.* When he fell, eighteen of the leaders and principal figures in his gang were also indicted by the federal government. Many of the small fry — including the children — were arrested and convicted in the local courts.

Mitchell was found guilty on federal charges of "operating a continuing criminal enterprise," conspiring to operate a drug ring, and tax evasion. He was sentenced

to life in prison without the possibility of parole and sent to Leavenworth.

After his conviction it was said that he began dealing in prison. Reportedly, when one customer failed to pay for ten dollars' worth of dope, Felix negotiated with another prisoner to act as his enforcer. The customer got wind of this and stabbed Felix ten times, killing him. He had been in prison less than a year.

Putting Felix and his major rivals away did not put an end to the drug scene in Oakland. His example continued to cast a spell over young kids. One morning an officer told us he was going to the juvenile division to "pick up a bad boy."

"How bad is he?" we asked jokingly.

"Very bad," the cop answered. "He's a twelve-year-old dealer, and he's been arrested twice before. I picked him up last night at two-thirty with six hundred dollars in his pocket."

Felix Mitchell and Frank Ragusa preyed upon different classes of people. Ragusa sold drugs to an upscale clientele, and he helped corrupt the judgment of a white artistic and intellectual elite. Felix

Above left: Two free-basing pipes, cocaine in powder and rock forms, cash, a .32 caliber revolver and two .25 caliber automatics.

Above: Cocaine, cash, and a food coupon.

---

* The primary Oakland police officer on the case was Everett Gremminger, a highly experienced narcotics investigator. In black English, *e*'s frequently sound like *i*'s, and he was known to the addicts as Grimminger. Before long, they shortened his name; the word would go out that "Grim is on the street again." They had it right.

Mitchell was a big man in the ghetto, a pied piper deceiving some of the most deprived children in our society.

The Mitchell and Ragusa cases illustrate the lack of finality that is characteristic of contemporary criminal jurisprudence. Reilly was tried for the Ragusa killings three times over a period of eight years, finally winning a reduction in his sentence, from first- to second-degree murder. Because Mitchell was murdered before he could make an appeal, his conviction was erased from the public record by an appellate court. The government is appealing this decision.

Surveillance

Most police surveillances are conducted to prevent the commission of a crime, to gather enough evidence to justify an arrest, or to apprehend a wanted person. Other purposes include locating the residence or hangouts of a suspect, clarifying the relationships between known criminals, establishing the routine habits of a person under investigation, and checking up on informants. Surveillance can sometimes help to locate a missing person, and it is essential in deciding on the best method for attempting a rescue.

Secret agents, spies, private detectives, and reporters apply many of the techniques of surveillance. Basically there are two types of surveillance: stationary and moving. The principles of each are the same: study the turf, study the person, and don't be seen. It is always best to reconnoiter before beginning the surveillance of a fixed location — a house, a store, an office — in order to learn what the best vantage points are, the condition of the streets in the area, what clothing to wear, and so forth.

It is essential to watch the right person. Fundamental as this is, some sophisticated operators have made this elementary blunder. In Scandinavia a few years ago, Israeli secret service agents tailed a man they thought was an Arab terrorist. Their preparation for the mission was sloppy. He was a harmless person — a dentist. They shot him to death.

Being noticed by the subject means, at the very least, that the surveillance burns up and becomes useless. At the very worst, the hunter becomes the hunted.

An example of a good stakeout by an investigative reporter occurred a while back when Marilyn Baker, an enterprising television newswoman, did a story on commercial sex businesses in San Francisco. She conducted a surveillance of a dirty-movie theater she knew was reporting receipts on the order of $30,000 a week. Using hidden cameras to cover the front and back entrances of the place around the clock for seven days, she discovered it had only fifteen patrons a day — good for a legitimate weekly gross of $700. The inference was drawn that the theater was a laundry, either for local drug money or possibly for syndicate money from out-of-state gambling, loan sharking, and extortion.

The Sergis Case

An investigation can be so completely botched that one can never be sure of the innocence or guilt of the suspects — or even of the existence of a crime. The Sergis case of 1890 was a classic example of this. Our information on it comes mainly from a long letter in defense of the Oakland Police Department by Police Chief John Tompkins, published in an Oakland newspaper of the time.

In May and June several arrests for child molestation had been made in Berkeley. The newspapers gave the arrests so much attention that people in the East Bay became jittery at the sight of strangers around young children.

The Sergis case began in Oakland on Saturday, June 21, 1890, when Mrs. Jones reported a possible case of child abuse at Levi's Boarding House. Captain Wilson interviewed her in "the private office" at police headquarters. She told him that on the previous Thursday a strange man had called at Levi's, where he had rented a room for one week for himself and his wife. Later in the day, instead of his wife, the stranger brought a five-year-old girl to the boarding house. He said the child was his daughter. They took up residence at Levi's, and the man watched the little girl closely.

The stranger's name was Sergis, and Mrs. Jones said that when he found the little girl playing with other children, she was instantly called into the house. He spoke to her in a foreign language, and Mrs. Jones thought "he was saying something to her he didn't desire to have others understand." She also said that the little girl "had no change of underclothing," "was covered with vermin," and "carried a change of underclothing into the bathroom to this man who was in a nude condition at the time."

After the inteview Captain Wilson walked down to Levi's Boarding House, which was a few blocks away, but Sergis and the little girl were not there.

On Sunday nothing was done, but on Monday morning, when Mr. Hunter — the head of the San Francisco Society for the Prevention of Crime — dropped in at police headquarters, he was told of the Sergis matter. He also went to Levi's but was unable to find the man or the girl. He spoke to Mrs. Levi, the landlady, and she confirmed what Mrs. Jones had said. By involving himself in the case, Mr. Hunter increased its importance.

On Wednesday, Captain Wilson returned to the boarding house and met with Mrs. Jones and her daughter. Miss Jones told him she had taken the little girl for a ride in her carriage on Tuesday and questioned her at length. What the little girl said convinced her that Sergis was not her father and that he had taken undue liberties with her. Miss Jones also said Sergis had invited her to San Francisco for a French dinner. (San Francisco's French restaurants were notorious places of assignation, and an invitation to dine at one was understood as a proposition.)

At about nine o'clock that night, Mrs. Jones sent a messenger to

Captain Fletcher, the night watch captain. The messenger said that the little girl was "full" from whiskey given her by her alleged father, and that they were going to leave the city early in the morning. Mrs. Jones thought they should both be taken into custody immediately or they would escape.

So Captain Fletcher, in his turn, followed Captain Wilson and Mr. Hunter to the boarding house. He found Mrs. Jones, Miss Jones, Mrs. Levi, and other adults clustered around the little girl, who was chattering away merrily enough. Mrs. Levi demonstrated how much whiskey the child had consumed by "taking up a tumbler and placing the end of her finger about two inches above the bottom of it." Captain Fletcher talked with the little girl, and she said she would rather stay with him than with her father. She also said she had another daddy far away.

At this point, the mysterious Sergis came home. Captain Fletcher, who was in "citizen's dress," was introduced to him under an assumed name. After a conversation with Sergis, Captain Fletcher took Mrs. Levi and Miss Jones aside and told them he did not see any necessity for immediate action. Mrs. Levi exclaimed, "Oh, he is going away on the six o'clock train in the morning and something must be done right away." Then she told Captain Fletcher that she had placed the matter before Mr. Hunter, the reformer from San Francisco.

On hearing Hunter's name, Captain Fletcher decided to seek guidance from the chief of police. He went up to the Seventh Street police station and telegraphed the city prison, asking Night Prison Keeper Swain to telephone Chief Tompkins at home. The chief instructed Captain Fletcher to use his own judgment.

Captain Fletcher called for the patrol wagon, and Sergis and the little girl were taken to the city prison and detained overnight. Sergis was not booked. He was held incommunicado. His name was put in "the small book," which, unlike the regular, huge police blotter, was not open to public view.

Thursday morning, Chief Tompkins interviewed Sergis. Like Captain Fletcher, he quickly saw that Sergis was not a dangerous man. Even though he could not understand Sergis very well, "in consequence of his speaking such broken English," Tompkins wrote, "I was favorably impressed with him, and after sending him below had the little girl brought up. She was a very pretty and bright little girl, and after assuring her I was her friend and simply wanted to ask her a few questions, she dried her tears and promptly and cheerfully answered them. She informed me that she had another papa, but could not tell me his name or where he lived. She said she had been five years of age a long time; that she slept with her father; that he gave her brandy the night before; and that he drank beer. She again exhibited an aversion to her father, expressing a desire to go home with me instead. The portion of her underclothing in sight and the dress she had on showed plainly she was not neatly or cleanly provided for.

"I promptly told Captain Wilson that I did not believe the suspicions well founded, and as soon as Dr. Crowley had made an examination, if he found no evidence of anything criminal, to promptly dismiss them both, which was done."

Though Chief Tompkins did not say so in his report, it seems clear that during the interrogation he confirmed what Captain Fletcher had learned the night before — that Sergis was actually Reverend Sergis, a Protestant missionary who had been invited to Oakland to preach at several local churches. While Reverend Sergis was being detained and questioned, his hosts were trying to contact him. But Tompkins had ordered that no one — including newspapermen and lawyers — was to see Sergis until he was ready to cut him loose.

Once the specters of kidnapping and child abuse had been exorcised, the detention became the center of controversy. Reverend Sergis, his sponsors, and the friends he had made by preaching complained mightily about the arrest. They gathered strong support from members of the community, as shown in this editorial, which appeared in the *Oakland Enquirer:*

It is safe to say that Chief Tompkins acted in the matter of the arrest of Sergis with a view as much as possible to save scandal and prevent injury to the character of a possibly innocent man. Nevertheless the use of . . . "the small book" or secret register is forbidden by law and is a most dangerous practice, which in the hands of an unscrupulous man might be used to do gross injustice. Although illegal, it has been quietly winked at here and in San Francisco because it sometimes facilitates the ends of justice by giving time to work up evidence. It can scarcely be pretended, however, that this was the case in the present instance. . . .

Chief Tompkins denied that "the small book" was illegal, and he defended the detention stoutly. "Too many cases of men taking liberties with little girls have been brought to light lately, as the Police Court records will show, and the circumstances and report led us to believe that if a felony had not already been committed, it was likely to occur, or perhaps a case of kidnapping was at the bottom of it.

"Supposing, for example, that matters had been as we supposed, and that this man and little girl had been allowed to escape — then there would have been a howl long and deep because the authorities . . . had not taken steps to investigate the matter. . . .

". . . Some might exclaim 'the profession of the man ought to convince anyone that he could not be guilty of such a charge.' To be sure, he wore the habiliments of a profession which, in itself, should place the wearer beyond reproach or suspicion, but when a man claiming to be a minister of the gospel drinks beer and invites a young lady to partake of a French dinner with him in San Francisco when he (as he says) has a sick wife in Ogden, is it surprising that he should be suspected of offenses more serious?"

In time, new sensations diverted attention from the rights and wrongs of this case, and nothing further was heard of Reverend Sergis or his daughter. He seems to have been a bumbling parent — a universal human failing but certainly not a crime. The anxieties over child abuse which led the women at Levi's Boarding House to be suspicious of him diminished when no new cases were reported in the East Bay.

The "small book" system lasted until after the turn of the century, when the courts put an end to it.

Today the Sergis case would be handled by the Oakland Police Department's Youth Services Division, which is staffed by officers trained to deal with problems involving children. After a preliminary investigation, it would probably be referred to Children's Protective Services, an Alameda County agency that has authority to intervene in cases of abused or neglected children or unfit homes.

The Eddie Lee Ferguson Case

On January 16, 1978, Super Bowl Sunday, Mrs. Beverly Snoddy reported that her seven-year-old son, Eddie, was missing. He had wandered off during an early morning rain storm, she said. Maybe he had been kidnapped. Oakland police, beginning an immediate investigation, searched the area where the Snoddys lived and canvassed people who knew the first grader.*

In the newspapers and on television Beverly Snoddy pleaded for help in finding her missing son. Published photographs of Eddie showed a really attractive little boy — blond, fresh-faced, and smiling. The public became concerned for the child's safety.

Then Missing Persons investigators found three witnesses who said they had seen Eddie shortly before he dropped from sight. He had "red and swollen whip marks on his face" and was "dragging one of his legs." (One of these witnesses, whom we shall call Nancy, became a central figure in the case.) Neighbors said they saw Eddie going to the corner store, "hanging on to the walls while he tried to walk."

"None of the people who saw this terribly injured little boy

called the police about it," said Officer Mary Hilliard of the Missing Persons Detail.

The information given by the witnesses changed the nature of the case. Because it was probable that the little boy had met foul play, the department's Criminal Investigation Division (CID) became involved. They decided to conduct a discreet, low-profile investigation into the possibility that he had been murdered.

"We played dumb with the Snoddys," Mary Hilliard remembered. "We let them go on television and ask for the return of their child. Beverly had Pacific Gas and Electric and the telephone company crying over her misfortune and letting her get away with not paying their bills."

Lieutenant Terry Green, the commander of the Homicide Section, assigned an experienced investigator, Sergeant Alex Smith, to work with Officer Hilliard. Together, they began a painstaking investigation.

A check of police files revealed that Beverly Snoddy, twenty-nine, was not the proper housewife and mother she seemed. Her long record showed her to be a prostitute and thief. Eddie was a "trick baby" (that is, a child fathered by one of her customers). Like her husband, Calvin — Eddie's twenty-seven-year-old stepfather — she was a drug addict. Both were on parole.

Earlier, when Beverly was sent to jail in Southern Caifornia, the courts had taken Eddie away from her and sent him to live with a fos-

---

* This account is based on interviews with the primary investigators, Officer Mary Hilliard and Sergeant Alex Smith, both now retired.

ter family. There he was happy and flourished. When she got out of jail, she moved north and married Calvin Snoddy. This was an interracial marriage, Beverly being white and Calvin black. They moved among those for whom colorblindness and worldliness were facts of life and a romantic stance; where, according to Mary Hilliard, "You never knew when you went to call on somebody whether the person would be black or white. They were very street smart, and were making it on the edges of the system."

In time, Calvin and Beverly had two children. Then Beverly petitioned the court to have Eddie returned to her. Despite the opposition of Eddie's foster family and against the recommendation of the social worker handling Eddie's case in San Diego, a juvenile court judge in Alameda County approved the petition as a routine matter.

Soon after Eddie returned to the Snoddy household, he began attending school irregularly, the officers learned. When he did go, he was no longer the extroverted, cheerful child his schoolmates and teachers had known. Then he stopped going entirely.

Although it was a condition of parole that they stay off drugs, both Snoddys had large habits. The reason Eddie stopped attending school, Smith and Hilliard found, was that the seven-year-old took care of the other children — a one-year-old and a three-year-old — during the day. That was when his mother and stepfather went out to commit burglaries for money to buy dope. The boy didn't meet Calvin's standards as a baby sitter, so he beat him.

Eddie was dead, Smith and Hilliard were by then convinced. But they did not have probable cause to arrest Eddie's mother or stepfather. Without the body, or with-

out a witness who had seen the body, they had no case. All they had was an unexplained disappearance.

An anonymous tip received through a telephone call led Smith and Hilliard to Nancy, a friend of Beverly Snoddy's. The tip said Nancy had actually seen the dead body. If she had, an arrest warrant could have been obtained immediately. When the investigators interviewed her, Nancy admitted hearing the Snoddys say that Eddie was dead, but she absolutely refused to say that she had seen the body.

Mary Hilliard remembered Nancy as "a hype, but not a hooker, although she may have turned a few tricks. She was mostly into running up bad debts." She was a parolee who had gone back to being a street person, and the courts were considering recommitting her to jail. She was on parole for bouncing bad checks all over the place. Nancy got her dope by buying it or stealing it, or both.

Smith and Hilliard kept her out of jail from month to month as the investigation progressed. In turn, she cooperated with them. She even went into the Snoddys' apartment wired for sound on a few occasions.

Before long, Smith and Hilliard became aware of yet another friend of the Snoddys' — a young, white ex-convict we will call Billy. He was, Smith said, "coming on hard to Nancy, which somehow did not seem right in the circumstances." The detectives believed that Nancy was holding out on them, even though she was giving them some help. And they thought the Snoddys knew how much she knew about Eddie. So, the detectives guessed that the Snoddys might be setting Billy up to hurt Nancy in order to keep her quiet.

They took Billy aside and found out that he was a childhood friend of Beverly's. His mother had taken Beverly in at one time and looked after her. She was almost a sister to him. Even so, Billy volunteered to help the police find Eddie's body. Like many ex-cons, he despised child abusers.

The detectives decided to create a situation that would cause the suspects to move Eddie's body and thereby lead the police to it.

The investigators wired Billy for sound, gave him instructions, and sent him in to talk with the Snoddys. Parked down the block, Smith and Hilliard and other detectives listened, ready to move in if he got in trouble. Billy engaged the Snoddys in long, sympathetic conversations about Eddie, about the troubles kids can cause, about the disappearance, and on other topics verging on the crucial one. Finally, the investigators heard the Snoddys confide that the little boy was buried in a country field. Now, to find a way to get the Snoddys to reveal where the field was.

The winter of 1978 was an exceptionally wet one, and Alex Smith thought of a way to turn this to the advantage of the police. Billy suggested to the Snoddys that the heavy rains might cause mud slides. Wouldn't it be too bad if the body got uncovered? Once he had the Snoddys hooked on this worry, Billy told them he had a plan. He had access to a vat of acid at a chrome-plating plant in Oakland (arranged for by the police, of course). He would help them dispose of the boy's body there.

Smith and Hilliard arranged a visit to the plant for the Snoddys and Billy — and for a surveillance team, who tape-recorded everything. When Billy threw a piece of scrap metal into the vat, it sizzled. "Oh . . . ," Beverly said to her companions and to the hidden microphone, "that'll take care of Eddie." And so the Snoddys asked Billy to help them move the body.

While Billy helped the Snoddys get ready for the run to the grave site, the department assembled a technologically sophisticated surveillance team to follow them. "Chips Stewart [the division commander] gave us everything we asked for," Smith remembered. But luck wasn't with the police that day: minutes after the trip began, the van that the police had furnished Billy broke down and caught fire. Everybody, police and criminals, canceled plans and went home.

Three nights later, the Snoddys made another attempt to drive to the grave site, this time in a van Alex Smith borrowed from a friend of the department. The surveillance team was even more sophisticated. It had a special tracking system and a helicopter equipped with a homing device for following the van from a distance. Before the Snoddys reached the city limits, a drunken driver smashed into the van. Plans were canceled again.

Despite these setbacks, Smith, Hilliard, and Billy again tried to get the suspects to lead them to the body. But the second accident had freaked the Snoddys. Trying to move Eddie's body was too risky. Afraid to leave it where it was, they were even more afraid to try to move it. They especially feared an automobile accident while they had the body in the car.

While Billy attempted to talk them into trying a third time, Smith and Hilliard were informed that Beverly Snoddy's parole was going to be revoked because of her continuing heroin addiction. They advised her parole officer (let's call him Laval) of the investigation going on and asked for his cooperation.

A parole officer we know once told us that he felt his main job was to keep his parolees out of jail. A lot of parole officers feel this way; a few take their feelings to a dangerous extreme. Laval was one of these. He had no intention of allowing Beverly to go back to jail. He warned her about the pending revocation of parole. He also told her that the police thought Eddie was dead and that she was being looked at as a suspect. He advised her not to worry, according to Alex Smith, because as long as the police "didn't have a ton of circumstantial evidence, or the body, or someone who had seen the body, there was nothing the police could do to her."

This leak put the Snoddys on their guard and Billy's life in danger.

As Alex Smith remembered it, the next time Billy — his clothes loaded with wires, batteries, and a microphone — went into the Snoddys' apartment, the listening officers, parked down the street and around the corner, got an unpleasant surprise. Beverly came out to use the pay phone and walked by the van with Smith and two other detectives in it and spotted them as the heat. She was paranoid from the dope. When she got back to the apartment, she accused Billy of being wired up and demanded that he lift the front of his shirt — right where the bug was. He refused, taking the line that he was very hurt by her suspicion: "What cops? What are you talking about? How could you think such a thing about me after what we have meant to each other all these years?" He made it clear that if they checked him out the relationship was over, and he was leaving for good.

Beverly wavered. Just as the detectives were entering the building to rescue Billy, she offered to show him that there really were cops outside. The detectives backpedaled real fast. When Beverly and Billy came out of the apartment and walked around to where she had seen the van parked, it was gone.

Smith and Hilliard gave up trying to get the Snoddys to lead them to the body. They fell back on interrogation, questioning everyone who knew the Snoddys, looking for someone who had seen something. This ultimately led them to another friend of Calvin's, the man who loaned them the car in which Eddie's body was taken out to the country. When this friend was questioned, he said that on the evening of the murder, when he delivered the car to Calvin, the Snoddys mentioned to him that Nancy had seen the boy's body.

The detectives called Nancy in for an interview. She tried to avoid it, breaking several appointments with them. It turned out that Nancy was withholding the information for fear that she would be implicated in the murder on a conspiracy charge. But, as Alex Smith emphasized to her, "we were not interested in that."

She finally came across when faced by the lie detector. According to the police report, she admitted that she "had observed Eddie dead in the apartment and attempted to render first aid, but the parents insisted she leave the apartment while they went to score some dope." This broke the case.

Smith applied for warrants for the arrest of the Snoddys. (Incidentally, by the time the warrants were served, the Snoddys had sold everything in their apartment, including the shower curtain, to buy heroin.) Once in custody, Beverly and Calvin soon admitted that Eddie was dead. They tried to persuade Smith and Hilliard that the cause was a skateboard accident. Smith told them, "We have one of the best pathologists in the country. If he examines the body and agrees, then you're free." With this promise they agreed to reveal the location of the body. "What else could they do?" Smith said. Together they led investigators to a cow pasture in Santa Rosa. Three hundred and fifty yards from the highway, in a gully next to a stream, was the little boy's grave. Under a pile of rocks, which Calvin placed over him to "keep the animals away," buried three feet down, they found the vinyl tote bag into which Eddie's bound body had been stuffed.

Following the autopsy, the pathologist advised the investigators that the child was black and blue over 40 percent of his body, and that in all his years of experience, this was by far the worst case of death by beating he had ever seen.

When the Snoddys learned (through a discovery motion) of the evidence that had been accumulated against them — the testimony of the informants and the tape recording of their visit to the chrome-plating plant where they tested the vat of acid — they waived a jury trial because they were afraid of what a jury would do to them. The prosecution put on its case and rested. Beverly then pleaded guilty and tried to take the blame herself, to shield Calvin, but it did not work. They were convicted of second-degree murder and sentenced to seven years in prison in December 1978. From the bench the judge regretted not being able to sentence them to more.

Beverly came out of prison in 1984 and soon got into trouble again. According to the newspapers, she and a friend held up a tavern owner in Southern Califor-

nia. After he gave them money, they shot him. She was convicted of attempted murder and sentenced to seventeen years in prison. Calvin was hanging out on an Oakland street corner one Monday evening in early October 1987 when someone in a passing car shot and killed him.*

Laval, the parole officer, was disciplined, and sometime later left public service. Alex Smith said, "He was never really in law enforcement anyway."

Nancy, recalled Mary Hilliard, "became quite attached to Alex and me. After the trial she went back to her home in the Midwest. I used to get four- and five-page letters from her, talking about how well she was doing. Once she came back out here, looking like a million dollars. She had cleaned up her act and gotten rid of the acne she had from using heroin. She was dressed in Dior fashions. Then after a while she began to write letters about her new boyfriend, who she said was involved in CIA activities in South America. Then she stopped writing. I am afraid that she went back to using dope and is either dead or doing some heavy prison time."

As a result of this case, the Alameda County grand jury conducted an investigation of the standards used by juvenile court judges in deciding petitions for the return of children to their natural parents. It recommended against routine approval of the petitions. Today the judges look more carefully at parents who request that custody of children be returned to them and at the homes to which the children would go.

---

* Calvin's murder is still unsolved, but most people think it was a drug-related hit.

Streetwalkers in the Neighborhoods

As elsewhere, street prostitution has been a problem in the East Bay for a long time. It has had a bad effect on life in a number of Berkeley and Oakland neighborhoods.

Fifteen or twenty years ago, efforts by Berkeley and Oakland police to curb street prostitution began to fail, primarily because the courts put prostitution, a misdemeanor offense, low on their list of priorities. The judges did not want to fill their calendars with prostitution cases at the cost of delaying the trials of more serious crimes.

In one twelve-month period, for example, fewer than 15 percent of the prostitutes arrested in Oakland were given jail terms. They could run up six or more arrests before being brought to trial. And when tried — sometimes well over a year after arrest — they were allowed to plea-bargain, copping to one offense instead of several. Although the law required the incarceration of prostitutes with previous convictions, only twelve out of forty-two streetwalkers with "priors" actually went to jail. The rest were released for the cost of their bail.

Since good-looking street prostitutes can make $300 or more a night, this style of enforcement did not give them a reason to avoid working the strolls along San Pablo Avenue and MacArthur Boulevard in Oakland or University Avenue in Berkeley. Arrest became an inconvenience, not a deterrent. An ironclad rule applies to all types of criminal vice: if it is not repressed, it increases.

The streetwalkers became a plague in the neighborhoods adjacent to the strolls. Flower beds were littered with used condoms, beer bottles, and other trash. Noise levels rose, particularly late in the evening, when loud, profane language echoed through the streets. Women who lived in the area — of whatever age or condition — found themselves being propositioned and subjected to verbal abuse from passing cars. Men on their way home from work, as well as relatives and friends visiting the area, were propositioned by the streetwalkers.

The owners of neighborhood mom-and-pop stores saw their business dwindling because of people's dislike and fear of doing business in the atmosphere created by prostitution and its related criminal activity. (Part of the reason the idea of prostitution as a "victimless crime" gained currency was a misunderstanding of what prostitutes do. Most people think they go out on the street, have sex with their customers, and go home again. Actually, most prostitutes are jills of all trades. They rob and steal, burglarize, kite checks, and do whatever else comes along.)

These neighborhoods were all working-class areas near freeway entrances; that is, on the routes followed by suburban commuters. The hookers walked, but the customers drove cars. When the residents began protesting the invasion of their neighborhoods, the police sympathized and increased the number of arrests. Given the revolving-door justice in the courts, increased enforcement did not slow down the trade. The courts held aloof, ignored the protests, and continued to follow their own priorities.

But the neighborhood groups persisted. In Oakland, the ministers of black churches came to the forefront of the movement. The churchgoing people, organized as the "Hooker Commission," bully-ragged the city council until a new antiloitering ordinance was passed. Then they put the municipal judges on notice: if they did not begin hearing the cases developed by the police department, they would face problems at election time. The police department enjoyed its rapport with the Hooker Commission and kept trolling for whores — that is, it continued to use plainclothes male officers to arrest the prostitutes. Many officers were privately

Prostitutes working a stroll.

Oakland Police Dept.

amused by the discomfort of the city council members and the judges.

In Berkeley, a Catholic priest, an activist with impeccable liberal credientials, took the lead. A "Hooker Patrol" was organized, in which the priest and his flock walked along University Avenue, following the girls at a short distance but not interfering with them — except by being present. They stayed close enough, however, to discourage customers who were shy about being seen and overheard negotiating with the prostitutes.

Then the pimps and prostitutes staged a counterattack against the neighborhoods. In Oakland, the prostitutes began defecating on the lawns of the churches, cursing the people as they came to attend services, threatening them, and making their lives as unpleasant as possible. In Berkeley, similar attempts were made to intimidate the Hooker Patrol.

Berkeley being Berkeley, the prostitutes went before the city council to complain that the Hooker Patrol was having a "chilling effect" on their constitutional right to free assembly. Besides, they said, they were only poor working women just trying to make a living. Some members of the council received these claims sympathetically.

This was fruitless, however. Like the customers, the prostitutes were out-of-towners — nonvoters.

The council members were told bluntly by the residents that prostitution would be *the* election issue if something was not done about it. As in Oakland, that settled the matter. Ultimately, some of the city council members even joined the Hooker Patrol.

When cases began to come up faster on the court calendars and when sentences made it clear that enforcement would take the girls off the street, cutting into their earning power, they disappeared from the strolls. Every now and then they have tried to make a comeback, but their number has never reached anything like its former size.

The police departments have been able to deal with the problem effectively with conventional enforcement measures. Oakland and Berkeley police employ a three-pronged approach to keep it under control: they arrest prostitutes and pimps for violating state and local laws (over 90 percent of prostitutes are managed by pimps); they initiate red-light abatement proceedings against motels and hotels that cater to the trade; and they arrest the customers.

The Berkeley and Oakland police departments have made thousands of prostitution arrests. In addition to the regular streetwalkers and their customers, the arrestees include drag queens and large numbers of juvenile prostitutes — some as young as thirteen. To help keep University Avenue clean, the Berkeley Police Department periodically holds what it calls John Nights. These are operations aimed at arresting the customers, not the streetwalkers.

On a John Night, patrol officers sweep the regular hookers off the street, and then the vice control unit puts female undercover officers on the corners. The police department's "girls" walk along the stroll and engage in encounters that follow a fairly standard protocol. The john cruises slowly along the street, and, after selecting the girl he wants, he pulls up beside her and stops. The dialogue goes something like this:

"Are you available?" (Some johns use the euphemism "Are you dating?")

"What do you want?"

"I want . . ." The john spells it out. He tells the girl what he wants to do and what he wants her to do. Then he says what he will pay her, or he asks her how much she wants. At this point, he is arrested.

In a recent seven-month period, Berkeley officers arrested 123 customers on four separate John Nights. Like other departments, they have found that arresting the johns has a stronger, more lasting deterrent effect than arresting the girls. The customers suffer embarrassment, especially when their names are printed in the newspapers. Most decide it is not worth it. Usually johns are released the same night they are arrested and eventually plea-bargain to "disturbing the peace."

This is a more humane method of making arrests, from the point of view of the police, than the routines that were followed earlier in the century. Then the courts required proof of the sexual act. An officer would hire two stool pigeons to have sex with the girl. Then the informers would testify against her in court. The "customers" were granted immunity for their testimony. Many officers considered it degrading to furnish this kind of proof, since they were forced to depend on men they considered worse than the prostitutes. Rather than play the game by those rules, they often turned a blind eye to what was going on on their beats.

POOR ALMA HOWARD

In the 1880s the following story appeared in an Oakland paper under the title "A Pretty Girl's Fall — Complete Degradation of Jaunty Alma Howard":

At 1 o'clock this afternoon John Tayler, a soda manufacturer, told Officer Felley that he had seen a young tough lead a girl into the old stable known as the Washington Riding Academy, which is just across the track from the narrow gauge depot at Fourteenth and Franklin Streets. As it was evident that the hoodlum meant the girl no good, the officer made a descent upon the place. As he approached a dogfaced sort of fellow slouched away. Then two young men, working in the stable, grinned as the officer went to the door of the room once used as the stable office. Forcing open the door Felley found the girl lolling on a filthy bunk, with a sneaking, dirty, unkempt opium fiend as her companion. The room reeked with the fumes of smoked opium. A question or two showed that the girl was either drunken with liquor or under the influence of opium. She was locked up. A prettier girl has never been behind prison bars. The rushing blood pinks her pale cheek and dyes her full lips like ripe cherries. A neat dress of light goods, with the skirt set off with figures in navy blue, gave effect to a good figure; and a jaunty hat of brown straw rolled up on one side added a grace to the carriage of her head which drunkenness could not overcome. She gave her name as Alma Howard, and burst into tears when a reporter asked her if she lived in Oakland. "No, you know I don't," she blurted out, and was led sobbing to a cell.

The police have watched with sad interest the fall of this girl. She had a home and a husband in Nevada City, but drifted away and into the maelstrom of sin. She became known as Myrtle Thompson. Her husband obtained a divorce. Then she was arrested as a vagrant, but Justice Henshawe, hoping he would make the last effort at reform, which she promised, let her go. The company in which she was found today indicates the last broglio of degradation.

This was a shocking story and was intended to be. What makes it particularly effective is the contrast between the loveliness of the girl ("the rushing blood pinks her pale cheek . . . a neat dress . . . a good figure . . . a jaunty hat") and the scum who made use of her (the "dogfaced" fellow slouching away, the "sneaking, dirty, unkempt opium fiend") as well as the sordid details of the crib in the riding stable.

But it was written to a formula. Stories on prostitution were regularly run under the heading, "One of Our Girls." The prostitutes were always described as looking like lost Pre-Raphaelite madonnas or George Meredith heroines. For example, there was "pretty dissolute Etna Carson"; "dainty wicked Etna," who "looked like an angel . . . as pure and gentle as a fawn" as she pled guilty to prostitution and was given a suspended sentence on condition that she leave town. She "tripped from the courtroom followed by a company of young roughs at whom she had been dimpling and smiling ever since she took her seat in the dock." But Etna was an old offender, and the reporter ended his story by asking and answering a question: "Will she go? Well, not very fast, nor very far."

Beneath the formula, however, poor Alma Howard seems to have evoked some genuine final sympathy before she was dismissed, with the sour joke about the "last broglio of degration," and left, as a bad woman, to the mercy of the double standard.

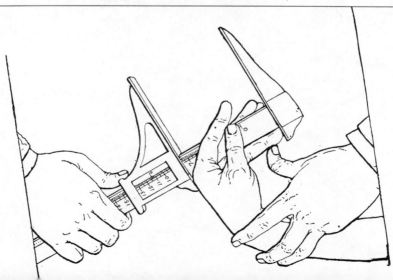

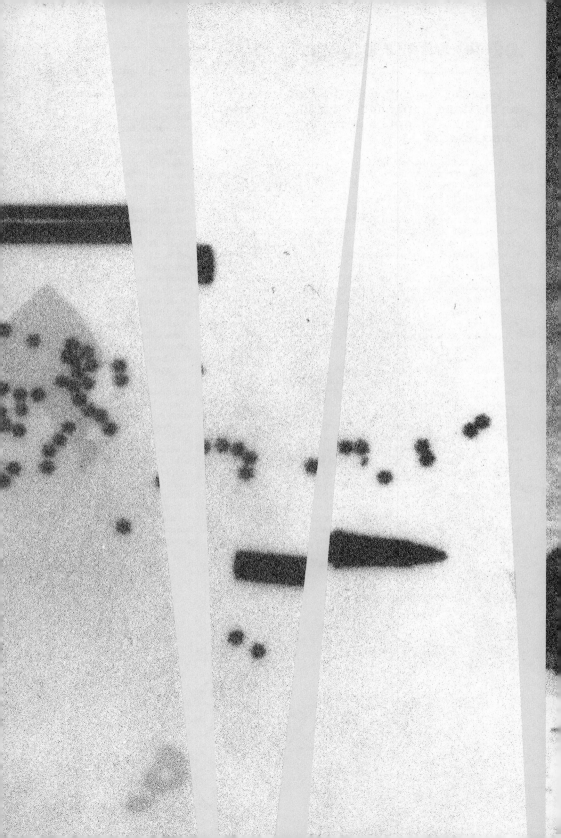

CLUES

Sir Bernard Spilsbury

. . . the life of Sir James Lub-bock, who had the misfortune to be a particular friend of Lord Peter's, was made a burden to him with daily inquiries as to the post-mortem detection of such varying substances as chloroform, curare, hydrocyanic acid gas and diethylsulphonmethylethyl-methane.

— Dorothy L. Sayers, *Unnatural Death*

Sir Bernard Henry Spilsbury was a tall, handsome man who always dressed well, usually wearing a carnation in his buttonhole. He became one of the most formidable expert witnesses of all time. His manner in testifying was detached, imperturbable, confident. And with reason. After attending Oxford, he trained at St. Mary's Hospital in London, where he studied under the founders of modern forensic medicine in England — Dr. A. J. Pepper, Dr. A. P. Luff, and Dr. William Willcox. In addition to their work as professors at St. Mary's, these three doctors also served the Home Office in criminal matters. Their pupil Spilsbury went on to make himself the finest forensic pathologist of his time. He came to the attention of the public in 1910, during the murder trial of Dr. Crippen.

Hawley Harley Crippen was an American doctor and surgeon. He and his wife went to England so that she could make a career as a singer. She failed, and their relationship deteriorated. Apparently they were mutually unfaithful. Crippen fell in love with his secretary, Ethel Le Neve. Three years after Ethel became his mistress, Crippen's wife disappeared.

After one of her friends informed Scotland Yard that Mrs. Crippen had not been seen for more than a month and that the doctor had installed his mistress in their home, the police began to make inquiries. Crippen told Chief Inspector Dew that his wife had left him, and that he had no idea where she was. Two days later, he and Ethel Le Neve (dressed as a man) fled the country. When the police learned this, the hunt was on.

An excellent follow-up investigation by Chief Inspector Dew led to the discovery of human remains — or what appeared to be human remains — in the basement of Crippen's house. The corpse, if such it was, had no arms, legs, bones, genital organs, or head. Whoever had mutilated it clearly intended to prevent its ever being identified.

This grisly find made headline news, and when Chief Inspector Dew used the new "wireless telegraph" to locate Crippen and Le Neve on the S.S. *Montrose*, bound for Quebec, the case became a sensation. Millions began to follow it intently.

The Home Office assigned the pathologists at St. Mary's — Drs. Pepper, Luff, and Willcox — to the case, and at their request they were joined by Dr. Spilsbury. Dr. Pepper identified the remains as human. Dr. Willcox and Dr. Luff

Topical Press

examined the remaining organs. Dr. Pepper and Dr. Spilsbury examined the skin.

While the pathologists did their work, Dew boarded the fast liner *Laurentic* and beat the *Montrose* to Canada. Once there, to avoid the newspaper reporters, he took a launch out to meet the *Montrose*, boarding it well up the St. Lawrence River. He arrested Crippen and Le Neve and brought them back to England. Crippen steadfastly and persuasively maintained that he and his mistress were innocent of any crime. They might be sinners seeking a little happiness, he said, but they were not murderers.

While the excitement of the chase was holding everyone's attention, the pathologists began piling up strong evidence against Crippen. Dr. Willcox determined

Sir Bernard Henry Spilsbury

that an overdose of hyoscine hydrobromide caused the death, and Dr. Pepper and Dr. Spilsbury identified an irregularity on one of the pieces of skin as an abdominal scar from an old operation. With this to go on, Chief Inspector Dew subsequently established that Crippen had purchased a large quantity of hyoscine hydrobromide, and that Crippen's wife had undergone major abdominal surgery in New York.

The trial was attended by dense crowds of people every day, and news of the proceedings was carried far and wide by the daily newspapers. Crippen's defense claimed the remains found in the basement could not be Mrs. Crippen's because she was still alive. Moreover, the remains, they claimed, could not even be shown to be female, and dated from some time previous to Crippen's occupancy of the house. Two doctors testified for the defense that the alleged abdominal skin was actually from the body's thigh, and that the scar was really a fold that had occurred after death.

What the jury would believe about the scar tissue became the crux of the case. If the jury thought the defense witnesses canceled out the prosecution witnesses, Crippen would go free.

During the analysis of the body, Spilsbury participated as an assistant to his seniors. Now he moved front and center. He testified clearly, simply, and impressively as to how he independently verified Dr. Pepper's finding that the tissue was from the abdomen and contained a surgical scar. "I have my microscopic slides here," he said, "and I shall send for a microscope in case it should be wanted." It was, and before long he was demonstrating his own findings to the members of the jury. The next day, after looking

at his slides and re-examining the tissue, the two defense witnesses conceded that Spilsbury's analysis was correct.

This removed any reasonable doubt that Mrs. Crippen was not dead, and it destroyed her husband's defense. Everything fell into place: the love affairs, the poisoning of the wife, the dismemberment of her body, and the lovers' flight. It took the jury only half an hour to convict. Ethel Le Neve was tried separately and found not guilty of being an accessory to the murder; shortly after Crippen's execution, she left England for Australia and then dropped from sight.

Spilsbury's reputation was made. He went from one success to another. And the case also established the reputation of forensic pathology: until the Crippen trial, British juries had had no faith in forensic evidence. In 1922, when he was forty-five, Spilsbury was knighted for his services to the Crown. But he was in no way ready to retire. He worked assiduously until his death in 1947.

Spilsbury became famous in England as the prosecution's pathologist of choice in the important cases of his time. He traveled the country, examining bodies and testifying in big cities and small hamlets. In one Welsh village where he was a witness, the proceedings were recessed at sundown, as the court — like the village — did not have electric lights. Spilsbury became something of a celebrity, and *Punch* wrote:

When arsenic has closed your eyes,
This certain hope your corpse may
    rest in:
Sir B. will kindly analyze
The contents of your large
    intestine.

More lasting evidence of his fame

can be found in Dorothy Sayers's mystery novels. Under the name of Sir James Lubbock, he is a person from whom Lord Peter himself seeks expert guidance. (Spilsbury was the Home Office pathologist; Sir James was the "Home Office analyst.")

Spilsbury performed his work with great intensity. He was highly skilled in the use of a microscope, but he could also recognize with his naked eye evidence that was invisible to his colleagues. There were numerous instances of his unaided observations being verified by their microscopes.

He also applied his acute sense of smell to the work. One Scotland Yard detective reminisced: "I well remember my first case with Sir Bernard. It was a particularly unpleasant corpse, an exhumation case. I walked into the room, and there it was all laid out ready for examination. I was terribly afraid I should make a fool of myself, which would never do for a C.I.D. officer, so I put on a cigarette and tried to think of something else. After a while Sir Bernard came in. He sniffed twice, looked round the room, and said, 'You mustn't smoke, please, Johnson. I can't smell the smells I want to smell.' He then bent down over the corpse and sniffed away as if it was a rose-garden."[*]

The story is told that at an exhumation in Croydon, Spilsbury arrived at the graveside dressed in his usual immaculate manner, and when the coffin was raised, he ran his nose along it, straightened up, and said, "Arsenic, gentlemen."[†]

Spilsbury accomplished a staggering volume of work during his forty-year career. He performed some 25,000 postmortems, 250 of which were for murder cases. It has been suggested that Spilsbury performed too many, and that, given the fallibility of human nature, in such a large number of autopsies errors must have crept in from time to time. Sir Sydney Smith, an eminent pathologist who testifed on the opposite side in a number of Spilsbury's cases, recalled Spilsbury as "very brilliant and very famous, but fallible like the rest of us — and very, very obstinate. . . . Spilsbury was scrupulously careful and painstak-

[*] Douglas G. Browne and E. V. Tullett, *The Scalpel of Scotland Yard*, p. 241.

[†] Ibid.

CRIMINALISTICS IN THE OLD WEST

"Perhaps you remember the trial of Arthur Brooke," said Officer Tom Downey one afternoon in May 1888, "who was accused of the murder of his father, Geoman Brooke. They lived at the point, and just before the old man was shot he had been drinking coffee. There was a suspicion that young Brooke had put arsenic into the coffee. We took a considerable stock of their coffee, but we did not want to pay the expenses of an analysis without cause, so we got Dallimore, who was then Poundman, to give us an old dog.

"We kept the dog for three days, until we thought he must be pretty well starved. Captain Pumyea and Detective Fuller took the dog out into the prison yard, and — the dog refused to touch the coffee.

"We afterward had some analyzed, and found that there was not a bit of poison in it. Brooke was acquitted, but is now serving three years in the San Francisco House of Correction for forgery."

ing in his work, but once he had given an opinion nothing would make him change it." When he was wrong, Smith said, he was "terrifying."*

For a rough comparison of Spilsbury's workload with that of a present-day pathologist, we can refer to Bill Davidson's fine study of a prosecutor's staff, *Indict and Convict*. In 1969, Dr. John Wallace Graham appeared as an expert witness for the prosecution in a murder trial. In testimony establishing his qualifications, Dr. Graham stated that he had performed 1,470 autopsies over a seven-year period, including 125 in homicide investigations. Spilsbury performed an average of 625 postmortems per year, compared to 210 a year for Dr. Graham. Where Spilsbury averaged 6 murder victims per year, Dr. Graham averaged 18.

Spilsbury's usual role as a pathologist was to uncover deception, but an interesting episode late in his career shows him abetting deceit. This was his contribution to Operation Mincemeat, the World War II intelligence exercise in misinformation involving "the man who never was."

After the Allies defeated Rommel in North Africa, the British prepared an elaborate ruse to convince the Germans that Sardinia and Corsica — not Sicily — would be invaded by the Allies. The plan called for the body of a British staff officer carrying secret messages to float ashore in Spain, apparently the victim of an airplane crash. This courier was actually the body of a noncombatant dressed in a uniform; the messages were false; and he had been launched toward the Spanish shore from a submarine. German sympathizers, it was hoped, would

recover the body and forward the misleading documents to Berlin. Lieutenant Commander Ewen Montagu, the author of the scheme, turned to Spilsbury for advice as to whether the plan was even possible:

I rang up Sir Bernard and we arranged a meeting at his club, the Junior Carlton. There, over a glass of sherry, I put our problem to him. After a moment or two of thought he gave me one of those concise, yet complete, expositions that had convinced so many juries — and even so many judges. His advice gave me hope. If the body was floating in a "Mae West" when it was recovered, we could use one of a man who had either drowned or died from any but a few of the "natural causes." . . . My opinion of Sir Bernard was fully justified; that extraordinary man listened to my questions and gave me his answers without ever for a moment giving vent to the curiosity which he must have felt. He asked me some questions which bore on the pathological problem that I was putting to him, but never once did he ask why I wanted to know or what I was proposing to do.

When the body of a man who had died of pneumonia had been obtained, and the operation was ready to proceed, Montagu went to see Spilsbury once more:

As a precaution I had another chat with Sir Bernard Spilsbury. He was quite satisfied: the pneumonia was a help. . . . If a post mortem examination was made by someone who had formed the preconceived idea that the death was probably due to drowning there was little likelihood that the difference between this liquid . . . and seawater would be noticed. Sir Bernard closed our talk with the characteristically confident statement:

---

* Sir Sydney Smith, *Mostly Murder*, p. 144.

"You have nothing to fear from a Spanish post mortem; to detect that this young man had not died after an aircraft had been lost at sea would need a pathologist of my experience — and there aren't any in Spain."★

★ Ewen Montagu, *The Man Who Never Was*, p. 21.

The operation went forward and was a complete success. German and Italian troops were moved out of Sicily, away from the coming battle, and many British and American lives were saved.

E. O. Heinrich, Criminologist

In October 1923, three bandits attempted to rob a Southern Pacific train in a remote mountain area near the Oregon-California border. It was a botched job. They set fire to the mail car and killed the mail clerk, the brakeman, the engineer, and the fireman. When they fled the scene, they left clues behind — a detonator and a pair of greasy old overalls. They also left behind all the loot.

The local sheriff in Oregon rounded up the usual suspects. Then he cut them loose for lack of evidence. Finally, he arrested a garage mechanic on the theory that, because the man had greasy hands, he could have left his mark on the overalls. But the mechanic refused to confess to the crime, and the investigation stalled.

Southern Pacific officials were determined that the case should be solved, and on their strong recommendation E. O. Heinrich was called in from Berkeley to analyze the evidence. He traveled north, was briefed on the investigation, and given the detonator and the overalls for analysis. Then he returned to his laboratory in Berkeley.

A few days later he wired the sheriff. "You are holding the wrong man. The overalls you sent me were worn by a left-handed lumberjack accustomed to working around fir trees. He is a white man between 21 and 25 years of age, not over five feet ten inches tall and he weighs about 165 pounds. He has medium light brown hair, a fair complexion, light brown eyebrows, small hands and feet, and he is rather fastidious in his personal habits. Apparently he has lived and worked in the Pacific Northwest. Look for such a man. You will be hearing more from me shortly."★

They let the mechanic go. And Heinrich did send more informa-

★ Eugene B. Block, *The Wizard of Berkeley*, p. 17.

tion: in the pencil pocket in the bib of the overalls he found a receipt for registered mail with the number 236-L. This broke the case. It provided the name of Roy D'Autremont, a left-handed lumberjack, white, in his early twenties, five ten, and about 165 pounds. The search was on. And went on for four long years. Finally, in 1927, D'Autremont and his brothers were arrested. During their trial, they confessed to the crime.

Edward Oscar Heinrich (1881–1953) practiced as a free-lance criminologist on the West Coast for more than thirty years. He was called "America's Sherlock Holmes." He did not like the comparison, but his fondness for oracular pronouncements (as in the railroad investigation) made the title irresistible.

As a young man Heinrich worked in Tacoma as the city's chemist and sanitary engineer. He began to do criminological work when the police department and the coroner's office called on him from time to time to assist their investigations. What began as an occasional involvement became a full-time preoccupation. He solved a number of difficult cases in Washington and became well known. He met Berkeley's Chief Vollmer, and they began a correspondence that led to Heinrich's being asked to teach and work in the Bay Area.

Heinrich was selected as chief of police of Alameda, California, in 1917, at the munificent salary of $175 a month. This brief interlude in his career sheds light on his personality and on his understanding of how law enforcement worked. When he took over, the newspapers made the usual noises about a shake-up in the department, and some officers may have feared for their jobs. The patron-

age system had been weakened by civil service reforms, but it could still be devastating in small departments where political influence remained paramount.

Heinrich assured the officers that he did not intend to make sweeping changes. "I am here," he said, "to take the department as I find it and to take advantage of the good points of the force. If there are any weak ones, I will do what I can to bring them up to the maximum of efficiency. There, however, will be no fireworks. We are all going to work together for the community good."*

As a free-lance criminologist, Heinrich had been a lone wolf. But the full range of police work, including investigations, requires teamwork, and Heinrich's declaration of intent when he took charge of Alameda showed an appreciation of this. He made some changes in the department, such as creating an improved record-keeping system, but what his long-term impact might have been will never be known. When the United States entered World War I, he was called into military service. At war's end, he accepted a position as city manager of Boulder, Colorado, but held it only for a short time. Late in 1919, he returned to California and set up the laboratory in Berkeley that became his life's work.

Eugene Block, Heinrich's friend and biographer, estimated that the laboratory handled well over a thousand cases in its thirty years of operation. They comprised civil as well as criminal matters, since his clients included insurance companies and state agencies that needed expert interpretation of evidence relating to disputed claims. Among the cases Heinrich mentioned in his *Who's*

* From an unidentified clipping in an Oakland police inspector's scrapbook.

Who entry were the Fatty Arbuckle trial (1921), the St. Francis Dam failure in Los Angeles (1928), and the suit for damages from the horrible explosion set off by saboteurs at Black Tom Island, in New York harbor, in July 1916 (*U.S. vs. Germany*, 1930–34).

In Heinrich's early days as a criminologist, very few police departments had their own laboratories. When the authenticity of a document was in question, for example, they would hire an outside expert on a temporary basis. In most instances, moreover, the role of experts was rather limited. They were not usually part of the investigative team.

Heinrich helped to change this. He was a notable pioneer in the use of scientific methods to investigate crimes. His success made him a transitional figure. As Block wrote, Heinrich "paved the way for many of the scientific procedures regarded today as routine in police laboratories throughout the country."

With the passage of time, and with the spectacular results produced by microscopes, test tubes, and other, more exotic instruments, law enforcement agencies moved to add scientifically trained personnel to their staffs. With this, the importance of the free-lance criminologists declined, although they still have a role. When a police department lacks a specialist in a particular area (serology, for example), it may hire the services of an outsider. But not very often — at least in California — and even then, the expert is often a retired law enforcement person.

HEINRICH'S THOUGHTS ABOUT HIS WORK

Every criminal episode in life is a succession of methods: entrance, approach, retreat, exit. Each separately must be analyzed. The facts must be determined for each phase and evaluated in order to determine their position in the mosaic. Thereby each fact so found becomes a clue.

The smaller the detail, the more likely it is that the criminal has overlooked it.

In newspaper reports of newly committed crimes there appears with monotonous frequency this statement: "The criminal left no clue." But I have always held that the criminal virtually labels every crime he commits. My procedure is to reconstruct the crime by visualizing the habits and actions of the criminal. I do this by using the debris that the criminal leaves behind and relocating it with respect to the criminal episode. So I make the natural sciences interpret what I have observed. You can see that no guesswork is involved — certainly no hunches.

The camera never lies but a camera in the hands of a liar is a dangerous instrument.

In its simplest aspect crime analysis is orderly procedure. Its guiding spirit is criticism. Its ever recurring questions are: Precisely *what* happened? Precisely *when* did it happen? Precisely *where* did it happen? *Why* did it happen? *Who* did it?

Strange though it may seem, only the last two questions, "why" and "who," seem to receive immediate attention from the average investigator.

Alas, nothing ever shoots so wide of the mark as a guess at motive. The true detective must analyze the method of the crime before he can analyze its purpose and discover the criminal.

One clue always is present after the commission of a crime. That one is the criminal's method. Every person in his every act in daily life leaves some impress of his method of procedure. So the criminal. Although he aims to keep his character and his identity his own secret, yet the mechanism of the crime, that is, precisely how it was committed, exposes his knowledge, his skill, and his habit. Among these, typical symptomatic actions appear that limit an investigation to a particular individual or to a small group.

Quoted by permission from E. O. Heinrich, "The Challenge of the Clue," *California Monthly*, February 1929.

IT'S A FALLACY

• Burying a body in quicklime will cause it to be quickly eaten away and destroyed.

Often the body will be preserved longer than if buried in earth. The lime combines with body fat to produce a hard soap that resists invasion by insects and bacteria, and retards putrefaction.

Bertillon, Ravachol, and the Mona Lisa

. . . we travelled down to Woking together . . . and I could not gather from his appearance whether he was satisfied or not with the position of the case. . . . His conversation, I remember, was about the Bertillon system of measurements, and he expressed his enthusiastic admiration of the French savant.

— Arthur Conan Doyle, "The Naval Treaty," in *The Memoirs of Sherlock Holmes*

Alphonse Bertillon was a vain, irascible, eccentric French genius who in 1879 invented anthropometry, or Bertillonage. This system of criminal identification was an enormous improvement over all previous methods employed by the police and was a pioneering application of science to criminology.

Before Bertillonage, police relied more on their memories than on records to identify recidivists ("old offenders," as the English call them). Because the penalties for second and third offenses were drastic, criminals had every incentive to use aliases and disguises to conceal their true identities. Police detectives, for their part, cultivated informers and their powers of recall. Agents of the Sûreté claimed they never forgot a face. They probably believed it too.

Even today, for a police officer a trained memory is a powerful professional tool. Many detectives develop an astonishing ability to recognize criminals months and even years after arresting them. Even so, in the nineteenth century large numbers of repeat offenders slipped through police lineups. But within the first six months of regular application of his system in 1883, Bertillon identified forty-nine recidivists the detectives had missed. In the first full year, he identified three hundred. He also went to the morgue and solved missing person cases by identifying corpses.

Bertillon based his system on the hypothesis that after reaching physical maturity no two human

120

Alphonse Bertillon

Bettmann Archive

beings have identical bone structure. A man might gain or lose weight, dye his hair or lose it, grow a beard or shave it off, or make any number of other changes in his appearance, but his bone structure would remain unchanged, and unique.

By taking eleven careful measurements of different aspects of the head, trunk, and limbs, a police clerk could create a numerical "picture" of the subject's skeleton. Bertillon calculated that if all the measurements were taken, the odds were better than 286 million to one against two people having identical measurements. When the clerk entered the numbers on the card, the criminal's identity was fixed for all time. Bertillon devised

a simple method by which cards could be located and compared.

When we describe Bertillon's system to police officers today, they immediately point out the same objections to it raised by French officers when the system was new one hundred years ago: the measurements they said, did not help the officer on the street to identify and pick up a suspect. Also, to be effective, the system demanded unrealistically high performance from the police clerks who took the measurements: they had to be exact. The problem was that measurements taken at different places and times, even within the same department, often differed.

To remedy this, and to improve

the system, Bertillon started the practice of taking full-face and right-profile photographs of prisoners at a standard distance and under uniform lighting. He also invented a technique of verbal description that, in a simplified form, is still used. He included tattoos and scars in a miscellaneous category labeled "special marks." The photographs were pasted on Bertillon cards, and the special marks were recorded in the space provided.

The Ravachol case, Bertillon's greatest triumph, illustrated the strengths and weaknesses of his method. It began in Paris on March 11, 1892, when someone set off a bomb in an attempt to kill a prominent judge; there were no clues to the perpetrator.

The first break the Sûreté got was a tip from an informer. This led them to a suspect who, to clear himself, implicated Ravachol, and the hunt was on.

Then another judge's house was bombed, and Ravachol became famous. The anarchist press hailed him as "an invincible hero," an avenger of the poor and helpless. By the time the Paris police arrested him on March 30, he was front page news and the topic of revolutionary propaganda throughout Europe.

The police considered Ravachol a thoroughly bad hat. But they could do nothing about the growing romantic myth surrounding his name until they could establish his true identity. But he wasn't talking, except to spout anarchist slogans. The question of the hour was, who is Ravachol?

The Paris police circulated a notice asking for information on anybody known to use the name Ravachol. A reply came from Saint-Étienne (near Lyon) that François Koenigstein, a burglar wanted for grave robbing and murder, went by that alias. Paris sent for Koenigstein's Bertillon card. Bertillon himself arrived at headquarters to measure Ravachol. The measurements matched! The identification caused an international sensation.

Eventually, Ravachol admitted that he was, indeed, Koenigstein. He also admitted the charges against him at Saint-Étienne. He *had* stolen jewelry from a grave and killed an old man for 35,000 francs (worth about $4,000 today). The anarchist hero turned out to be a very common criminal. The

The Bertillon card for Koenigstein, a.k.a. Ravachol.

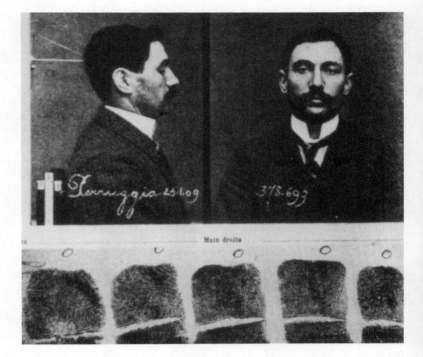

Vicenzo Perugia, the man who stole the Mona Lisa.

propaganda legend of Ravachol was dead even before he was marched to the guillotine.

Bertillon's great accomplishment in this case was a triumph of scientific method.* But it was also an organizational success: Koenigstein was an old offender, and the Sûreté's network of informers (which the veteran detectives still used to reinforce their memories) had supplied his name.

The Ravachol case gave the Bertillon system international prestige and led to its adoption by the German, Austrian, and Russian police, Scotland Yard, and the New York Police Department. From New York it spread across the United States. Police departments everywhere set up "measuring

rooms" and invested in calipers and measuring tapes. Millions of Bertillon cards were printed and laboriously filled out. Bertillonage seemed a permanent addition to police work.

But at the turn of the century, Scotland Yard began to rely on fingerprinting for identification purposes. Outside England it was not fully realized how absolutely individual fingerprints were, and there was debate within law enforcement circles as to which method was best, fingerprinting or Bertillonage. Bertillon recognized fingerprinting as an accurate tool, but he also saw that it offered a dangerous challenge to the primacy of his system.

To protect his procedures, Bertillon did his best to muddy the waters. He added fingerprints to his system as a subordinate element, another type of "special mark" to reinforce the measurements that he insisted had to be the primary means of identifica-

---

* In 1894, he became involved in a very unscientific piece of work. He was a prosecution witness, testifying as a handwriting expert, against Captain Dreyfus. He firmly believed Dreyfus was guilty. That he should have made such an error remains, as one of his biographers put it, inexplicable.

A class in Bertillonage
at the Berkeley Police
Department, around
1909.

tion. To limit fingerprints to a sec-
ondary place, he provided space
on the Bertillon card for the prints
of only one hand, the right.

Then, in 1911, came a theft that
shocked the world: the Mona Lisa
was stolen from the Louvre. There
were no eyewitnesses, and the
Sûreté's informers could not provide a lead. Bertillon was asked to
find the thief.

At the scene of the crime he
found a great clue — a clear
thumb print on a glass case that
the thieves had moved. A thrill of
hope went through France. There
were over 750,000 cards in his
files, thousands of them with criminals' fingerprints on them. But

the fingerprint he had found was
from the thief's *left* thumb. Bertillon could not solve the case.

The defect this revealed in Bertillon's system was deeper than a
failure to take complete sets of fingerprints. Even if the thief's left
thumbprint had been taken, Bertillon had no way of retrieving it
without previously knowing the
name or measurements of the suspect.

When the man who stole the
Mona Lisa, Vicenzo Perugia by
name, tried to sell the painting in
Florence, in December 1913, he
was arrested. Afterward, it was
discovered that he had an arrest
record in Paris and that his mea-

surements — and fingerprints — were in Bertillon's files. With the fingerprint system used by Scotland Yard, Perugia would have been quickly identified. This underlined the fact that Bertillon failed in this case because of his prejudice against fingerprints. As realization of this spread through police circles, the prestige of Bertillonage declined. Nevertheless, Bertillon argued with increasing bitterness against complete reliance on fingerprinting until he died in 1914.

As long as it could be claimed that Bertillon measurements were unique to the individual, some doubt remained about whether to rely on Bertillonage or fingerprinting. But it began to be demonstrated that the measurements were *almost* but not quite singular. This was discovered in the case of mistaken identity involving Adolf Beck, in England, and in the United States, at Leavenworth in 1903, when two prisoners who looked enough alike to be twins were found to have essentially the same measurements. What is more, they had the same name. Only their fingerprints differed. No two sets of identical fingerprints have ever been found.

But even while the issue was being threshed out, police realized that the utility of fingerprints does not depend on existing records. Fingerprints have the supreme advantage of being evidence that can prove a person was at the scene of a crime. Bertillon measurements, as shown decisively in the case of the Mona Lisa robbery, cannot do that.

For another dozen years or so, many police departments maintained dual sets of files. For example, in 1914 the files of the Bureau of Identification in Oakland contained 28,000 Bertillon cards and 17,600 sets of fingerprints, as well as 120,000 photographs. Wanted posters listed Bertillon measurements along with fingerprint classifications.

Within limits, after all, Bertillonage did work. On April 13, 1911, in a classic use of the system, Oakland Inspector Harry Caldwell matched the measurements of an arrestee who called himself William Smith with those of one William Searcy, who was wanted in Los Angeles. When Detective Captain Walter Petersen confronted Searcy with Caldwell's results, Searcy confessed his identity.

As a practical matter, Bertillon files were kept active because they were the only files on certain criminals. But crooks get old, and policemen retire. As time went by, the information contained on Bertillon cards became less and less useful, and the number of people who could decode it diminished. Then the whole system vanished as though it had never existed.

Bertillon's life was dramatic. His great contribution to criminology was scientific, but his temperament was not. He made a science of identification and freed it from the vagaries of personal memory. But the bitterness with which he resisted fingerprinting, a superior method for achieving the same purpose, is a lesson in intellectual pride.

The Distinctive Mark

While Bertillon was developing his method, erratic progress on the problem of identification was being made in the Far East and elsewhere.

Fingerprints had long been used as identifying marks in Japan and China. In *Fingerprinting*, Charles Chappel quotes a Chinese contract found by the British explorer Sir Aurel Stein which concluded, "The two parties have found this just and clear and have affixed the impressions of their fingers as a distinctive mark." The date was A.D. 782! The Chinese used hand- and fingerprints to seal contracts and bills of divorce, and in orphanages took the fingerprints of abandoned children. In Japan, handprints were used to sign documents and official petitions as well as to sign hotel registers and acknowledge the receipt of mail.

Traders carried the practice of fingerprinting with them throughout the Far East, but no one anywhere thought to apply it systematically to criminal matters. This was left to two British subjects.

The first, Sir William Herschel, began his career as an assistant in the old East India Company. In 1853, he was sent to Jungipoor, on the upper reaches of the Hooghly River, and placed in charge of the district. After five years there, he wrote later, "My executive and magisterial experience had . . . forced on me that distrust of all evidence tendered in Court which did so much to cloud our faith in the people around us. . . . The time of which I am speaking was the very worst time of my life in this respect."* Like other administrators, he was frustrated by the fact that the Indians did not share the British sense of the sacred, binding nature of a contract.

In July of 1858, he remembered, "I was starting the first bit of road metalling at Jungipoor, and invited tenders for a supply of 'ghooting' (a good binding material for light roads). A native named Rajyadhar Konai, of the village of Nista, came to terms with me, and at my desire drew up our agreement in his own hand, in true commercial style. He was about to sign it in the usual way, at the upper right-hand corner, when I stopped him in order to read it myself; and it then occurred to me to try an experiment by taking the stamp of his hand, by way of signature instead of writing. There was nothing very original about that, as an idea. Many must have heard of some such use of a man's hand. . . . I was only wishing to frighten Konai out of all thought of repudiating his signature hereafter. He, of course, had never thought of such an attestation, but fell in readily enough. I dabbed his palm and fingers over with the homemade oil-ink used for my official seal, and pressed the whole hand on the back of the contract, and we studied it together, with a good

* Sir William Herschel, *The Origin of Finger-printing.*

deal of chaff about palmistry, comparing his palm with mine on another impression."

And that is how modern fingerprinting began.

Sir William soon became fascinated by his impulsive experiment. "Trials with my own fingers soon showed the advantages of using them instead of the whole hand for the purpose then in view, i.e., for securing a signature which the writer would obviously hesitate to disown."

He knew fingerprint signatures were not binding in the courts and could not be used as evidence of perjury because "that was not settled, and could not have been settled . . . till, after many years, abundant agreement had been reached among ordinary people. The very possibility of such a 'sanction' (to use a technical expression) to the use of a fingerprinting did not dawn upon me till after long experience, and even then it became no more than a personal conviction."

But he began collecting fingerprints as a hobby, and found that even after long intervals, people's fingerprints did not change. He taught his staff to take fingerprints, being careful not to offend the Hindu sense of caste. "The clerks," he wrote, "took to it unhesitatingly, and enjoyed the fun of explaining the 'Sahib's hikmat.' " The fingerprints were kept "for my own inspection rather than as evidence."

At the jail, however, where he also began using fingerprint records, it was a different matter. "The common device of hiring a substitute to serve out a term was not unknown, but it involved a long risk of detection. A safer but very costly, and therefore rare, device was sham death and a purchased corpse, affording comparative safety after escape. . . . The precaution I adopted was to

take the fingerprints of each offender when passing sentence of imprisonment, both on the records of the Court and also on the warrant to the jailer."

Herschel kept files of fingerprints for almost twenty years, and in 1877 reported to his superior, the registrar general and inspector of jails, that he had discovered "a method of identification of persons which, with ordinary care in execution, and with judicial care in the scrutiny is . . . for all practical purposes far more infallible than photography. . . . I have taken thousands . . . and am prepared to answer for the identity of every person whose 'sign-manual' I can produce if I am confronted with him." He suggested that the methods he had developed and tested in his district might be used throughout India. However, the registrar general failed to appreciate the suggestion, and nothing was done with it.

The second British subject to advance the systematic use of fingerprints in criminal matters was an adventurous Scotsman, Dr. Henry Faulds. In the late 1870s, while teaching physiology in a Japanese hospital, he became fascinated by the ridges, whorls, and loops on human fingertips. He began collecting fingerprints and developed skill in distinguishing those of one person from those of another.

In two brilliant investigations, Faulds gave the first practical demonstrations of how to use fingerprints to solve crimes. In the first case, as a thief climbed through a window, he had left a clear, sooty handprint on a recently painted white wall. The local police had arrested a suspect. Faulds took a set of fingerprints from him and compared them with those left on the wall. They did not match. Faulds explained his results to the police convinc-

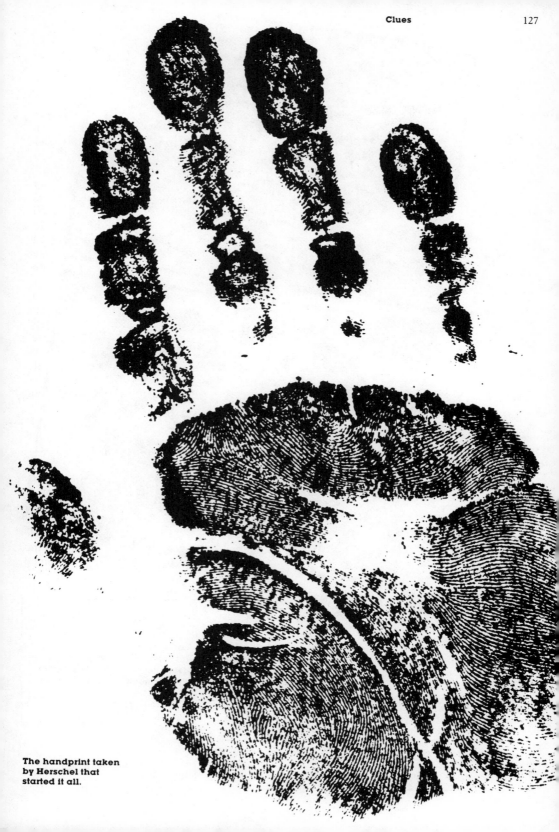

The handprint taken
by Herschel that
started it all.

Flaws in Bertillonage: Cases of mistaken identity. Right: William West and Will West. Facing page: Adolf Beck and William Thomas.

PUDD'NHEAD'S CASE

I beg the indulgence of the court while I make a few remarks in explanation of some evidence which I am about to introduce, and which I shall presently ask to be allowed to verify under oath on the witness-stand. Every human being carries with him from his cradle to his grave certain physical marks which do not change their character, and by which he can always be identi-fied — and that without shade of doubt or question. These marks are his signature, his physiological autograph, so to speak, and this autograph cannot be counterfeited, nor can he disguise it or hide away, nor can it become il-legible by the wear and muta-tions of time. This signature is not his face — age can change that beyond recognition; it is not his hair, for that can fall out; it is not his height, for duplicates of that exist; it is not his form, for dupli-cates of that exist also, whereas his signature is each man's very own — there is no duplicate of it among the swarming populations of the globe!

This autograph consists of the delicate lines or corrugations with which Nature marks the in-sides of the hands and the soles of the feet.

From *Pudd'nhead Wilson* by Mark Twain (1894)

ingly, showing them the points of difference between the prints, and the suspect was released. Later, when the police found another suspect, Faulds repeated his earlier procedures, and this time the prints did match. The thief confirmed the demonstration by confessing.

In the second case, also a theft, there was no known suspect. Faulds found a handprint on a glass mug at the scene and compared it with those in his own collection. The thief turned out to be a servant whose prints Faulds had taken for his files sometime earlier.

Faulds immediately realized the significance of his investigations. In a letter in the October 28, 1880, issue of *Nature*, he wrote, "When bloody finger marks or impressions on clay, glass, etc., exist, they may lead to the scientific identification of criminals. . . . There can be no doubt as to the advantage of having, besides their photographs, a nature-copy of the forever-unchangeable finger furrows of important criminals." This was the first article on the criminological applications of fingerprints.

Herschel and Faulds made their discoveries independently. After returning to England, they quarreled, in letters to *Nature*, about whose should be given the honor of precedence. But between them, they had done everything necessary to inaugurate the age of the fingerprint except devise a system of classification. There the matter rested until Sir Francis Galton became involved in it.

A cousin of Charles Darwin's and the founder of eugenics, Galton was a scientist who engaged in a wide range of studies. Through his fieldwork as an anthropologist, he became interested in human measurements and was the recog-

nized English expert on anthropometry. In 1888, the government asked for his opinion of the Bertillon system. This turned his attention to the problem of criminal identification. He went to Paris, came back dissatisfied with Bertillon's methods, and began exploring the problem himself.

Galton's doubts about Bertillon's system were not resolved by his own additional work on human measurements. When he remembered reading the letters Herschel and Faulds had sent to *Nature*, he contacted Herschel, who shared everything he knew with him. Herschel had collected fingerprints as a hobby. Galton now collected them systematically and on a large scale. He proved what Herschel had guessed: that human fingerprints are unique and unchanging. Galton calculated that the chance of any two persons having the same fingerprints were 64 billion to one.

Next, Galton addressed himself to the problem of classifying fingerprints so that they could be retrieved from files. After considerable labor, he developed a method based on four categories (arches, left loops, right loops, and whorls) and published it in 1892 in his book *Fingerprints*. The book impressed the home secretary, Herbert Asquith, who directed a police committee to see whether fingerprinting might be a better system than Bertillonage.

The committee was also impressed. But they agreed with Galton that his system had defects and was not quite suitable for the type of filing and retrieval required by police work. It was easier to find records filed according to the Bertillon system. The committee recommended a compromise — a modified form of Bertillonage accompanied by the taking of complete sets of fingerprints — in the

THE THUMBOGRAPH

"... It then occurred to me [testified Sergeant Bates of the Criminal Investigation Department] to try if I could get any help from Mrs. Hornby, and on the fifteenth of March I called at Mr. Hornby's private house and saw her. I explained to her what was wanted to clear her nephews from the suspicion that rested on them,

and she then said that she could dispose of those suspicions at once, for she could show me the thumb-prints of the whole family: she had them all in a 'Thumbograph.'"

"A 'Thumbograph'?" repeated the judge. "What is a 'Thumbograph'?"

Anstey rose with the little red-covered volume in his hand.

"A 'Thumbograph,' my lord," said he, "is a book, like this, in which foolish people collect the thumb-prints of their more foolish acquaintances."

He passed the volume up to the judge, who turned over the leaves curiously....

From *The Red Thumb Mark* by R. Austin Freeman (1911)

---

hope that a better method of classifying fingerprints would be found.

In 1891, Juan Vucetich, the talented head of the Statistical Bureau of the Argentine police in La Plata, was instructed to install the Bertillon system for the Argentine police and also to review the articles Sir Francis Galton had published on fingerprints. In far less time than it took Galton, he devised a practical classification system. Soon he and other officers were using fingerprints to solve crimes. In 1896, the Argentine police abolished Bertillonage. That country thus has the distinction of being the first in the world to base its system of police records on fingerprints.

From Argentina, fingerprinting spread to other South American countries, but not to North America or Europe, which failed to benefit from Vucetich's spectacular success. But the general adoption of fingerprints as an aid to identification was clearly only a matter of time. The breakthrough for the non–Spanish speaking came, once again, from the Indian police service.

Sir Edward Henry, who had been appointed inspector general of the Bengali police in 1891, supervised the installation of Bertillonage in India. Within a few

years, Calcutta alone had accumulated over one hundred thousand Bertillon cards, a completely unmanageable number. News of Vucetich's accomplishments failed to reach Henry, but he did read Galton's book. Intrigued, while home on leave he sought out Galton and discussed the problem with him. Galton did for Henry what Herschel had done for him: shared everything he knew.

Late in 1896, Henry hit upon the solution that had eluded Galton of how to file and retrieve fingerprints efficiently. He divided them into five broad categories, labeled "A" for arch, "T" for tented arch, "R" for radial loop, "U" for ulnar loop, and "W" for whorl. The departure from Galton's categories may seem slight, but it made all the difference. Within these major divisions there were many subdivisions. To this he added a method for counting the ridges on the skin. From all of this he derived an alphanumeric code that was flexible enough to accommodate millions of fingerprints and yet allow one set of prints to be retrieved from the files within minutes.

The Indian police dropped the Bertillon system in 1897 and began to rely exclusively on fingerprints. Three years later, Henry was appointed police commis-

Left to right:
Sir William Herschel
Sir Edward Henry
Dr. Henry Faulds

sioner of London and brought his system with him. This marked the end of Bertillonage at Scotland Yard. Henry repaid Galton's kindness by insisting on sharing credit for the innovation, and for many years the English method of fingerprinting was referred to as the Galton-Henry system.

Two celebrated cases led to the acceptance of fingerprinting in England, earning for its validity what Sir William Herschel had described as "abundant agreement . . . among ordinary people." The first involved mistaken identity. An honest, innocent man named Adolf Beck was twice mistaken for a con man named William Thomas. Beck was convicted of swindling women out of their money in 1897 and imprisoned. When released in 1904, Beck was promptly arrested and convicted of the same offense again. Thomas's victims mistook Beck for him, and so did detectives who had ar-

rested Thomas years earlier. Beck was finally freed — before being sent to prison a second time — when Thomas was arrested for fencing stolen goods and an officer connected with Beck's case saw him in jail. This dreadful episode pointed up the shortcomings of the older methods of identification, including Bertillonage.

The second case, a double homicide, occurred the following year, 1905, and was known as "the case of the Deptford murderers." Brothers Alfred and Albert Stratton killed an elderly couple named Farrow and robbed their money box. Alfred left his thumbprint on the box. There was a lot of evidence against the Strattons, and the prosecutor presented it all. Then he brought the thumbprint in as the final, conclusive proof. This was the first time a fingerprint was ever used in a capital case, and the prosecution was in suspense over how the judge

Bettmann Archive

**Above:
Sir Francis Galton**

would react. Would Justice Channell, a conservative jurist, allow the print to be introduced? He did, and a major precedent was established. The Strattons were convicted.

Similar triumphs for fingerprinting soon followed on the Continent and in the United States. At Leavenworth in 1903, the convicts Will West and William West, unrelated despite the similarity of their names and the fact that they looked like twins, were discovered to have identical Bertillon measurements. When it was found that their fingerprints clearly differed, Leavenworth abandoned Bertillonage for fingerprinting.

The St. Louis Police Department was the first to begin using fingerprints in the United States. Its officers learned about them from bobbies stationed with the British exhibit at the world's fair. Within a short time, the St. Louis

department's example was followed by the New York Police Department. In 1908, the Oakland Police Department became the first on the West Coast to use them.

For more than seventy years now, fingerprints have been the standard method of identification. As an investigative aid they are unsurpassed. They are a more reliable means of identification than photography. The presence of a person's fingerprint at the scene of a crime is one of the most powerful forms of evidence.

From the investigator's point of view (rather than that of the identification specialist), there are four types of fingerprints: visible, plastic, latent, and elimination prints. Visible prints are those found in plain sight. Classic examples are the sooty handprint left on a wall and the sweaty print on a glass mug — the kinds that enabled Dr. Faulds to help the Japanese police

FINGERPRINT POWDER ALLERGIES

The ideal latent fingerprint is one that can be brought up in sharp contrast to the surface on which it was imprinted.
    To develop a print, the officer or technician brushes fingerprint powder on the surface being examined and, if he finds a print, lifts it by covering it with tape, carefully raising the tape, and transferring it to a latent fingerprint lift card. The card is sent to fingerprint examiners. (If the fingerprint is in a spot where it might be damaged during the lift, it is photographed before lifting. A specially designed Polaroid camera is used so that the quality of the picture can be judged immediately.)

Fingerprint powders are black, white, gray, silver, and red. The choice of color depends on the color of the surface being examined — usually white powder for a dark surface and black powder for a light surface. The other colors are used if they can provide better contrast.

Fingerprint powders are carbon-based products made from lampblack, graphite, or willow charcoal, with a filler added to keep the powder from clumping up. They are all fine-grained dust. Since they are designed to adhere to the salt in the perspiration that makes the fingerprint mark, they will also adhere to the officer's hands and arms and lodge in his nasal passages. "If you have been working with a lot of it," a technician told us, "you will still be blowing it out of your nose two weeks later."

Fingerprint powder affects different people in different ways. Two technicians we know developed allergies to it. The lungs of one of them filled up with goo. The other's nasal passages became swollen shut. "I was using the same nasal decongestants the coke addicts do," the latter told me, "just to keep my nose open." He began wearing a mask to reduce the amount of fingerprint dust he inhaled, but it did not help. He told us that some old-timers' sinuses were so affected by the stuff that eventually it began coming to the surface of their skin as "real long blackheads."

In recent years, several new methods of raising fingerprints have come into use. Perhaps the most widely employed are chemical sprays containing ninhydrin that are applied to paper, cardboard, and certain wood surfaces. These are fairly toxic, and the user has to be careful to keep the spray out of his eyes and lungs. In Oakland, sprays are not used in the field. Objects are sent to the crime lab and sprayed there, in a well-ventilated space designed for the purpose.

Ninhydrin differs from fingerprint powder in that it reacts to the amino acids in the skin rather than to the salt in perspiration, but as something to work with, it is not a solution to the discomforts of fingerprint powder.

solve two crimes. Plastic prints are those impressed in a surface, as when a fingerprint is left on clay, soft soap, or wet paint. They are visible, but they alter the surface on which they were made. Latent prints are invisible (or practically so) and must be "brought up" by dusting with fingerprint powder. The vast majority of fingerprints found at crime scenes are latent.

The final category, elimination or comparison prints, is not based on visibility. It includes all the prints taken from nonsuspects known to have been at a crime scene. A typical room is full of fingerprints made by people who have a perfect right to be there. To determine which belong to an intruder, those belonging to the nonsuspects must be identified and eliminated from consideration.

The Henry system of filing fingerprints is almost infinitely expandable. But as with any system based on manual search, retrieving information from the files is extremely time consuming. Today a "cold" search (that is, a search in which there is no known suspect) of the files of a large police department by an expert fingerprint analyst can take days. No department can afford to devote weeks or months to it.

To speed up the process, computers are being used more and more frequently. The FBI took

LATENT FINGERPRINT LIFT CARD
Oakland Police Department

DATE REC'D IN LAB:	LCF:	RD #

SEARCHED: ☐ YES ☐ NO   ☐ COMPUTER ☐ MANUAL   QUALITY:

FOR LAB USE ONLY

CRIME: DATE:

COMPLAINANT:

ADDRESS:

LOCATION OF LIFT(S).   (Do not exceed two lifts per card.):

536-457 (6/75)   TECHNICIAN

Oakland Police Dept

Latent fingerprint lift card

Oakland Police Dept.

Latent fingerprints, brought up by fingerprint powder and ready for transfer to a fingerprint lift card.

the lead in developing electronic search techniques, and state, county, and municipal agencies are following along as quickly as they can. In California, the state's Department of Justice began using the Automated Latent Print System, which was usually referred to by its acronym, ALPS.

ALPS contained the fingerprints of more than 151,000 convicted felons. Oakland used ALPS with considerable success in cases of murder, rape, and armed robbery where there were no known suspects. In 10 percent of the cases Oakland submitted to it, suspects were located and convicted. The San Francisco Police Department has had similar success with its own system.

In 1985 a new statewide computer system for fingerprints went on-line as a successor to ALPS. It includes the ALPS data base and is continually growing. In its first operation, a fingerprint from the scene of one of the "Night Stalker" killings was fed into it. In three minutes it came up with a print belonging to Richard Ramirez, who was subsequently arrested and charged with this terrifying series of murders.

Fingerprinting has come a long way from Jungipoor on the upper reaches of the Hooghly, but it is still helping to put away criminals who thought they were home free.

Black Bart's Laundry Mark

Black Bart's specialty was robbing Wells Fargo stages as they made their way through the thinly populated back country of Northern California. His first robbery took place on August 3, 1877, near Point Arena. Over the next five years he struck at irregular intervals over a wide range of territory north and east of San Francisco. By the end of June 1883, he had committed twenty-seven successful holdups.

He stood out from ordinary bandits because of the verses he left in a few of the strongboxes he emptied. Investigators found these lines at the scene of one of his early robberies:

> I've labored long and hard for
>   bread,
> For honor and for riches,
> But on my toes too long you've
>   tread,
> You fine-haired sons of bitches.

After another robbery he deposited this verse in the strongbox:

> Here I lay me down to sleep
> To wait the coming morrow,
> Perhaps success, perhaps defeat,
> And everlasting sorrow.
> Let come what will I'll try it on,
> My condition can't be worse;
> And if there's money in that box
> Tis munny in my purse.

He did not always leave poems. But when he did, they seem to have been composed before the robberies while he waited for the stage. Joseph Henry Jackson, an authority on California history, said the two verses quoted above were the only ones Bart actually wrote. Most students of Bart's career agree that the following poem was by one of his imitators, partly because it seems to have been written after a holdup:

> So here I've stood while wind and
>   rain
> Have set the trees to sobbing,
> And risked my life for that damned
>   stage
> That was not worth the robbing.

Bart was a businesslike robber who did not stick around after the crime. He made his getaway immediately.

Here's another verse attributed to Bart that is almost certainly not his:

> I rob the rich to feed the poor,
> Which hardly is a sin.
> A widow ne'er knocked at my door
> But what I let her in.
> So blame me not for what I've
>   done,
> I don't deserve your curses,
> And if for any cause I'm hung
> Let it be for my verses!

There was nothing of the Robin Hood about Bart, and it is thought that some newsman composed this poem, since it fits so completely into the sentimentality of the time.

All of his poems were signed "Black Bart the Po8." "Po8" is to be read "poet," as with current license plates that mix numbers and letters to form approximations of words (such as the famous "6UL DV8," which turned up in San Francisco a couple of years ago).

Bart's M.O. was clear-minded. He chose locations where he could stay hidden until the stage came along, which put the element of surprise strongly in his favor. These were places where the stage had to move slowly, where it was far from any kind of help, and where the robbery would not be interrupted by passersby. To prevent the driver from identifying him later, Bart wore a flour sack over his head that had eye holes cut into it. He wanted to rob the stage, not kill the driver, so he carried an enormous and powerful double-barreled shotgun, not a six-shooter. Looking down the barrels of that gun, nobody ever resisted him.

Even so, over time detectives developed a small fund of reliable information about Black Bart. His M.O. was consistent, and people interviewed in the area of the holdups added to the descriptions furnished by the stage drivers. He was of medium height, a middle-aged or elderly man with a deep voice and gray whiskers. He had vividly blue eyes.

All good things come to an end. In November 1883, Bart set out for Funk Hill, near Copperopolis, a town due east of San Francisco. He made camp as usual, cleaned his gun, shook the dust from his flour sack, perhaps scribbled a few lines of verse. Then, satisfied with his preparations, he spread out his bedroll for a night under the stars.

In the morning, as stage driver R. E. McConnell was driving into Copperopolis, he spotted a young friend tramping along the road and pulled up the horses to give him a lift. The youngster, Jimmy Rolleri, was on his way out to the

Oakland History Room, Oakland Public Library

countryside to try his new repeating rifle on small game. Halfway up Funk Hill Jimmy got off the stage, and McConnell watched him push off into the brush. The driver yelled "Giddup" and the stage climbed on.

Just below the crest of the hill Black Bart stepped into view. Bold with head in flour bag and shotgun in hand, he told McConnell to unhitch the horses and lead them on over the top of the hill. Looking at the gun, McConnell was willing. As soon as the driver and the team were out of sight, Bart took an ax and set to work on the strongbox.

On the other side of the hill, who should McConnell find but his friend Jimmy. They very carefully climbed up to a vantage point from which they could see the stage. McConnell took the rifle

Sheriff Harry Morse in 1868.

and, as Bart climbed out of the stage ("exited the vehicle," an officer might write in a crime report today), opened fire on him. He missed and Bart fled into the underbrush, taking the money with him.

A posse was organized. Poking around the scene of the robbery, they found Bart's camp. He had abandoned various odds and ends, including a derby hat, a pair of field glasses, and a handkerchief with a laundry mark on it that read "F.X.0.7." This handkerchief was turned over to Harry Morse.

Morse was one of the outstanding peace officers in California. Six months before, Wells Fargo had engaged him on special assignment to run down Black Bart. Morse is little known today, but he was famous in his time and deserves to be remembered. Hiring him was like hiring Palladin or Hopalong Cassidy.

Born in New York, Henry Nicholson Morse came to California in 1849 as a boy of fourteen, did some mining, settled in Oakland in 1854, and served there briefly as a deputy U.S. marshal.

In 1862, at the age of twenty-eight, he was elected sheriff of Alameda County. Young for the job, he held it fourteen years, a remarkably long run in a government office in California in those days. During the same years, Oakland had seven different city marshals and captains of police.

Morse was elected over and over again because he was such a remarkably efficient sheriff. Almost singlehandedly he eliminated the bandits and rustlers who infested the hinterlands — the canyons, foothills, and mountains in the eastern and southeastern ends of the county.

A contemporary writer, J. M. Guinn, said of Morse, "From the day he entered the office it became evident that he was a calm, cautious, patient, persistent, highly educated detective. His aim was always to find and capture his criminal by the exercise of skill and sagacity, avoiding but not shrinking from a conflict. . . . He was stern and terrible in the discharge of his duties, carrying the weight and burden of its responsibilities in something of the spirit of an old Scotch Covenanter." Morse killed several outlaws who had the temerity to challenge him face to face.

After he cleaned up Alameda County, Morse went across the bay to establish a private detective agency in San Francisco. It became the best known on the West Coast. He was the logical choice for Wells Fargo when it got fed up with Black Bart.

The evidence found on Funk Hill was brought to Wells Fargo's San Francisco office. The derby and the field glasses were kept by the company's chief of detectives, but the handkerchief was turned over to Harry Morse to see what he could make of it. Morse quickly found that there were almost a hundred laundries in San Francisco, and he decided to find out whether one of them was the source of the laundry mark. If, after checking them all, he did not get results, he would begin inquiring outside the city. In less than a week, however, he located the laundry that put "F.X.0.7." on Bart's handkerchief.

From there he traced the handkerchief to a cigar store that doubled as a laundry agency. He learned from the proprietor, a man named Ware, that the handkerchief belonged to one C. E. Bolton, and that Bolton was a mining man and one of his best customers. "In fact," he said, "Mr. Bolton makes my shop his headquarters when he is in town." Morse

THE WASH-AND-WEAR BURGLAR

In 1985, the Fort Lauderdale Police Department captured a burglar with a clue that resembled the one Harry Morse used to track down Black Bart.

The burglar in this case broke into houses, took what he wanted, and then, before leaving the premises, washed himself and changed into clothing belonging to his victims. He left his own dirty clothes behind. The burglar's dirty laundry became a trademark as distinctive as the verses Black Bart left in the strongboxes. Before long, the cops were calling this fellow "the wash-and-wear burglar."

Eventually he got careless. Just once he did not empty everything out of his pants pockets. He left behind a rent receipt with his name and address on it.

Well, case solved.

Even though the receipt was easier to run down than the laundry mark on Bart's handkerchief, it was the same type of clue: the record of an honest transaction.

Black Bart's M.O. appears to have been chosen freely, in a way reasonable for what he had in mind. One has the impression that if something better had occurred to him, he would have seized upon it immediately and changed his way of committing robberies. His verses were odd, but only in that highway robbery is a strange occasion for such playfulness. Not so with the wash-and-wear" burglar's M.O. His seems to belong in the murky class of methods generated by compulsions and fetishes. It implies unspoken and unacted violations of the victim.

---

replied. "I, too, am in mining. I want to see Mr. Bolton on a matter of business."

Just then Bolton came strolling along the street. Ware greeted him and introduced him to Harry Morse. For Morse it was like a religious moment, an epiphany — one of those instants of revelation in which things that have been shadowy and indistinct become clearly visible and known with certainty.

"He was elegantly dressed," Morse told a reporter, "carrying a little cane. He wore a natty little derby hat, a diamond pin, a large diamond ring on his little finger, and a heavy gold watch and chain. He was about five feet, eight inches, in height, straight as an arrow, broad-shouldered, with deep-sunken bright blue eyes, high cheekbones and a large handsome gray moustache and imperial; the rest shaven clean. One would have taken him for a gentleman who had made a fortune and

was enjoying it. He looked anything but a robber. I knew he was the man I wanted, from the descriptions."

In short order, Bolton was being interviewed at Wells Fargo. He claimed to be a mine owner, but could not tell them where his mine was located. He was detained by authority of the San Francisco police, taken back to Copperopolis for identification, and questioned there in detail by Harry Morse about the latest robbery. Before long he confessed and led Morse and the local sheriff to the spot where he had hidden the loot — $500 in gold coins, $65 in gold dust, and 228 ounces of gold amalgam (unsmelted ore).

Some students of this case think that the laundry mark clue made Bart's capture a foregone conclusion. Maybe. But good detective work often appears later to have the quality of inevitability.

(text continues on page 142)

**Tuolumne County,
Black Bart country.**

Alameda County Sheriff's Department

Harry Morse in the
1880s.

A mug shot of Black
Bart, probably taken
at San Francisco City
Prison after his trip to
Copperopolis with
Harry Morse.

Bancroft Library

Nobody knows what became of the derby and the field glasses found in Bart's abandoned hide-out. It is possible that either of these would have led to Black Bart if properly developed. But they were not. It is equally true that in the hands of another investigator the laundry mark could have been an unproductive clue.

C. E. Bolton, alias Black Bart, the expert miner of strongboxes, was sentenced to six years in San Quentin. He was released with time off for good behavior on January 21, 1888. Soon afterward he disappeared from view, and his whereabouts were never reliably reported again.

Harry Morse died at his home in Oakland on January 13, 1912, leaving an estate valued at half a million dollars, mostly from his investments in mining stocks. Morse really did know the mining business.

A SUSPICIOUS DEATH

When the red light on the police box at Twelfth and Franklin went on, the crisp, authoritative voice of the phone operator told me to go across the street to the St. Marks Hotel and investigate a body in one of the rooms. "I can't locate the homicide detail," he told me, "so you make a suspicious death report, wait for the coroner and have him sign for the body."

I wrote down the all-important time — 11:42 A.M. — in case I was called to testify before a jury in a homicide case. It was the first time I had handled a death. It could be a murder, suicide, accidental or natural death.

In my head I reviewed my recent lessons on the first officer's duties at the scene of death from unknown causes. If foul means were suspected, all evidence and the scene were to be preserved as found. In all strangulation cases, the knot was not to be disturbed but the rope was to be cut away from the knot and the rope or cord preserved intact. I was to look for suicide notes, the instrument of death, position of body, anything out of the ordinary. I should note room temperature, condition of body, wounds, extent of rigor mortis and even if any

flies were present. The coroner made all of these notations but a policeman's notebook should also contain all possible information relating to a case.

The desk clerk at the hotel told me that the body was in room number 508. I could take the slow elevator or I could go up the stairs which were faster. I went up the stairs and was out of breath when I reached the fifth floor.

There was already a news photographer on the floor, Doc Rogers from the *Tribune* across the street. He wanted a picture and story so he accompanied me to number 508. The door was locked. The clerk had said that it would be open. Besides we heard voices in the room, a couple quarreling. So we tried several doors down the hall. Number 518 was open with our body and an awful stench.

The body on the hotel bed was a male Caucasian, probably in his fifties, thin and white-skinned. He was lying on his back naked. He felt cold and clammy. The body must have been there for some time as there was an occasional escape of body gas. In school we had been informed about this phenomenon of life ac-

tivity caused by the bacteria in the stomach and the intestinal tract. His stomach seemed to have a greenish tinge consistent with the process of decomposition. Also the appearance of rigor mortis had set in. His male organ was erect — held in position by a spasm of the fenestra muscle. This indicated a probable heart attack — or a crime of passion.

Doc wanted to take a picture but he did not want the penis standing up like that. "Do something about it," he said.

I took out my baton and gave it a hard knock to dislocate the fenestra muscle. We had been told about this after-death condition in school.

Then all hell broke loose! The old guy came alive and ran into the bathroom slamming the door. Later, no one would believe his story about a man with a camera and a cop with a big club. He was a drunk who often had the DTs.

The correct room was number 508. The maid who had discovered the body locked the door, but she did not turn off the radio.

Death was from natural causes.

From "Six Gold Stars: On the Beat with Dexter H. Mast, OPD," in *The Express*, August 22, 1980.

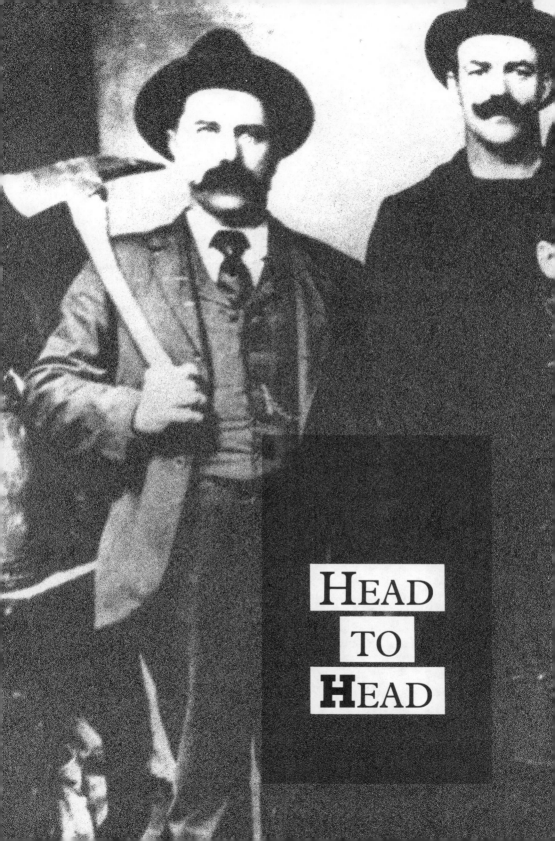

HEAD
TO
HEAD

*A*rrest

An arrest is defined by the California penal code as "taking a person into custody, in a case and in the manner authorized by law. An arrest may be made by a peace officer or by a private person." This definition was enacted in 1872, and while its terms have been litigated, it has never been changed. It is typical of statutory definitions of arrest in use around the country.

The power of arrest is a serious one, since it involves depriving a person of his or her liberty, and it must not be abused. Consequently, it is a crime to conspire to "falsely and maliciously" indict a person for a crime or to "procure" another to be arrested falsely.

**All right, please.
Name and date of
birth?"**

The Thriller Confrontation Scene

One of the standard scenes in detective stories of the old school occurs when the detective assembles all the suspects in a living room or some other social setting (a splendid dinner party, as in the movie of Dashiell Hammett's *The Thin Man*) and begins, "I've asked you all here this evening . . ."

We asked a veteran homicide investigator whether there was any basis in fact for this classic scene. "It might have been done in the old days," he said dubiously, "but you couldn't do it today. Can you imagine giving their *Miranda* rights to a whole roomful of people?"

Nick and Nora Charles, played by William Powell and Myrna Loy.

Bettmann Archive

Right and facing page: The real Nick and Nora, Dashiell Hammett and Lillian Hellman.

Bettmann Archive

The scene violates sound procedure, which is to isolate everyone, witness or suspect, who knows anything about the crime. This is done so that they cannot compare notes and alter their accounts. As an example of how stories might change, the investigator suggested a situation with a man and a woman, in which the man is the dominant personality. The man may convince the woman that what he is saying is the truth — and he may be lying. Or they may

Lillian Hellman

argue about what happened, confusing their own recollections.

Furthermore, if the confrontation is not used to generate new information but to reveal the solution of the crime and if the suspect is armed, he may actually get his gun out and shoot somebody. Then you've got two homicides to account for instead of just one. The murderer in *The Thin Man* did pull a gun, as you may recall, but Nick Charles put the arm on him.

The Liar's Puzzle

"Interesting puzzle, the VanDorn murder case," Sergeant McGuffy remarked to his lieutenant one day after it was all over. "The way I reconstruct the crime, the innocent people were so excited when they first talked to us, they each got one fact wrong. But the killer wanted to confuse our trail — and so coolly lied from beginning to end."

Knowing this much, can you figure out who is the killer?

Egmont VanDorn has been found dead in his apartment. From the beginning, it is pretty clear to the police that it is murder dressed up to look like suicide. Before they can be separated, the four young people who found the body — Arnold, Betsy, Charles, and Daisy — eagerly begin to tell their story.

"If, as the police say, Egmont was killed between four and five," said Daisy, "that must let us all out. We all arrived here at the apartment at six. And we were all together having dinner for at least two hours before we came over here."

"We got here at seven," said Charles.

"Arnold said that it was six o'clock at the time, just before we opened the door. Didn't you Arnold?" said Daisy.

"I said it was just seven on the nose," said Arnold. "Sorry, honey."

"I have no idea what he said or what time we got here," declared Betsy. "The thing I remember is the gas in the hall. We rang the doorbell, and no one came and no one came, and then I smelled the gas. My heart turned over. I thought to myself, he's dead. I just know he's dead."

"Don't dramatize yourself," said Daisy coolly. "There is no way that you could have smelled the gas before we opened the door. The place was locked up, and sealed too, tighter than a drum. We'd still be in the hall if Eggy hadn't given me a key last week."

"There was gas in the hall, all right," said Charles. "I smelled it before we opened the door. You seemed to take forever getting your key out. When you finally got the door opened, the gas just streamed out."

"That was a pretty dangerous thing you did, Charles," said Arnold, "turning on the lights the way you did. Didn't it occur to you that a spark at the light switch could have blown us all up."

"The lights were already on, Arnold," Charles replied.

"For my part, I'm sorry about pulling him out of the oven — tampering with the evidence and all that," said Arnold. "Murder never crossed my mind. Locked room, you know. All I could think of was that maybe he was alive and we could still save him."

"I don't believe this," said Daisy. "*You* didn't pull him out of the oven. I did. You ran and opened the window. Very good move, too, I thought at the time."

"*I* opened the window!" cried Betsy. "I was dizzy from the fumes, and I knew I needed to do something fast."

"The only things you opened were the door to the liquor cabinet and a bottle of Scotch, Betsy." Charles laughed at her. "And I thought they were good moves."

"That was Arnold who got out the Scotch," said Betsy. "Don't you remember our sitting there after you called the police, and Arnold passing out the glasses."

"It couldn't have been me. Must have been you," said Arnold. "I've never been here before. I didn't even know where he kept the stuff. Charles, what did you do?"

"Do you know what? I don't think I did anything. I remember quite clearly, walking over here with you after that long dinner we had together, and then seeing poor Eggy's feet through the door. But after that, I don't think I did a thing, except stand there gasping."

Who did it? Read on.

Solution to the Liar's Puzzle

Each innocent person had one fact wrong, and the killer lied all the time.

Who did it?

Charles?

Charles and Daisy agree that they all had a long dinner and arrived together. If Charles is the killer, he is lying about this, and Daisy is mistaken. If Daisy is mistaken about this, she must be right that Arnold opened the window. If Arnold opened the window, then Charles must be telling the truth that Betsy didn't open it. But if Charles is telling the truth, he can't be the killer.

Daisy?

If Daisy is the killer, she lied about their having arrived together after the long dinner, and Charles is mistaken there. If Charles is mistaken there, he must be right in everything else. But Charles disagrees with Betsy twice — about whether Betsy opened the window and whether she opened the Scotch. That would make Betsy mistaken twice, and that can't be.

(Why is it that the reasoning that proves Charles is not the killer won't work to prove Daisy isn't? Suffice it to say that if Daisy lied when she said that Arnold opened the window, it wouldn't necessarily mean that Betsy opened it. Daisy could have opened it herself.)

Betsy?

If Betsy is the killer, Charles is mistaken about whether there was gas in the hall, and right about everything else. So when Arnold and Charles disagree about whether the latter turned on the lights, it must be Arnold who is mistaken. Arnold would be right about everything else. But Arnold disagrees with Daisy twice: about what time Arnold said they arrived, and about who pulled poor

Eggy out of the oven. If Arnold is right about both, Daisy is wrong twice, and that can't be.

Arnold?

So is Arnold the murderer? Yes. Let's take it from top to bottom.

Charles and Daisy are both right about the long dinner and everybody's arriving together.

Arnold lies when he quotes himself as saying they had arrived at seven on the nose — and Daisy is right that he had said six.

Betsy and Charles are both right about the smell of gas in the hall. Daisy has made a mistake.

Arnold lies about Charles's turning on the lights, and Charles is right that they were already on.

Arnold lies about pulling Eggy out of the oven, and Daisy is right that she did it.

Daisy is right that Arnold opened the window; Charles is right that Betsy did not open the window; and in thinking she did, Betsy is mistaken.

Arnold lies about Betsy's opening up the Scotch; Betsy is right that Arnold opened it; and in thinking it was Betsy who did it, Charles is mistaken.

Postscript: You may wonder why Charles and Daisy are not in disagreement as to when they arrived. Let us point out that Daisy's statement about this begins with an "if." It is a hypothetical statement, and logically true at that.

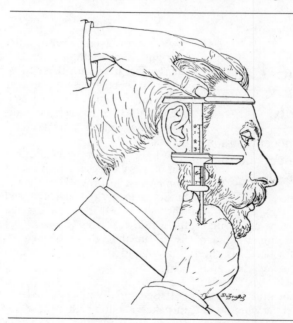

"Officer Richard Mooney . . . had so far stopped at eight resorts without success. He was not disappointed, as he had expected nothing. In police work, he knew, much time and effort had to be futilely spent. It was part of his responsibility to do his share."

John Ball, *The Cool Cottontail*

*F*act into Fiction

George Roberts   June 4, 1842
Notion Magazine
Boston, Mass.

My Dear Sir.

It is just possible that you may have seen a tale of mine entitled
'The Murders in the Rue Morgue' and published, originally, in
'Graham's Magazine' for April, 1841. Its theme was the exercise of
ingenuity in the detection of a murderer. I have just completed a
similar article, which I shall entitle 'The Mystery of Marie Roget
— a Sequel to the Murders in the Rue Morgue.'

The story is based upon the assassination of Mary Cecilia
Rogers, which created so vast an excitement, some months ago, in
New York. I have, however, handled my design in a manner
altogether novel in literature. I have imagined a series of nearly
exact coincidences occurring in Paris. A young grisette, one Marie
Roget, had been murdered under precisely similar circumstances
with Mary Rogers. Thus, under pretence of showing how Dupin
(the hero of The Rue Morgue) unravelled the mystery of Marie's
assassination, I, in reality, enter into a very long and rigorous
analysis of the New York tragedy. No point is omitted. I examine,
each by each, the opinions and arguments of the press upon the
subject, and show that this subject has been, hitherto,
unapproached. In fact, I believe not only that I have demonstrated
the fallacy of the general idea — that the girl was the victim of a
gang of ruffians — but have indicated the assassin in a manner
which will give renewed impetus to investigation.

My main object, nevertheless, as you will readily understand, is
an analysis of the true principles which should direct inquiry in
similar cases. From the nature of the subject, I feel convinced that
the article will excite attention, and it has occurred to me that you
would be willing to purchase it for the forthcoming Mammoth
Notion. It will make 25 pages of Graham's Magazine; and, at the
usual price, would be worth to me $100. For reasons, however,
which I need not specify, I am desirous of having this tale printed
in Boston, and, if you like it, I will say $50. Will you please write
me upon this point? — by return mail, if possible.

Yours very truly

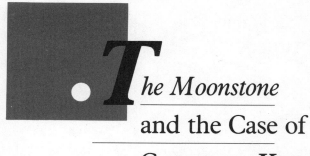

The Moonstone
and the Case of
Constance Kent

BBC. Hulton Picture Library

Constance Kent

Wilkie Collins's *The Moonstone* is the first and one of the best modern English detective novels. Dorothy Sayers, who once planned (but did not write) a biography of Collins, called it "the very finest detective story ever written."

Published in 1868, *The Moonstone* is loosely based on the real life case of Constance Kent. The circumstances were as follows.

The Kent family lived in Wiltshire, southwest of London. Samuel Saville Kent, the head of the household, had been married twice. His first wife gave him ten children: of the six who lived, four were still at home, including Constance, at the time a pretty girl of sixteen. After his wife died, Kent married the children's governess. They had three children, among them little Francis, who was three.

Although Samuel Kent was a rising man in his field, the neighbors did not like him. He lived beyond his station, local gossips agreed. He kept a larger house and more servants than his position justified. They noted, as a newspaper put it, that an "unusual number of servants have been discharged from [his] establishment." The older children were jealous of the attention given to the younger ones, some said. Although the Kents had friends who took a more kindly view of their situation, it was clear that the household had its share of problems.

In the early morning hours of June 29, 1860, little Francis was stabbed in the chest with a knife. Then his throat was cut. The killer wrapped the boy's small body in a blanket and stuffed it into the servants' privy.

Superintendent Foley of the Wiltshire constabulary botched the investigation. He found valuable clues. And then he lost them. He made it known that he suspected Elizabeth Gough, the children's current nurse, but he could not develop information against her. His investigation stalled. The district judge asked Scotland Yard to intervene.

Detective Inspector Whicher, a highly regarded investigator with more than twenty years of experience, was assigned to the case. Superintendent Foley resented Whicher's presence, so he withheld information from him.

Nevertheless, Whicher soon learned that one of Constance Kent's nightgowns was missing. He also discovered that Foley had found a blood-spattered "woman's shift," disregarded it, and lost it. Whicher put two and two together and concluded that Constance Kent was the murderess. (Foley's astonishing blunder actually occurred. Conan Doyle's Inspector Lestrade never fell so low!)

Despite the fact that the evidence amounted to little more than hearsay, thanks to Foley, Inspector Whicher arrested Constance and interrogated her. She refused to make any admissions. A week later she was held to answer before the court. The local gossips were outraged that a maiden of unsullied reputation should be charged with such a hideous crime. The Victorians simply refused to believe that an innocent young girl could behave so cruelly. Scotland Yard was widely criticized for the arrest. The court agreed. Constance was discharged.

Whicher resigned from Scotland Yard a little less than three years later, in March 1863. Though he stated that his resignation was due to ill health, people believed it resulted from the clamor that followed his arrest of

Constance Kent. After leaving the Yard, Whicher became a successful private detective and helped to solve several important cases, including the once-famous Tichborne fraud.

A year after Whicher's resignation, Constance Kent confessed to the murder. She was tried, convicted, and sentenced to death, but her sentence was commuted to life in prison. She served twenty-one years.

The resolution of any famous murder case is often challenged later by writers who profess to have found serious mistakes in the investigation or in the trial. The case of Constance Kent was no exception. Several writers have offered hypothetical reconstructions of the case that purport to show Constance's innocence and her father's guilt. In opposition to these hypotheses, as Douglas Brown noted dryly in his history of Scotland Yard, "stands the opinion of an experienced, intelligent, and unbiased police officer, and a confession of guilt. As against guess work, this sort of testimony will usually be accepted in the ordinary affairs of life."

The Moonstone, as fiction, triumphantly carries us far away from "the ordinary affairs of life." Clearly using the Kent case as a point of departure, it soon leaves the factual situation behind, even though fascinating pieces of it are embedded in the story.

To begin with, *The Moonstone* is not principally a murder mystery, although a murder does occur. It centers on the investigation of a theft — the theft from Rachel Verinder of a fabulously valuable jewel known as the Moonstone.

The situation of the Verinder family differs considerably from that of the Kents. Members of the nobility, Lady Verinder and her daughter Rachel enjoy unchallenged social and financial pre-eminence in their neighborhood. Not for them the wobbly status of the Kents! The servants are deeply devoted: Betteredge, the butler, has spent his life with the family, and Rosanna Spearman, the maid, gives her life for it.

As the investigation of the Moonstone theft begins, a nightgown that is an important clue disappears. It is a clue very different from the one in the Kent case, however. The Kent nightgown was bloody; the *Moonstone* nightgown has a small paint stain on it. Just as Wilkie Collins changed the type of stain on the nightgown, he also changed its ultimate meaning. By hiding the nightgown, Rachel Verinder protects not herself (as, in all probability, Constance Kent protected herself) but the man she loves, and whom she suspects of the theft. And she takes a selfless risk, becoming the primary suspect. Though why she should have stolen the jewel from herself remains an inexplicable part of the mystery.

The Moonstone abounds in parallels to the Kent case, but each of them has been magically transformed. It is anything but a *roman à clef*. It is in fact an absorbing demonstration of the power of a novelist's imagination.

Sergeant Cuff, who is based on the character of Inspector Whicher, is a great creation. He is a world-weary, patient, knowledgeable man who sees deeply into human beings. Here is how he appears to Betteredge on arriving at the Verinder estate:

A fly from the railway drove up . . . and out got a grizzled, elderly man, so miserably lean that he looked as if he had not got an ounce of flesh on his bones in any part of him. He was dressed all in decent black, with a white cravat round his neck. His face was as sharp as a hatchet, and the skin of

it was as yellow and dry and withered as an autumn leaf. His eyes, of a steely light gray, had a disconcerting trick, when they encountered your eyes, of looking as though they expected something more from you than you were aware of yourself. His walk was soft, his voice was melancholy; his long, lanky fingers were hooked like claws. He might have been a parson, or an undertaker, or anything else you like except what he really was.

Sergeant Cuff's presence in the Verinder household is at once unobtrusive and extremely disturbing. When, after conducting the opening phase of his investigation, he announces his preliminary results and indicates that he suspects Rachel Verinder, it is with what Betteredge describes as "a horrid clearness that forced you to understand him; with an abominable justice that favored nobody." Even so, the butler and everyone else is shocked and outraged that Cuff has ventured to accuse her. Rachel is not only well loved by the family and servants, she is a young lady.

Lady Verinder has Sergeant Cuff removed from the case: "Circumstances," she says, "have fatally misled him." But, as the story later shows, Cuff had correctly recognized Rachel as a liar despite her social standing, just as clearly as Whicher saw that young Constance Kent had slain her little stepbrother.

So in these cases both detectives saw through one of the great pieties of their age, that of the innocence of young maids, and each suffered for it by being taken off the case. As we have seen, Inspector Whicher was vindicated by Constance Kent's confession; however, he received no official credit for his part in the affair. Ser-

John Welsh as Sergeant Cuff in the *Masterpiece Theatre* production of *The Moonstone.*

geant Cuff fared better. He was called back into the investigation and helped wrap it up.

There is something claustrophobic in the moral atmosphere of Constance Kent's crime, a narrowness and blunt intensity in her concentration on precedence in her father's affections — for hers was surely a crime of jealousy. By contrast, *The Moonstone* occurs in a morally spacious world, one in which many degrees and varieties of affection are displayed.

Two characteristics of mystery fiction were established in *The Moonstone*: the fictional crime, be it a murder or a theft, is more complex than most real crimes, and the cast of fictional characters has a higher social standing than their opposite numbers in real life.

Chinatown, Fu Manchu, and Charlie Chan

In San Francisco and Oakland in the late nineteenth century, Chinatown was a tough beat. Gambling, opium, male and female prostitution, slavery, and other profitable crimes flourished in the midst of Asian immigrants trying to adjust to a harsh, new, and tremendously different world than the one they left behind.

The society outside Chinatown,

WHOSE BODY? #1

Murder is common in history and fiction. Bodies abound. Here are some of the more memorable ones. Can you identify them?

1. Murdered he was, but drowned in a butt of malmsey? So legend has it. Who was he?
2. For refusing to reveal the whereabouts of two young women, this devoutly Christian man was flogged to death by a degenerate planter. Who was he?
3. He has long been thought to have died of a guilty conscience, but recent re-examination of the evidence shows he was probably poisoned by a jealous husband. Who was he?
4. He was reading an unfinished article when its writer drove an ice ax through his skull. Who was he?
5. Shortly after his wife visited this smallpox-stricken man, the house was blown up with gunpowder. A mess? Not to worry. He was found in the yard in one piece — strangled. Who was he?
6. He was stabbed in the bath by a woman who disapproved of his political excesses. Who was he?
7. A nice lady gave this fugitive

food, drink, and shelter, and then hammered a nail through his head. Who was he?
8. A swinging pot of cactus bashed in his poor head something awful. Who was he?
9. Though it followed a longstanding custom in his country, his fall in 1948 made "defenestration" a household word in America. Who was he?
10. He was murdered in the cathedral. Who was he?
11. This poor woman's corpse was found in her fourth-floor apartment in Paris, stuffed feet first up a chimney. Who was she?
12. Poisoned, shot, dropped into the river through a hole in the ice, fished out and buried in a silver casket, he was dug up and burned by the mob. Who was he?

Answers to Whose Body? #1

1. Clarence, the third duke of York, secretly killed in the Tower of London in 1478.
2. Uncle Tom, killed by Simon Legree in Harriet Beecher Stowe's antislavery classic, *Uncle Tom's Cabin*.
3. The Reverend Arthur Dimmesdale, secret lover of Hester Prynne, in Nathaniel Hawthorne's *The Scarlet Letter*.
4. Leib Davydovich Bronstein. We know him as Trotsky. Killed in Mexico in 1940.
5. Henry Stewart, Lord Darnley — the second husband of Mary, Queen of Scots — at Kirk o' Field, Edinburgh, in 1567.
6. Jean Paul Marat, the French revolutionary and terrorist, by Charlotte Corday in 1793.
7. Sisera, the Canaanite general, who was fleeing defeat by the Israelites under Barak. The lady with the hammer was Jael the Kenite (Judges 4:17–22).
8. Mr. Noakes, in Dorothy L. Sayer's mystery novel *Busman's Honeymoon*.
9. Jan Masaryk, foreign minister of Czechoslovakia. Found spread-eagled in the courtyard of Czernin Palace, Prague.
10. Thomas à Becket, the archbishop of Canterbury, in 1170 by four overzealous knights.
11. Mme. L'Espanaye, in Edgar Allan Poe's "The Murders in the Rue Morgue," published in 1841.
12. Grigori Efimovich (called Rasputin or the Debauched One), in 1916.

which was mostly white, was ambivalent about their presence, and sometimes quite hostile. In Chinatown itself, of the burdens the Chinese had to bear, one of the most difficult was the tongs. The tongs were modeled on the social associations that have played an important role in Chinese life for centuries. Some associations were (and still are) publicly known and served benevolent purposes. Others were secret or semisecret political, or even revolutionary, organizations; still others had criminal purposes.

In the United States and England the tongs were simultaneously benevolent social organizations and criminal conspiracies. In their beneficial aspect, they were of great value to the Chinese. But when the tongs fought each other for control of the rackets, the highbinders (professional assassins, also known as hatchet men) came into their own, and honest men and women were not safe. Highbinder murders were quick, brutal, and unpredictable. As long as the highbinders were an active menace to residents and visitors alike, Chinatown remained isolated and was looked on by the majority community mainly as a vice district.

The special Chinatown squads, along with the regular beat officers in San Francisco and Oakland were an important part of the effort to control routine crime in Chinatown. But they performed an even more important function that was vital to the assimilation of the Chinese into American society: they helped to suppress the violence of the tongs. For many of the years that he ran the central district (downtown) in Oakland, Captain J. Frank Lynch had a magnificent Oriental rug in his office — alas, long since disappeared. It was a gift he had been given by the Chinese merchants in thanks for his part in negotiating peace among the local tongs. He was very proud of that rug.

Interacting with the Chinese was not without cost to the reputations of the police departments. This was especially true in the area of gambling enforcement. The tongs never really bought the idea that gambling should be illegal; instead, they bought a lot of the police officers, and paid them off to allow the lotteries to function.

When the highbinders disappeared and Chinatown grew quiet, the Chinese and their outside neighbors began to come to terms with one another. Chinatown underwent a transformation from a red light district into a tourist attraction. Chinese culture rose in the estimation of the majority population. Chinese people began moving into the surrounding society and absorbing as much of its culture as was valuable to them.

The racial and cultural turmoil of the tong war days is the background against which the dramas of Fu Manchu and Charlie Chan were enacted in the world of thrillers and mystery stories. Fu Manchu, the great master of the tongs, came first.

Sax Rohmer, the English Orientalist and student of the occult, created Dr. Fu Manchu in 1913. He published thirty novels about him, the last of which appeared in 1959. Villains of Fu Manchu's stripe are out of fashion nowadays. Mystery writer Bill Pronzini summed up the current opinion of him and his creator when he wrote, "Dr. Fu Manchu and the other Oriental supercriminals were a product of the 'Yellow Peril' hysteria of the first quarter of this century, and certainly do not bring credit to writers . . . who saw little except evil in ethnic and racial groups different from their own."

Sax Rohmer was an avid student of Middle Eastern and Far Eastern culture. Maybe he was a racist, but if so, not in the ordinary way. In an autobiographical sketch he wrote, "I cannot doubt that I spent at least one incarnation beside the Nile. Throughout my school days I studied hieroglyphics. . . . The Middle East . . . enthrall[ed] me — especially Egypt. Interest in the Far East was to come later. When I took up the study of art, my own paintings were almost exclusively Oriental in character." It seems that his involvement with China and the Chinese was a rather complicated and idiosyncratic mix of attraction and repulsion.

But he was also a professional writer who had the luck to create a notable character. Dr. Fu Manchu belongs to the melodramatic tradition of ingenious weapons, trap doors, secret hiding places, wild chases, hairbreadth escapes, and plots to conquer the world. He is a brother to Professor Moriarty, projecting the same qualities of malevolent omnipresence: in the early years of the century any unsolved crime in London must have been committed by one or the other of them. In Sax Rohmer's novels the reader gets a full dose of what Robert Corrigan has called "the overriding tone of paranoia which informs melodrama. . . . For melodrama's greatest achievement is its capacity to give direct objective form to our irrational fears."

For of course the Fu Manchu stories depend on a circumstance that generates paranoia: Fu Manchu can never conquer the world, nor can he ever be finally defeated and disposed of by Nayland Smith. Fu Manchu must survive if the stories are to continue. Consequently, in one story after another, the brilliant Nayland Smith and the fiendishly clever, infinitely re-

Bancroft Library

sourceful, and deadly Fu Manchu behave, by any realistic standard, like bumbling nitwits. The tales are really chains of non sequiturs. If someone is late for an appointment, Nayland Smith knows to a certainty that Fu Manchu is responsible. Fu Manchu spends years training exotic animals to kill his enemies, when any competent tong master would hire a highbinder, who would dispatch the target in a minute.

Sax Rohmer kept writing Fu Manchu stories up to the time of his death. By then, the world had changed enormously. Asian nations had grown powerful beyond anyone's expectations back in 1916, but fear of the Yellow Peril had largely abated by 1959. And Fu Manchu's place in popular en-

tertainment had been taken by Charlie Chan.

Earl Derr Biggers wrote his novels of Charlie Chan, the Hawaii-born detective, between 1925 and 1932. Charlie Chan became an almost mythic figure — like Sherlock Holmes or, at a more serious level of literature, Babbitt or Elmer Gantry — a character whose life transcends the stories in which he appears. There were so many Charlie Chan movies (at least thirty) that it is surprising to realize that Biggers actually wrote only six novels. In the movies Charlie Chan — as played by Warner Oland (who had also played Fu Manchu) and Sidney Toler — was a man in whom you could place absolute confidence.

Biggers said of him, "Sinister

Night Scene in San Francisco's Chinatown at the turn of the century.

and wicked Chinese are old stuff, but an amiable Chinese on the side of law and order had never been used. . . . If I understand Charlie Chan correctly, he has an idea that if you understand a man's character you can nearly predict what he is apt to do in any set of circumstances."

In the 1925 novel *The Chinese Parrot*, Charlie Chan made his first visit to San Francisco's Chinatown. It was Chinese New Year's Eve:

At a little after eight, the detective from the islands left the friendly glow of Union Square and, drifting down into the darker stretches of Post Street, came presently to Grant Avenue. A loiterer on the corner directed him to the left, and he strolled on. In a few moments he came to a row of shops displaying cheap Oriental goods for the tourist eye. His pace quickened; he passed the church on the crest of the hill and moved on down into the real Chinatown.

Here a spirit of carnival filled the air. The facade of every Tong House, outlined by hundreds of glowing incandescent lamps, shone in yellow splendor through the misty night. Throngs milled on the narrow sidewalks — white sightseers, dapper young Chinese lads in college-cut clothes escorting slant-eyed flappers attired in their best, older Chinese shuffling along on felt-clad feet, each secure in the knowledge that his debts were paid, his house scoured and scrubbed, the new year auspiciously begun.

Provisions Market in Chinatown, about 1895.

The Highbinder's favorite Weapons

WONG AH BANG.

CHU AH LUNG.

CHUNG AH KIT.

Highbinders and their weapons.

Boris Karloff and Myrna Loy in *The Mask of Fu Manchu.*

Cinemabilia

Sidney Toler and Benson Fong as Charlie Chan and his number one son.

Cinemabilia

At Washington Street Chan turned up the hill. Across the way loomed an impressive building — four gaudy stories of light and cheer. Gilt letters in the transom over the door proclaimed it the home of the Chan Family Society. For a moment the detective stood, family pride uppermost in his thoughts.

In an obituary of Earl Derr Biggers, *The Nation* said that Charlie Chan symbolized the sagacity, kindliness, and charm of the Chinese people, and that "his epi-

grams redistilled the wisdom of the ages in a new and captivating fashion."

Today, with large numbers of new Asian immigrants in the United States, law enforcement officials have expressed apprehension about rising crime rates in Chinatown. The triads, crime syndicates from the Far East, have made an appearance. Their representatives are almost as sinister as Fu Manchu. They will come up against excellent Asian-American police officers.

Dot King and the Canary

The Canary Murder Case is one of the most widely known of S. S. Van Dine's mystery stories. It was a best seller in 1927, quickly outselling all previous mystery novels. Translated into several languages and made into a movie, it is still reprinted in new hardcover and paperbound editions. The case it is based on, the March 15, 1923, murder of a young woman named Dot King, was a real life "locked room" puzzle.

Dot King was a demimondaine, a kept woman. She was born Anna Marie Keenan, the only daughter of working-class, immigrant Irish parents. Her father was a night watchman and her mother a laundress. She had two brothers, a "taxicab chauffeur" (as cab drivers were known then) and a truck driver. A discontented adolescent, she married at eighteen but soon left her husband.

She became a model in New York and took Dot King as her name. Russel Crouse, the journalist, said, "Her skin was fair, her hair corn yellow, and her eyes clear and blue. . . . She had the hard beauty that was softened by dim lights." Before long, men were taking her to dinner, the theater, and the speakeasies, a new element of Broadway's night life.

She left modeling to become a speakeasy hostess.

One afternoon she was picked up by a wealthy, elderly, married gentleman from out of town who introduced himself to her as Mr. Marshall. Within a few days she became his mistress. Marshall's name was actually J. Kearsley Mitchell, and he was a multimillionaire. Mr. Marshall, as we shall continue to call him, set Dot up in an apartment, paid her bills, and in the first year of their relationship gave her over $30,000 worth of cash, bonds, and jewelry.

When Mr. Marshall was out of town, Dot passed a lot of the money he gave her to the love of her life, a Puerto Rican named Albert Guimares. Although part of the reason Dot loved him was for the beatings he gave her, Guimares was not just a sadist. He had also been indicted in Boston for selling fraudulent stocks and bonds.

On the fifteenth of March, Mr. Marshall spent the evening with Dot, leaving for Boston at about two-thirty in the morning. By then Dot was probably tired, but something unexpected happened, and when she did go to sleep, she went to her eternal rest.

The next morning, around eight or nine o'clock, the maid came to work, unlocked the door, and let herself in. Finding Dot's body cold, she screamed and then called the police. Dot had been dead approximately five or six hours. At first, the officers and the medical examiner thought the young woman had committed suicide. Soon, however, the position of her body, the scraps of chloroform-soaked cotton scattered here and there on the floor, and the discovery that all of her jewelry and her best clothes were missing made it clear that she had been murdered.

In mystery fiction, a homicide victim found in a locked room signifies a fiendishly clever crime. In real life, however, it does not immediately indicate to the police that a clever murder has been committed. Usually it means that one of the residents committed the crime — a boyfriend, a girlfriend, or some other person close to the victim — and that the killer locked the door on the way out.

The first police theory was that Dot had been killed by the unknown Mr. Marshall, or that after his departure, she had unlocked the door and let the murderer in. Either way, the preliminary indications were that she knew her killer.

An unknown intruder seemed unlikely because of the location of her apartment. According to Russel Crouse, "Dot's apartment was on the top floor of a five-story building. It contained only two windows. One, a bay window in the living room, was completely inaccessible unless the thief had let himself down to it from the roof by a rope, and there was no evidence of that. The other, a small one in the kitchenette, could have been reached only by a dangerous swing from the fire escape." As a practical matter, the only way into Dot's apartment was through the locked front door.

Dot's building had been combined with the one beside it to make a very large apartment house. The hallways of the buildings had been joined. Dot's half had an elevator; the other half did not. A person could walk up the stairs of the other side of the building and along the hall to Dot's door without being seen by the el-

evator operator. For this reason the police did not rule out the possibility of an unseen, unknown intruder. Still, the lock on Dot's door had not been tampered with, and there was no reason for her to let a stranger in at that time of the morning.

On learning of Dot's death, Mr. Marshall contacted the police and came to New York to be interviewed. He was candid about their relationship and convinced the police that she was alive when he left her.

Dot's mother fingered Albert Guimares as a suspect, but he was able to establish a firm alibi for the night and morning of the murder.

Once the living occupants of the locked room had been cleared as suspects, the police turned to other possibilities. One was that Dot might have been killed to keep her and Guimares from practicing extortion. The weakness of this theory was that although jewelry and clothing had been taken from the apartment, Dot's correspondence was still there.

No new leads turned up, and the investigation stagnated. Newer cases superseded it at the center of attention, and then it was relegated to the limbo of open but inactive cases.

This tantalizing jazz-age mystery is what S. S. Van Dine chose as the basis of Philo Vance's second case.

S. S. Van Dine was considered by his friends to be one of the most enigmatic of American writers. His career divided neatly in half: in the first part, he produced nine serious intellectual studies under his given name, Willard Huntington Wright, and in the second half, he wrote the Philo Vance mysteries under the pseudonym S. S. Van Dine (an alias based on an old family name).

Educated in Southern California

at St. Vincent's College (now Loyola-Marymount) and Pomona College, he came out of the West to continue his studies in Munich and Paris. He returned to the United States to do some work at Harvard and then began a career in journalism with a stint at the *Los Angeles Times*, soon to be embroiled in heavy union problems.

One night in October 1910, while he was working at the *Times*, he had a headache and filed his copy early. A few minutes after he left the building, bombs exploded. They had been set by the McNamara brothers, infamous anarchists. Twenty-one men were killed, including the reporter who worked at the desk next to Van Dine's.

Offered an editorship at *The Smart Set*, he soon left the *Times* to join H. L. Mencken and George Jean Nathan in their campaign to remake American culture. By this time he had begun to develop his own style. Ernest Boyd, who met him in 1913, remembered him as "suavely and sardonically cosmopolitan. . . . He looked as if he had just left the Café de la Paix — not a trace of the Dôme or the Deux Magots. . . . A Right Bank American, if ever there was one." He was "a brilliant talker and a good listener, as only people who really understand the art of conversation are." As Wright and as Van Dine, he tended to understate his achievements. He pulled his own weight at *The Smart Set*, but Boyd wrote, "It was not until I came to know him intimately that I discovered that George Moore, D. H. Lawrence, Wedekind, Strindberg, Schnitzler, James Joyce, and James Stephens got their first hearing [in the United States] through [his] editorial perspicacity."

He became known as a dandy because he wore a Vandyke beard and wing collars, and preferred a monocle to spectacles. He affected some Americans the way Claude Rains did: his European taste and his obvious intelligence seemed sinister.

In 1913 he went to Europe once again, this time with Mencken and Nathan, and they collaborated on *Europe after 8:15*, a portrait of European night life on the eve of World War I. Mencken and Nathan returned to the United States, but Van Dine lingered on to write *What Nietzsche Taught*. He stayed until the war was well under way and came home on the last westbound voyage of the *Lusitania*, bringing with him the manuscript of *Modern Painting: Its Tendency and Meaning*. This book, a study of painting from Manet through Picasso and the cubists, created a sensation in the art circles of two continents.

Wright left *The Smart Set* in 1915 and entered a period of intensely hard work. He published several books in short order. They were, said Ernest Boyd, "all pioneering work of their kind, never making any concessions to popularity," and they were all commercially unsuccessful. Looking back, another friend wrote, "when Wright was Wright, he tried to do more than was humanly possible. He had been a football player on one of the roughest teams in the Southwest, but no physique was equal to the strain he placed on [his own]. . . . Suddenly he disappeared from New York and it was nine years before he again engaged in sustained work. In the barren years he knew illness and poverty."

He emerged from them as S. S. Van Dine. The first Philo Vance mystery, *The Benson Murder Case*, appeared in 1926. Following its success, he wrote nothing but mysteries — twelve in all — and

Brown Brothers

edited a well-regarded anthology, *The Great Detective Stories.*

Those who hoped he would write books like *Modern Painting* again were disappointed, but the qualities he showed in those earlier works did not entirely disappear. They surfaced for brief moments when Philo Vance, who was to some degree a self-portrait, became his spokesman.

In Philo Vance's asides ("But most popular truth is mere ingenuity — that's why it's so wrongheaded"), Van Dine speaks his mind. Vance's tendency to disappear into art galleries when he goes off-stage shows Van Dine's continuing interest in the subjects that preoccupied him when "Wright was Wright." Van Dine's extensive knowledge of Broadway's half-world in the early twenties was the perfect background for writing *The Canary Murder Case*.

In his role as narrator, Van Dine tells us that on Broadway in the early twenties Margaret Odell, a Follies star known as the Canary, was "a scintillant figure who seemed somehow to typify the gaudy and spurious romance of transient gaiety. . . . She impressed me then as a girl of uncommon loveliness, despite the calculating, predatory cast of her features. She was of medium height, slender, graceful in a leonine way. . . . There was in her face that strange combination of sensual promise and spiritual renunciation with which the painters of all ages have sought to endow their conceptions of the Eternal Magdalene. Hers was the type of face, voluptuous and with a hint of mystery, which rules man's emotions and, by subjugating his mind, drives him to desperate deeds." Alas, even before this provocative description occurs early in the novel, the Canary has been bumped off. The circumstances of her death strongly resemble those of Dot King's.

The door to the Canary's apartment was locked. There was only one entrance, through a door that opened into the main hall of the apartment building and was in full view of the telephone switchboard operator. The switchboard was open when the murderer made his escape, but the telephone operator didn't see a thing.

The investigation, led by District Attorney Markham, turned up five suspects:

Kenneth Spotswoode, a manufacturer descended from wealthy old Yankee stock, who was sowing a few late wild oats along Broadway. According to District Attorney Markham, he was "a highly respected member of society." His wealth and position were rather similar to those of Dot King's Mr. Marshall. He was the Canary's last conquest.

Tony "Dude" Skeel, a flashy dresser, professional burglar, and former lover of the Canary. She hadn't quite gotten free of him, and he was still demanding money from her. It is not stated that he beat her, but he does resemble Albert Guimares.

Dr. Ambrose Lindquist, "a fashionable neurologist" who ran a private sanatorium. He had fallen hard for the Canary, and in a fit of jealousy he threatened to shoot her.

Louis Mannix, a rich man who occasionally backed Broadway shows. He differed from Spotswoode in that he represented new, immigrant blood and new money. He had a taste for showgirls and had a fling with the Canary.

Charles "Pop" Cleaver, a former Tammany politician, gambler, and man about town. He had the same motive for murder as Louis Mannix, since the Canary had blackmailed both of them.

Philo Vance's problems are essentially the same ones faced by the police in the Dot King case: to identify the killer, account for how he got into the apartment, and show how he got away afterward.

One of the conventions of the detective story with an amateur sleuth is that the hero or heroine is invited to participate in the investigation and is given access to all the information the police have. District Attorney Markham, Vance's close friend, asked him for help. This does not happen often, but very few people would refuse such a request.

District attorneys do not usually lead homicide investigations, at least not in Alameda County. In important cases a D.A. may be involved from the outset (as Markham is in this one), but more often it is an *assistant* district attorney, and his or her role is to provide legal information for the detectives. In cases developed by the D.A.'s own investigative staff, a D.A. might interrogate the suspects, as Markham did, but this would be unusual. Different jurisdictions have different structures, and the setup Van Dine created for his novel is easy to accept.

Today, and perhaps even in the 1920s, the amount of information from the police files given to Philo Vance by the district attorney might easily raise civil liability issues, especially if it could be claimed that a suspect's right to privacy had been violated.

However, when Vance accompanied the D.A. and the detectives on their rounds, the people they interviewed accepted his presence as legitimate, and this effect is lifelike. They simply assumed that he was another plainclothes officer. Basically, they were correct. Most of what Vance did during the investigation would in reality have been done by a regular detective. From this angle, and within the conventions of the genre, *The Canary Murder Case* works as a study of police procedure. Its rich circumstantial detail gives a clear picture of how the NYPD must have operated in the 1920s.

With Vance's help the Canary murder case was solved in eight days. This seems about right. A hard case will either be solved while it is hot or probably not be solved at all. The correct procedure would be to assign a large number of officers to it, which is what Markham did.

Vance and Markham doubled up on interrogations, taking the well-known good cop/bad cop roles. Markham leaned on the suspects, quizzing them thoroughly and at length. He was tough and, when necessary, abrasive. Vance let the suspects relax and, when they dropped their guard, drew damaging information from them.

Their interrogation of Dude Skeel, who was under arrest, was what is now called a custodial interrogation. Today it would require a *Miranda* warning. It is interesting to see that even though the Dude had been put through the third degree and handled it without flinching, when Vance scored with his questions, the Dude immediately invoked his right to a lawyer.

Under today's rules they would not have had to give the *Miranda* warning to the other four men because, although there was probable cause to think they might be involved in the crime, none of them had been "focused on" as probably guilty. Markham and Vance handled these sessions as detentions for the purpose of obtaining information.

Van Dine mixed people of different classes together in a much more sinister way than Wilkie Collins did. Through his involvement with the Canary, Spotswoode, for example, lost his claim to moral and social superiority to Skeel and the others. Van Dine also made the Canary more interesting than Dot, clothing her in stardom and celebrity while depicting her as more ruthless and ambitious.

Vance's solution of the Canary's death is psychologically — and physically — possible. It fits the given circumstances, shows the crime as direct, bold, and simple, the product of intense premeditation. If true, it reveals the murder as the intentional deed of a desperate man. The murderer admitted that Vance's solution was correct.

But it seems unlikely. It makes the crime too complicated.

An important difference between the Dot King case and the Canary murder is that the real crime was never solved. The police eventually developed a plausible explanation as to how it was done, but that did not lead to an arrest. The theory was inspired by another unsolved murder, one that had an eerie resemblance to the King case. This one, though, had a witness. From what he said, the police deduced the M.O. behind the Dot King murder. There were two killers, not just one. They were robbers who chose kept women as their victims. One of them dressed in a messenger's uniform, and they sneaked into apartment houses without being seen. Then the messenger rang the doorbell, telling the victim he had a package for her from her sugar daddy, probably even giving the right name. So, when Dot King opened the door, they overpowered her, putting the chloroform to her mouth and dumping her on the bed. They robbed her and left her apartment, thinking she was still alive. Robbery *was* the motive; the murder was accidental.

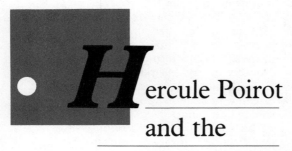

*H*ercule Poirot and the Lindbergh Kidnapping

At approximately nine-fifteen on the evening of March 1, 1932, the baby son of Charles Lindbergh, America's Lone Eagle, was kidnapped. Seventy-two days later, after Lindbergh had left over $50,000 ransom in a quiet graveyard, the baby's body was found. To many Americans and Europeans feeling pain and sorrow for their hero and his young wife, this became the crime of the century.

In February 1934, seven months before Bruno Hauptmann was arrested for the crime, Agatha Christie's *Murder in the Calais Coach* was published. In it Hercule Poirot finds himself involved in the Armstrong kidnapping case, a fictional crime transparently based on the then still unsolved Lindbergh case. But in Christie's book the crime has already been solved by the police; the killer has been tried and acquitted. The mystery at hand for Poirot is a different one. In a railway carriage snowbound somewhere north of Belgrade, in Yugoslavia, he discovers and reconstructs to the reader's satisfaction how the killer, Samuel Edward Ratchett, has been punished.

It took the New Jersey and New York police a little longer to wrap up the Lindbergh case. They did not arrest Bruno Hauptmann until September 19, 1934, two and a half years after the kidnapping. It was another eighteen months before Hauptmann was tried and executed.

At the time of the kidnapping, Hauptmann was a young carpenter with a pregnant wife. He was also an illegal immigrant who had been convicted as a second-story man (that is, a burglar who enters homes by climbing in through upstairs windows) in his native Germany. He lived in a plain working-class neighborhood by necessity, not by choice. He collected the $50,000 ransom one night, and the next morning he quit his job and never went to work again. After seeing him in the courtroom, Lindbergh described him as "a magnificent looking man, very well built," who had eyes "like the eyes of a wild boar — mean, shifty, small and cruel."

But Hauptmann was moved to commit his crime by more than the desire for easy money. As Alexander Woollcott observed, Hauptmann was "a smoldering megalomaniac who, in his grandiose daydreams, nourished a consuming jealousy of the world's hero whom he especially resented on behalf of his own boyhood hero, Richthofen, the wartime German ace. It was for Richthofen he was to name his own son, born after he had killed Lindbergh's. And it was the life of Richthofen that he read in his cell as he awaited trial."

Christie's villain Ratchett is somewhat different. To start with, he is not a young man. He is rich and sophisticated. It is interesting, however, to note how Poirot's impression of him foreshadows the comments of Lindbergh and Woollcott on Hauptmann: Ratchett was "a man perhaps of between

sixty and seventy. From a little distance he had the bland aspect of a philanthropist. His slightly bald head, his domed forehead, the smiling mouth that displayed a very white set of false teeth — all seemed to speak of a benevolent

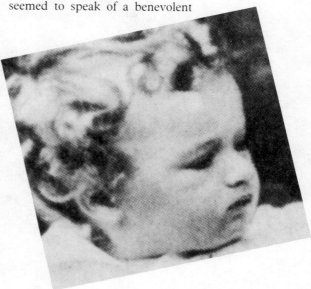

personality. Only the eyes belied this assumption. They were small, deep-set and crafty. Not only that. As the man . . . glanced across the room, his gaze stopped on Poirot for a moment and just for that second there was a strange malevolence, an unnatural tensity in the glance. . . . His voice was slightly husky in tone. It had a queer, soft, dangerous quality." When Ratchett passed Poirot in the restaurant car of the Orient Express, the detective observed, "I had a curious impression. It was as though a wild animal — an animal savage, but savage! you understand — had passed me by."

Ratchett has the attributes of a master criminal, of one of the lords of the underworld. Even so, standard police work had led to his arrest for the Armstrong kidnapping. When brought to trial, however, "by means of the enormous wealth he had piled up, and owing

Lindy and Anne

Associated Press

The Little Eagle

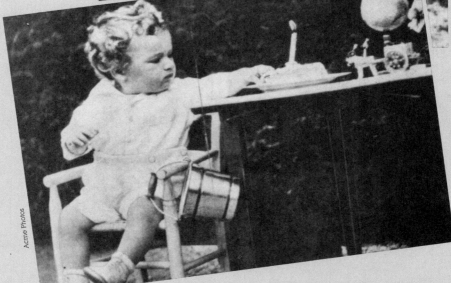

Acme Photos

International Newsreel Photo

The ladder, being inspected by a New Jersey detective.

International Newsreel Photo

Re-enacting the crime.

to the secret hold he had over various persons, he was acquitted on some technical inaccuracy."

Murder in the Calais Coach offers an interesting instance of the tendency of crime fiction to upgrade the social status of the characters. Wealthy from the fruits of his crimes, Ratchett lives on an altogether grander scale than the petty thug Hauptmann ever aspired to. Agatha Christie invests Ratchett's victims, the Armstrong family, with wealth, popularity (which the Lindberghs had), and noble connections (which they had not). Throughout the story they remain vague and shadowy figures — undoubtedly partly due to a kind of delicacy of feeling on Christie's part for the ordeal of the people upon whom they are based. Also, perhaps, any fictional characters would look pale when placed beside the unassuming grandeur of Charles and Anne Morrow Lindbergh.

In its principal lines, the real investigation of the Lindbergh case was as elegant as any of Poirot's.

A number of different agencies were working on the case, and at first their efforts were not well coordinated. Even so, in the early stages two critically important decisions were made. When the two lines of investigation started by those decisions converged, they provided evidence that clearly established Hauptmann's guilt. First, Elmer Irey, the chief investigator for the U.S. Treasury, decided to pay off the kidnappers, using marked money.

The use of marked money is a standard procedure, but not a simple one. It is not always successful. Irey proposed to pay the ransom with the easiest type of money to trace, gold certificates which (like the two dollar bills) were legal tender but not widely circulated. Only J. P. Morgan had $50,000 worth of these certificates, and the police assembled the ransom in the Morgan vaults in New York City. The danger in the method was that the kidnapper might recognize the gold certificates as a trap while he still had the baby at his mercy. With the courage that marked his behavior through this horrible ordeal, Lindbergh agreed to take that chance.

The second important decision was made by Colonel Norman Schwarzkopf, the head of the New Jersey State Police and leader of the New Jersey end of the investigation. At that time thousands of people were volunteering to help solve the Lindbergh kidnapping. At times it must have seemed to the police that everyone in the country was on the case. Most of the volunteers were harmless and well intentioned. Some were malicious crooks like Gaston Means and Al Capone, and others, like John Hughes Curtis, were probably mentally unbalanced. The red herrings they started consumed an enormous amount of investigative energy.

Colonel Schwarzkopf was a professional and, like many pros, not very fond of amateurs. Yet, he accepted the services of a volunteer detective, an expert on wood named Dr. Arthur Koehler. This action led to what one commentator described as "a piece of scientific detection at which one can only marvel."

Found at the scene of the crime was a homemade wooden ladder used by the kidnapper to take the baby from his bedroom on the second floor. It became a clue that led to Hauptmann and a major piece of evidence at the trial. Koehler traced the wood in the ladder from a planing mill in South Carolina to the National Lumber and Mill-

Dr. Koehler testifies.

Culver Pictures

work Company in the Bronx
(where Hauptmann had been an
employee), and from there to
Hauptmann's garage, and then to
where it was found after the kidnapping.

The reports on the marked
money came in slowly at first.
Then, for reasons related to high-
level economics — not the Lindbergh case — President Roosevelt
withdrew gold certificates from
circulation. It was a piece of luck
for the investigators. A form of
currency that had really not been
in general use became even rarer.
Circulating the list of serial numbers on the certificates began to
pay off when they started showing up in the Bronx. Eventually a
gas station attendant, wondering
whether a bill really was legal
tender, wrote down the license
plate number of a car whose driver
had given him one. When the cer-
tificate was sent to the bank, an
alert clerk recognized it as part of

the ransom money. In very short
order, Hauptmann was arrested.
Fourteen thousand dollars in
marked certificates was found in
his garage.*

Murder in the Calais Coach was a
great success when it first appeared in 1934. Much of this was
due to not only the general popularity of Christie's novels and the
freshness and ingenuity of this
particular plot but also the rage
people felt at the Lindbergh kidnapping and their wish to see the
murderer brought to justice.
Christie provided a surrogate

---

* As in other famous cases, there have been
writers who remain skeptical of the evidence or
the verdict. A recent example of this is Ludovic Kennedy's *The Airman and the Carpenter*, which argues passionately — and, in the
end, unconvincingly — that Hauptmann was
the innocent victim of a conspiracy with which
Lindbergh cooperated. Kennedy has also presented this thesis in the PBS documentary *Who
Killed the Lindbergh Baby?*

upon whom those desires were carried out.

Unlike Hauptmann, who was to be found guilty by a jury, his appeals listened to by the higher courts, and then executed, Ratchett beat the rap. We are not told how, but we can guess that he got off on a point of due process. But he did not escape justice. His punishment was unofficial, meted out vigilante style.

The question of justice is an interesting one here. The quality we associate with Agatha Christie and her detectives is rectitude. She establishes and re-establishes Hercule Poirot's moral authority. "I do not approve of murder," he says in more than one book. In *The Labors of Hercules*, when an inoffensive little man is killed by mistake, and the murderer suggests that it is not important because, after all, the victim was a nobody, Poirot replies by saying, "It is important to me."

It is surprising, therefore, when Poirot agrees to allow Ratchett's killers — his second jury and his executioners — to escape. Evidently Agatha Christie did not believe law and justice to be synonymous, but that when there was a conflict between justice and due process, substantial justice should be done. Other stories point to the same conclusion.

In *Ten Little Indians*, one person murders nine others for the same reason; the victims were all killers who had escaped punishment by the law. In Poirot's last appearance — in *Curtain*, published

The Lindberghs in search of peace.

after Christie's death — the principle is extended to punish not only the criminally wicked but one whose crimes are unintended.

The desire to cut through due process to administer due punishment is not uncommon. Julian Gloag's recent novel, *Blood for Blood*, is a masterly treatment of the theme. And a police captain once told us he had had a dream that he was fatally ill and decided to use the time he had left by going around town and bumping off all the people he knew who had gotten away with really bad crimes.

Did Bruno Hauptmann chance to read *Murder in the Calais Coach?* Probably not, but if he did, it told him the fate he had earned, and it also told him what civilized people would always think of him.

"In one series of interviews I spoke to four convicts, each of whom implied that he had committed more than a hundred muggings. I did not find these men to be irrational, violent, impulsive, or sadistic, but experienced them (remember, I saw them in a prison setting) as quiet, rational, and not psychotic. They were, however, singularly lacking in insight and frightening in their inability to relate to anyone's needs but their own. One man said, "I am not a sadist. I don't beat people — only if they are slow in giving me my money."

Dr. Martin Symonds, "Victims of Violence"

**INTER-
ROGATION**

The Telephone

Most people, and all television writers, do not understand how much the police rely on the telephone.

In certain circumstances the telephone — or "land-wire," as it is called — is preferable to and safer than the radio. The news media listen to police broadcasts, and so do members of the general public. News of a barricaded gunman, for example, can go public very quickly if the main radio frequencies are used too often in the initial response to the incident. The neighborhood grapevine always produces a local crowd in any case, but the longer the arrival of even more people from outside the area can be delayed, the better the chance of resolving the situation early, One broadcast on an "instant news" radio station can multiply the problems of crowd control. Furthermore, there is always the possibility that the gunman is listening to the police radio too. (Some hostage takers become more difficult to deal with if they "make" the local news. They listen avidly to the broadcasts, and are reluctant to give up the attention and sense of power it gives them.)

Telephones let detectives stay in touch with the victims of crimes. That is an important function. An excellent sexual assault investiga-tor in Oakland, now retired, used to spend hours on the telephone talking to rape victims. Many of them were poor young girls who grew up in unstable households and who were, outside the family circle, quite friendless. He became their father confessor, helping them pull themselves back together. He was genuinely kind, and his compassion helped them put up with the ghastliness of trial procedures.

Suspects can also be reached by telephone. As another former investigator said, "I just used to call them up — not go out looking for them — and they would come in. I would say to a guy, 'I've got a case on you that needs to be resolved one way or another, so come on downtown and let's talk about it.' So he would come in and try to burn someone else on it, and at a certain point I would say, 'That's all. Come on, you're going to jail.' "

Police receive phone calls too. It is safer for an informer to telephone the narcotics detail, say, than to come to the station or meet an officer on the street.

There is an episode in the *Mannix* television series that illustrates why the telephone should be used in emergencies. A bomb has been wired to the ignition of a syndicate gangster's automobile, and, just after dawn, Mannix learns of it. To save the man from being blown up, Mannix hops in his car and sets out across Los Angeles to warn him. A series of cross-cut scenes follow, switching back and forth from Mannix whipping through commuter traffic to the gangster leisurely eating breakfast, getting ready to go to the office, kissing his wife and daughter, strolling to his car, and getting in. In a long shot, we see Mannix round the corner as the gangster's car explodes.

Any responsible private detective would have telephoned the man rather than trying to drive to the rescue, no matter what time of day he got the information. If the telephones were not working for some reason, he would have notified the police, who would have dispatched the beat officer to warn the intended victim.

Confessions

The 1912 edition of Oakland's police regulations contained a brief discussion of confessions. It said, "Confessions are received, if free and voluntary, as deserving of the highest credit, because they are presumed to flow from the strongest sense of guilt, and therefore they are admitted as proof of the crime to which they refer."

The operative words were "free and voluntary," "strongest sense of guilt," and "proof."

The statement proceeds from the assumption that when a person commits a foul act, unless he is a sociopath, it will become an intolerable burden on his conscience. To seek relief, he will confess to someone, somewhere. If he has been arrested, the confession will be to a police officer.

This does not mean, however, that the guilty confession will be complete. It may be, but then again it may not be. Remorse does not extinguish the instinct of self-preservation. A guilty person will often confess to a crime but withhold information about the details in order to soften the picture of what happened.

Suppose, for example, Dick is suspected of the murder of his girlfriend, Jane. During interrogation he confesses that they quarreled, and, after intense provocation, he knocked her down with a single glancing blow. He says she was alive when he left the scene.

This is a confession, even though Dick did not really come clean. It omits a major fact known to him and his interrogators — namely, that Jane's skull was fractured by repeated blows. But the one-punch story is easier to tell. And it is self-preserving: it considerably reduces his culpability for her death. In fact, it leaves room for a jury member to find a reasonable doubt as to whether he really is responsible.

There are experienced felons who try to build the basis for an appeal into their confession. Knowing that the police can prove their crime, whatever it was, they do not confess to seek relief from guilt. Rather, they use the confession to try to distort or weaken the meaning of the evidence and to improve their chances of beating the rap.

Whenever a big crime hits the headlines, the news will draw mentally unbalanced confessors to police headquarters. These are people who have a pathetic craving for attention and who will confess to the most degrading crimes to get it. In Oakland several years ago a malicious lunatic made a bomb, placed it in a paper bag, and left it on a bench at a bus stop. Two young boys came along, and, out of curiosity, one picked up the bag, which exploded and maimed him. This hideous crime has never been solved, but fifteen men and women lined up to confess to it.

Usually the detectives hear such people out and then send them on their way. Once in a great while, though, one of them actually knows something about a crime — or seems to. In these instances, a statement is taken. "If you don't listen to them," a homicide investigator says, "you aren't doing your job."

Detectives routinely withhold facts from the public during their investigations. This information, known only to them and to the criminal, is used to distinguish true confessions from false ones. With true confessions, the information is used to assess how much of the confession is accurate and how much of it is intended to be misleading.

So, while a confession can be important evidence, may even be proof of guilt, every effort must be made to evaluate it correctly and to corroborate it from other sources — accomplices ("other responsibles"), demonstrable guilty knowledge, witnesses, circumstantial evidence.

A confession usually ends a mystery novel, but for a real detective it means there is still a lot of work to do.

THE MURDERING WIFE PUZZLE

The body of a sinister-looking man was found on the sidewalk of the international quarter, shot through the heart. The police talked to six witnesses, including the murderer. The six were very open about what had happened. The only trouble was that none of them spoke any language the police could understand. Nevertheless, the police were able to piece together the following information:

1. The witnesses were three men and three women: Fred, John, and William; Gloria, Gilda, and Barbara.
2. The men were married to the women, though not necessarily in the order listed.
3. William's wife was the murderer.
4. Fred speaks and understands only Basque.
5. John is bald.
6. The couple who live next door to Gilda and her husband have the same color hair she does, and speak both Spanish and Basque.
7. William's wife recently gave Barbara a home permanent.
8. Gilda's husband speaks only French.

What is the name of the murderer?

Solution

If you can identify William's wife, you'll know the murderer.

William's wife isn't Barbara, because the former gave the latter a permanent. William's wife must be either Gilda or Gloria.

Fred's wife isn't Gilda, because he speaks only Basque and her husband speaks only French. So Fred's wife is either Gloria or Barbara.

If John is bald, he doesn't live next door to Gilda and he doesn't speak Spanish and Basque. Therefore, John must speak French and be married to Gilda. Only Gloria can be William's wife and the murderer.

Reading the Rights

A generation of law enforcement officers has come and gone since *Miranda* was announced in 1965. The decision is older than the careers of most of today's police detectives and has always been a standard part of their procedure.

This is also true for suspects; the warning is older than their involvement in crime. They expect to have their *Miranda* rights read to them, if only because they have seen it done on television. Suspects who have been around the block a few times know that if the beat officer does not (as they say) *Mirandize* them, a detective will come along later and do it.

Although *Miranda* has reduced the total number of confessions, lots of confesssions are still made. Most of the time, the *Miranda* warning is treated simply as a formality the officer and the suspect must get through before they can do their real business. One investigator described his *Miranda* routine this way:

"I come in and say, 'I am Sergeant Flynn. I'm here to investigate the charge of burglary that has been placed against you. Do you want to talk about it?'

"If the suspect says no, I leave him immediately. If he says he is willing to talk, I give him the warning and then interrogate him.

"I try to get him to think positive and focus his attention on the interview, not the warning. I say, 'You are going to use this interview to establish your alibi, right? And show me that you couldn't have done that burglary, right? You're a smart guy, and you understand all this. So let's do it.

"And then I get an affirmative for each of the phrases:

" 'You have the right to remain silent. O.K.?'

" 'Anything you say can and will be used against you in a court of law. O.K.? Got it?' I keep it moving firmly, not blurring it but not lingering over any of it.

" 'You have the right to talk to a lawyer and have him present with you while you are being questioned. Right?'

" 'If you cannot afford to hire a lawyer, one will be appointed to represent you before questioning if you wish one. Right? O.K. Sign here.' and I give him the form. 'Now, we can talk about this burglary. What did you want to tell me?'

"If I think he is guilty and I really want to put him away, I lean on him and use all the techniques in my power—leading questions, body English, and so forth. You try to develop intensity and momentum that keeps him talking and leads him to crack.

"But as soon as he asks for a lawyer, that's it."

Once the suspect asks for a lawyer, interrogation ceases and the prospect of a prompt confession fades away. No lawyer worth his salt ever advises a client to confess.

The *Miranda* warning has produced a not always recognized benefit for the police: it has become harder for defense attorneys to plead abuse of their clients, and the general credibility of confessions has increased.

WHO DONE IT?

1. Who killed Cock Robin?
2. Who shot Dan McGrew?
3. Who killed his girlfriend by wrapping her golden hair three times around her throat?
4. Who, tempted by a new love and visions of wealth and luxury, drowned his pregnant mistress?
5. Who killed his half-brother for raping his sister and, incidentally, thereby made himself the heir to the throne?
6. What twins mortally wounded each other in a fight, each recognizing the other only after it was too late?
7. Who beat his wife to death when she refused to share with him $5,000 she won in a lottery?

8. Who killed her two small sons to get even with her husband for deserting her?
9. Who killed an old lady and then pulled off an improbable impersonation?
10. Who shot his friend through the head while describing to him once again the farm of their dreams?
11. Who stabbed a doctor at midnight in a graveyard and framed the town drunk with the crime?

Answers to Who Done It?

1. The sparrow, with his bow and arrow (from Mother Goose).
2. An unnamed miner, the wronged husband of "the lady that's known as Lou," in Robert Service's poem "The Shooting of Dan McGrew."
3. Porphyria's lover, in the poem of the same name by Robert Browning.
4. Clyde Griffiths, murderer of Roberta Alden, in Theodore Dreiser's *An American Tragedy.* Two movies were made of the novel, one with the title *A Place in the Sun.*
5. Absalom, the son of King David, killed Amnon, his half-brother and heir to the throne (from 2 Samuel 28).
6. Balan and Balin, in *Idylls of the King* by Tennyson.
7. McTeague, in *McTeague* by Frank Norris.
8. Medea, in the play by Euripides.
9. The wolf, in "Little Red Riding Hood."
10. George Milton shot Lennie Small, in *Of Mice and Men* by John Steinbeck.
11. Injun Joe, in *Tom Sawyer* by Mark Twain.

Where fiction meets fact: Mary Pickford and Officer W. H. ("Bow Wow") Goodwin strike a pose during the Armistice Day Parade in Oakland, 1927. Did he give America's Sweetheart a ticket? Did she give him an autograph?

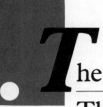

The Third Degree

At one time "the third degree" was a method of interrogation widely used by local law enforcement agencies, and especially by municipal police departments. From the mid nineteenth century through the 1930s, large numbers of police detectives — perhaps even a majority — considered it a useful way of getting confessions.

Webster's defines the third degree as a "severe examination or treatment of a prisoner by the police to extort a confession," but this definition is not satisfactory. It is too abstract and clean. The third degree could be a long, harsh, exhausting, and ruthless interrogation carried out under bright lights by teams of interrogators. At times it degenerated into beatings and torture.

When the third degree was attacked by critics, some police officials defended it. In 1912, for example, Walter J. Petersen, Oakland's captain of detectives, gave a speech at a Berkeley church where he described it as "a severe form of questioning, but not generally of a physical nature." This was not fully responsive: people did not mind the severity, it was the "physical nature" of the thing that bothered them.

By the standards of the time

Captain Petersen was a humane and progressive officer. He was a skillful interrogator, and while he subjected many suspects to the third degree, he did not stoop to beating or torture. There were officers and detectives who did, however, and without shame. About the time of Petersen's speech, Los Angeles police officers were trying to solve a bombing case by stabbing sharpened pencil points into the feet of a suspect who was — according to reporter Hugh Baillie, a disinterested witness — clearly insane.

Most private detectives and federal agents in those days did not use the third degree to get confessions. Their ability to work efficiently without relying on extreme duress or brute force showed how little justification there was for anyone to use the third degree.

The third degree did not end with the gaslight era. It continued into the 1930s, 1940s, and 1950s. It came under prolonged attack from *within* law enforcement as well as from without. Reform-minded progressives, like Berkeley's Chief Vollmer, decided the third degree had to go. They campaigned against it on these grounds:

1. It did not produce the truth. An exhausted suspect might confess anything simply to end the questioning, and a tortured suspect was even more likely to do so.

2. A confession, as one old formulation put it, "forced from the mind by . . . the torture of fear" could not be considered as freely

given and would — and should — be thrown out of court.

3. It brutalized the officers who administered it and brought them into contempt among their fellow citizens.

4. When a defense attorney could convince a jury that police officers had beaten a defendant, the jury invariably set the defendant free, guilty or not. Juries imposed that penalty on the police as a way of expressing disapproval of the third degree.

By the late 1950s the reformers had largely won the battle: even before the *Miranda* decision, physical torture had been eliminated in all but extremely backward or corrupt jurisdictions. Although the third degree is obsolete in American law enforcement and no police official would venture to defend it today, it is alive and well in many countries throughout the world. The courts, the police, and our citizens should remain alert to keep it from reappearing here.

HOW GOOD A COP ARE YOU? #3

Responding to a call, Officer Jones has found Susie, a teenager, bruised and sobbing. She says her date, a young man named Joe, raped her in her home while her parents were away. Unfortunately, Susie felt dirtied by the act and has reacted by taking a bath.

You are now at headquarters interrogating Joe, who has so far waived his right to have an attorney present. You are aware that with much of the physical evidence of rape down the drain, Joe's confession is necessary for a conviction.

Joe, who has started out being cocky, has become more cautious as you take him over the ground again. He pauses to think before he gives answers. He is also getting more nervous — sweating, swallowing to relieve his dry throat, picking at his nails.

Joe is guilty; you feel confident of that. Experience tells you that he is approaching the edge: as he gets more tense, a part of him wants to confess and get it over with. Here is the place where you can obtain a confession, or lose the chance forever. Supposing you had only the four choices of action below. Which would you do?

1. Sit down beside Joe and sympathize with him about how Susie probably dressed and acted provocatively, acting as if she wanted it, leading him on and getting him aroused until he really needed it — that any man would have had a hard time not to do what he did.

2. Go away and leave Joe to stew in his own juice for an hour. Then return and take him over the same ground as before.

3. Put on the pressure. Stand over him and let him know in an angry voice that he is taking up your time, that you know he did it, and that it will go worse for him if he doesn't come clean now.

4. Break him down by telling him how revolted you are at what he did. Impress upon him the moral seriousness of what he has done; how it is condemned by society and religion. Tell him that he has probably ruined the girl's life, and how he has hurt his parents and himself in the eyes of the community.

*T*wo Versions of the *Miranda* Case

An interesting facet of appellate cases, including those of the Supreme Court, is how different the same set of events can look in two separate opinions. The *Miranda* case provides a wonderful example of this. Here, Justice Earl Warren's concern is for correct process, and Justice John Harlan's is for the substance of the issue — Miranda's guilt or innocence.

Justice Warren:

On March 13, 1963, petitioner, Ernesto Miranda, was arrested at his home and taken in custody to a Phoenix police station. He was there identified by the complaining witness. The police then took him to "Interrogation Room No. 2" of the detective bureau. There he was questioned by two police officers. The officers admitted at trial that Miranda was not advised that he had a right to have an attorney present. Two hours later, the officers emerged from the interrogation room with a written confession signed by Miranda. At the top of the statement was a typed paragraph stating that the confession was made voluntarily, without threats or promises of immunity and "with full knowledge of my legal rights, understanding any statement I make may be used against me."

At his trial before a jury, the written confession was admitted into evidence over the objection of the defense counsel, and the officers testified to the prior oral confession made by Miranda during the interrogation. Miranda was found guilty of kidnapping and rape. He was sentenced to 20 to 30 years' imprisonment on each count, the sentences to run concurrently. On appeal the Supreme Court of Arizona held that Miranda's constitutional rights were not violated in obtaining the confession and affirmed the conviction. In reaching its decision, the court emphasized heavily the fact that Miranda did not specifically request counsel.

We reverse. From the testimony of the officers and by the admission of respondent, it is clear that Miranda was not in any way apprised of his right to consult with an attorney and to have one present during the interrogation, nor was his right not to be compelled to incriminate himself effectively protected in any other manner. Without these warnings the statements were inadmissible. The mere fact that he signed a statement which contained a typed-in clause stating that he had "full knowledge" of the "legal rights" does not approach the knowing and intelligent waiver required to relinquish constitutional rights. . . .

Justice Harlan:

On March 3, 1963, an 18-year-old girl was kidnapped and forcibly raped near Phoenix, Arizona. Ten days later, on the morning of March 13, petitioner Miranda was arrested and taken to the police station. At this time Miranda was 23 years old, indigent, and educated to the extent of completing half the ninth grade. He had "an emotional illness" of the schizophrenic type, according to the doctor who eventually examined him; the doctor's report also stated that Miranda was "alert and oriented as to time, place, and person," intelligent within normal limits, and competent to stand trial, and sane within the legal definition. At the police station, the victim picked Miranda out of a lineup, and two officers then took him into a separate room to interrogate him, starting about 11:30 A.M. Though at first denying his guilt, within a short time Miranda gave a detailed oral confession and then wrote out in his own hand and signed a brief statement admitting and describing the crime. All this was accomplished in two hours or less without any force, threats or promises and — I will assume this though the record is uncertain — without any effective warnings at all.

Miranda's oral and written confessions are now held inadmissible under the court's new rules. One is entitled to feel astonished that the Constitution can be read to produce this result. These confessions were obtained during brief, day-time questioning conducted by two officers and unmarked by any of the traditional indicia of coercion. They assured a conviction for a brutal and unsettling crime, for which the police had and quite possibly could obtain little evidence other than the victim's identifications, evidence which is frequently unreliable. There was, in sum, a legitimate purpose, no perceptible unfairness, and certainly little risk of injustice in the interrogation. Yet the resulting confessions, and the responsible course of police practice they represent, are to be sacrificed to the Court's own fine-spun conception of fairness which I seriously doubt is shared by many thinking citizens in this country.

Miranda's case was sent back for retrial. Further investigation by the Arizona police led them to Miranda's common-law wife. She testified in court that he had admitted the rape to her. Miranda went to jail for nine years.

When he came out of prison, Miranda became a barfly. He carried business cards that identified him as *the* Miranda, and traded them for drinks. In February 1976, he was stabbed to death in a cheap bar during a quarrel over a $3 poker bet.

"A lawyer has no business with the justice or injustice of the cause which he undertakes, unless his client asks his opinion, and then he is bound to give it honestly. The justice or injustice of the cause is to be decided by the judge."

Dr. Samuel Johnson

THE COURTROOM SCENE

Defense Lawyers

In *Final Verdict,* a biography of her father, Earl Rogers, who was an extremely well known defense attorney, Adela Rogers St. Johns wrote:

To defend the innocent, as Bill Ballon once said to me, is every criminal lawyer's ideal. It can't come to him too often. Leibowitz [the defense lawyer] drove members of the New York press crazy for years wanting them to write a play about the only man, we all decided, he ever defended he was sure was innocent. Under our laws, our expert investigation, our highly trained personnel, our grand juries, not too many innocent men can be falsely arrested and charged. Even the magnificent work of the Court of Last Appeal, which tries to save those who have been, doesn't show a large percentage of injustices. More often the reverse is true. Corruption and graft and political influence allow the guilty to escape punishment.*

A detective we know takes a disenchanted view of the court system. He thinks judges and lawyers — prosecutors as well — all belong to the same club. If you press him on it, he will concede that if this is not 100 percent true, it is close to it. He points out that de-fense attorneys are often paid with the proceeds from the criminal's loot. To be certain they are paid, they make every effort to induce the judge to turn over to them money that was in the suspect's possession at the time of arrest. This is especially true in drug cases. There was a local judge with whom the detective had a number of unpleasant encounters. The detective says the judge, a former defense attorney whose clients were dope dealers, transfers drug money to defense attorneys. "It's just the fraternity at work," says the detective.

If you hang around the courts for a period of time, you'll get to know the names of the local defense attorneys who specialize in criminal matters. Their clients have invariably been accused of — and often have committed — mean crimes. After a while you begin to assume automatically that anyone who hires one of these lawyers is guilty. If a police officer accused of breaking the law hires one of them, you take that as prima-facie evidence that the officer is in deep trouble.

"We don't sentence criminals. We catch them," [Sergeant] Terry Flynn said.

Joe Gash, *Priestly Murders*

A lawyer's opinion is worth nothing unless paid for.

English Proverb

---

* Adela Rogers St. Johns, *Final Verdict,* p. 76.

Juries

The average person's experience of jury duty is a dull disappointment. After hurrying to obey the summons by getting to the court on time and then sitting around with nothing to do while the morning drags slowly along, by noontime, when the judge announces that the matters on the calendar have been settled and the panel is dismissed, the potential juror is ready to go home. Or even back to work.

If the judge is courteous, he will thank the panelists for answering the summons and tell them they have played an important part in the proceedings. And they actually have, though the reason is rarely given: the desire to avoid a jury trial is the fuel that runs the plea-bargaining system. Trials are expensive for the government and risky for the defendants. Something on the order of 90 percent of the cases brought before the criminal courts are settled through plea-bargaining.

In headline cases, however, the atmosphere is different. Most members of the panel positively want to serve. During such a case in Oakland, we watched the examination of potential jurors and found it absorbing to see them matching wits with the attorneys. To avoid disqualification, the panelists weighed each question and responded in terms of what they thought the attorneys wanted to hear, at the same time trying not to betray their own beliefs. Sometimes their difficulties were transparent. The prosecutor and the defense attorney phrased their questions carefully, obviously trying to choose jurors advantageously while not revealing what they were looking for. The selection procedure was complicated — a three-sided duel.

This process, in which the members of the panel try to get on the jury while the attorneys try to assess whether they are sympathetic or antagonistic, is hardly ever exploited by writers or dramatists; in plays and novels, the jury is taken as a given. It is anything but: a trial can be won or lost during jury selection. (One of the rare portrayals of the jury selection process from the point of view of a prosecutor's staff can be found in Bill Davidson's *Indict and Convict*.)

The selection process is a fairly well defined arena. In California, the prosecutor and the defense attorney can each dismiss twenty jurors without giving a reason, although the appellate courts have begun to limit the rights of prosecutors to challenge jurors — especially where racial discrimination might be a factor in the trial. The judge plays a role in selection, too, excusing panelists for whom service would be a hardship.

So many people have sought to avoid jury duty in recent years that efforts are now being made to ease the burden of service. Recorded telephone messages tell jurors whether they need to report the next day. Jury rooms are less grungy than they used to be. Some cities and counties have even increased the amount of money paid to jurors.

What happens after the jury is chosen, after the attorneys have presented their case, after the judge has explained the law, and after the jury retires to make its decision is always, to some degree, a secret. Like voters at the polls, jurors make a decision they do not have to explain to anyone. They become the sovereign people.

Reginald Rose's *Twelve Angry Men* is a skillful drama based on a jury's deliberations. The toughest jury on record was the one Daniel Webster faced when he defended Jabez Stone, in Stephen Vincent Benet's story "The Devil and Daniel Webster."

JURY SELECTION IN THE 1880s

An anonymous *Oakland Tribune* reporter looked into the selection of municipal court juries and made the following report.

Juries are selected in the Police Court in a peculiar way. A venire is issued by Clerk O'Brien and forthwith Captain Wilson or Officer Quackenbush proceeds to skirmish around for jurors. The most prolific source from which men are unwittingly yanked before Judge Laidlaw is the free reading room. A great many men when they have a day of leisure go to the reading room to get caught up on the papers and magazines. A mechanic, tired of limb, glad to escape for the moment from the din of his trade, sits down to enjoy Matthew Arnold's criticism of American civilization, and he no sooner gets absorbed than an official places gratis his name on a jury slip and tells him to be in court at such an hour.

The man goes. Probably he sits in the lobby while the stream of crime slowly drags its length along Clerk O'Brien's calendar. Then his name is called. Perhaps after standing the fusillade of questions showered upon him by Prosecuting Attorney Church and some other attorney, it is found that the stranger, ruthlessly torn from his reading, is not on the assessment roll. It takes sometimes half a day to procure a jury. It makes a dreary desolate waiting for such as happen to have the necessary qualifications. Thursday afternoon in the Police Court, there was a shortage in the assortment of probable jurors from which selections were to be made. It happened that Attorney Chapman was merely a visitor to the courtroom. Church suggested that Chapman serve on the jury. The legislator had addressed innumerable juries in the past but had never served upon one himself; so for the experience, just as a man would make a trial of smoking opium, the counsellor-at-law took his place in the jury box.

The case involved John Davis, who was arrested some time ago by J. F. Ambacher on a charge of battery.

"How long will this case be likely to last?" said Chapman, who had legal business away from there in the afternoon.

"Oh, about fifteen minutes," said Church.

"All right," replied Chapman, "but when this jury goes out to deliberate, if they don't settle to some conclusion in ten minutes I want to be let out."

The testimony was produced. In place of being short and concise it strung out like an article in an eight-page daily in a city where four pages surfeits him who reads. Chapman forgot himself, yawned, took out one of his Havanas, lit it and was about to enjoy himself when Church roared, "No smoking in the jury box."

The testimony showed that Davis' boy had caused Ambacher considerable trouble, who in retaliation whipped the boy. The father had Ambacher arrested, who was tried and convicted. Later Ambacher had the father arrested, charging him with battery. At 5 o'clock the jury retired. Chapman was mad. He had temporarily lost faith in mankind and especially in Church. The jury locked horns; it argued and contended and, after it had been in there several hours, grew furious. Then above the clamor could be heard the deep-chested thunderings of Chapman, whose voice was like the bellow of a Durham bull in the midst of a wild stampede on the Llano Estacado. Just before 9 o'clock last night the jury came to an agreement. Hunger drove it to it. The judge asked the jurors if they had agreed upon a verdict. The answer broke from a dozen throats, "We have." It was that Davis was guilty. The jurors left, making a bee line for the nearest restaurant, and Attorney Chapman reviled the jury system in trenchant terms.

REVERSIBLE ERROR

Courtroom, **Quentin Reynolds's biography of Samuel Leibowitz, supplies a fine example of how an alert lawyer can take advantage of opportunities to create the grounds for rever-**sal on a judicial error. Leibowitz was the famous New York criminal lawyer who defended Al Capone, Bugsy Siegel, "Kid Twist" Reles, and many other notable racketeers. (In his non-gangster practice, to his ever-lasting glory, he defended the Scottsboro Boys.)

On one occasion, Leibowitz defended Vincent "Mad Dog" Coll, a gangster and known killer, when he was accused of a drive-by shooting. Allegedly, Coll had fired a submachine gun from a moving car at another gangster. The spray of gunfire missed its target but killed a five-year-old boy who happened to be nearby. The public was enraged. A $30,000 reward was offered, and subsequently Coll was fingered as the murderer by a man named Brecht, who said he saw the shots fired.

Early in the cross-examination, Leibowitz asked Brecht where he lived. Brecht asked the judge for permission not to answer the question. "I have a wife and family, and although I can take care of myself, I am afraid that gangsters might harm them if I reveal my home town." The judge replied, "I quite understand. No, you do not have to answer that question."

As Reynolds wrote, "Leibowitz bowed to the Judge, but he was very happy about the ruling. A very recent Court of Appeals decision had stated that

a witness must reveal his background and his residence, so that his character could be investigated by defense counsel. This quite clearly was reversible error."

Leibowitz knew of the decision and, if he had chosen to, could have brought it to the judge's attention. Doing so, he would have assured his client of due process and protected the integrity of the trial as a forum in which to assess Coll's guilt or innocence. But as much as he wanted to impeach Brecht and as much as he needed information on his character and background, Leibowitz chose to withhold his knowledge of the change in case law from the judge. Now, if Coll was convicted, he would have a basis for upsetting the result.

Leibowitz's ploy ultimately became a moot point. A day or so later a probation officer came to his office to give him a rundown on Brecht. Brecht was an ex-convict, a con man with an unusual racket. He collected reward money by offering false testimony as a prosecution witness. The New York police had been so eager to get Coll off the street and so sure he had killed the little boy that Brecht gulled them. With the information provided by the probation officer, Leibowitz demolished Brecht and Coll beat the rap. A short time later

somebody shot Coll to pieces in a public telephone booth.

The issue here, whether to reveal a witness's "background and residence," is a vexing point because in criminal cases retaliation is a real danger. Consistency on this has not been achieved anywhere, in case law or statutory law. Currently, in California courts a police officer has a right to refuse to divulge his home address. He is allowed to give the name and address of his employer instead, to protect his family from harassment. (Similar protection has recently been extended to rape victims.) In a federal court not long ago, when an Oakland officer invoked this right, the judge, who was from out of state, ruled that if the complainant must give his name and address, the police officer must surrender his.

The "Mad Dog" Coll case, as reported by Reynolds, is as full of odd angles as a hall of mirrors and shows why the law is unsteady on this issue. Coll was actually innocent of the murder for which he was on trial. That he was a killer there was no doubt, and, given a chance, he would have done in Brecht. The judge's ruling that Brecht could withhold his address was humane and sensible. But the judge's decency was manipulated by both Brecht and Leibowitz for their own ends. Brecht, as a perjurer, wanted to keep the truth about himself from coming out. Leibowitz, as a good lawyer with a poor case, wanted the option of being able to cancel the results of the trial if he lost.

When the famous Lucius Cassius Longinus Ravilla, regarded by the Romans as a judge possessing flawless integrity and wisdom, was president at a trial, he always used to ask the same question: *who benefitted by what was done?* And such a question is very realistic. No one attempts to commit a crime unless he is hoping it will do him some good.

Cicero, "In Defence of Sextus Roscius of Ameria" *(translated by Michael Grant)*

What Makes a Big Case?

The criminal justice system handles thousands upon thousands of cases every year. The vast majority begin and end without ever being mentioned in the newspapers or on television; others get a few lines at the bottom of a page of newsprint — if there is room. Of course, cases not reported by the media are important to the participants — defendants, victims, judges, lawyers, probation officers, social workers, and police officers. They just are not news.

But a big case is *news*. When one breaks, it is covered by newspapers and television for days, even months, on end. Tens of thousands of dollars are spent informing the public of the proceedings, and the participants are subjected to intense scrutiny. We once saw a defendant, a judge's wife on trial for minor drug charges, pursued into an elevator by television reporters carrying huge microphones and cameras. They pinned her against the back of the elevator, and it looked as if one of the female reporters was going to jam the microphone into her nostrils.

To become a big case, a crime has to have elements that command the attention of people who are not directly involved — the reporters and their audiences. They respond to crimes with dramatic rather than legal value. A really newsworthy crime should be passionate, bloody, or spectacular, involving sex, gobs of money, political power, or famous people. It should provide a series of sudden, surprising revelations: someone's private secret life, hypocrisy in the church, corruption in government, greed in high places.

These qualities can be seen in some of the biggest crime stories of recent years. The von Bulow case of attempted murder featured wealthy, socially prominent people, and control of a fortune was at stake. The principals in the Harris murder case were the apparently prim headmistress of an exclusive school for girls and a "diet doctor" who had become a celebrity. The Dan White murders turned on the distribution of political power in San Francisco and involved antagonisms between the heterosexual and homosexual communities.

Sometimes the center of attention in a big case is not the deed but the accused person: a judge or police officer, a celebrity, a socially eminent or wealthy person. A case may attract publicity because the victim's fate is particularly touching. A key element in making the Lindbergh kidnapping so moving was the cruel treatment of the helpless baby.

A big case poses different challenges for the lawyer and the reporter. For the defense attorney, it is a professional challenge. His (or, increasingly, *her*) reputation is on the line. A successful defense will attract clients; a loss will send them away. For the prosecutor, the prize may be a promotion or a career in politics. With so much at stake, both sides get psyched up to win. This has led some students of the law to compare media trials to sports events, with the lawyers as competing teams and the judges as umpires. This is an insider's view, which sees the trial as a test of skill and stamina, a contest rather than a search for truth. It attaches great importance to technical issues. Professionals admire a prosecutor who frames charges with finesse or a defense lawyer who finds new ways to win an acquittal or a reduced sentence. The White case made the reputation of his attorney, Douglas Schmidt.

From the point of view of the defense, a big case has three important elements: money, strategy, and time. Big cases are always expensive, even "political" ones involving a cause — civil rights, foreign policy, nuclear power — or alleged persecution by the government. Jury selection in big cases calls for the specialized services of sociologists, market researchers, psychologists, and psychiatrists who carry out in-depth studies of potential jurors.* This is critical, because a trial is often won or lost when the jury is selected. (Clarence Darrow was noted for his skill in choosing jurors.) Courtroom tactics receive infinite attention, since the defendant usually starts from a weak position. Lawyers scrutinize fine points of law and courtroom procedure to find a basis for an appeal in the event that the defendant is convicted.

Every delay in the trial helps the defense. The longer it can be postponed, the better chance the defendant has of winning in court. Over time, evidence gets lost, witnesses move away or die or forget precisely what happened, and changes take place in the prosecutor's staff. (Big cases are usually tried by senior prosecutors; when they retire or enter private practice, they are replaced by less experienced lawyers.)

For the prosecutor, major cases have to be exceptionally strong.

---

* "Jury work," as it is called, began in the 1970s, in conjunction with the trials of various left-wing activists. Although the originators of the field frequently worked *pro bono*, that, like much else, has changed. A prominent jury work firm has charged major corporations as much as $1.5 million for its services.

THE VICTIM

When one person kills another, there is an immediate revulsion at the nature of the crime. But in a time so short as to seem indecent to the members of the personal family, the dead person ceases to exist as an identifiable figure. To those individuals in the community of good will and empathy, warmth and compassion, only one of the key actors in the drama remains with whom to commiserate — and that is always the criminal. . . . He usurps the compassion that is justly his victim's due. He will steal his victim's moral constituency along with her life. — Willard Gaylin, *The Killing of Bonnie Garland*

HOW GOOD A COP ARE YOU? #4

You are driving in your patrol car down Main Street when Fred Kussik runs out of his cigarette and candy store and flags you down. You pull over and get out. Fred is raging mad.

"Dan," he says, that being your name, "I've had it up to here. Two, three times a week Joe Blot comes into my store, grabs a handful of Snickers bars, and runs off home. He's not crazy. He just thinks it's funny. I haven't complained before — I went to school with his wife — but today he knocked over the jellybean jar. I've got twenty bucks' worth of jellybeans all over the floor and a new jar'll cost fifteen. He ran out just before you drove up. I'll sign a complaint. I want you to arrest him."

You enter the store to take a look at the jellybeans and glass on the floor. You take down the necessary information, call in where you are headed, and drive to Joe's house. There, on the front porch, are sitting three people. One, Jones Jones, you already know because you went to school with him yourself. The other two, you soon learn, are Joe Blot and his wife, Helen Quincy Blot.

Later, having issued Joe a misdemeanor citation and released him in the custody of his wife, you go over what you have written in your notebook.

In preparation for writing your report for the D.A.'s office, and because you may have to testify, you put a check mark by each entry that can be used as evidence in court.

These are some of the entries. Which of them do you check?

1. As I approached the porch, the suspect stood up and stated, "Oh damn, I didn't think Kussik'd tell on me."
2. I observed that the suspect had chocolate smeared on all the fingers of his right hand and on the index finger and thumb of his left hand. He also had chocolate smeared around his mouth.
3. I told the suspect what he was accused of and read him his rights.
4. I then asked the suspect if he wanted to tell me about taking the candy and breaking the jellybean jar. He grinned and remained silent.
5. I talked with the suspect's wife, Helen. She said, "Joe came home with the candy ten minutes ago and wolfed it down in front of me. I'll testify to that."
6. Jones Jones volunteered, "When Joe came in with all that candy, I said, 'I bet you stole that from Fred, right?' But he just looked at me. He didn't answer me."

Answers

1. Check. This spontaneous exclamation of Joe's, though self-incriminating, is admissible. Statements made in shock, surprise, or excitement are said before the person saying them has had a chance to reflect or fabricate. Thus, they are considered *res gestae* — things that happened — rather than testimony.
2. Check. You may testify as to your observations.
3. Check. Since you are required by law to do this, you will testify to assure the court that the accuser's rights have not been violated.
4. No. The accused has the right to remain silent, without that silence — or any implication of guilt associated with it — being used against him in court.
5. No. In criminal law a woman may not testify against her husband except in actions he has committed against her or her child. Similarly, a husband may not testify against his wife.
6. Check. Though you cannot testify as to the suspect's silence when you invited him to confess, Jones can attest to his silence when he accused him earlier.

Money is not often a problem, but time is — for exactly the same reasons as for the defense — and so is legal precedent.

Rules of procedure, on the whole, tell more heavily against the prosecution than against the defense. "Acting up" in court rarely costs a defense lawyer more than a contempt citation (usually vacated at the end of the trial, when tempers cool), but improper procedure by the prosecutor or the police can be the basis for a dismissal.

A major problem for the prosecution is the quality of the witnesses. With the exception of police officers, witnesses generally have little courtroom experience. They must be convincing throughout the trial; if the defense can cast doubt on their testimony, the case may fall. Protecting the witnesses' credibility can be especially hard if they are underworld characters

— prostitutes, drug addicts, confessed thieves, or murderers — who have been granted immunity for their testimony.

Finally, if the defendant is convicted but the judge has made a judicial error, there may be grounds for a reversal or a new trial.

So the analogy with sports has a degree of validity. But the concerns of the expert insiders and the outsiders — that is, the public at large — overlap in the more easily reported elements of big cases. Here, the bottom line is whether the accused is found innocent or guilty, or, in a small proportion of cases, if guilty according to the law, whether the deed was justifiable in some extralegal sense.

The outcome, like justice itself, is a moral issue. But the subject of morality makes the legal profession uncomfortable. Many lawyers are more interested in procedural issues than in the substantive question of whether justice is done. Indeed, some even equate proper procedure with morality. An increasing number of observers suspect that this is why big cases reach final judgment in the appellate courts and *not* the trial

"Now then, the public prosecutor is saying some very nasty things to you. . . . Try to cry a little, at least from one eye . . . that always helps!"

Lithograph by Honoré Daumier

courts, where the public watches the law at work. The appellate courts, safely out of view, deal entirely in procedural issues — not whether Jones is guilty of killing Smith but whether (or how precisely) the legal process was followed all the way from arrest to trial. Appellate courts are a perfect insider's game.

Moral issues change from time to time, but the conflicts they provoke are inherently dramatic. The public is unlikely to lose its fascination with the big cases, but it will never take an expert's interest in them, and the professionals will always be a little uncomfortable with this.

Two men face the court: the apprehensive defendant and his lawyer.

Rod Lamkey

WHOSE BODY? #2

Test your knowledge. Here are some more bodies — all from fiction this time. Can you recognize them from the authors' descriptions?

1. The body which lay in the bath was that of a tall, stout man of about fifty. The hair, which was thick and black and naturally curly, had been cut and parted by a master hand, and exuded a faint violet perfume, perfectly recognisable in the close air of the bathroom. . . . On the dead face the handsome pair of gold pince-nez mocked death with grotesque elegance; the fine gold chain curved over the naked breast.

2. Blown to bits: limbs, gravel, clothing, bones, splinters — all mixed up together. I tell you they had to fetch a shovel to gather him up with.

3. The sleeper was covered over from head to foot with a white sheet and the limbs were vaguely defined; all that could be seen was that a human figure lay there, stretched at full length. All around in disorder at the foot of the bed, on chairs beside it, and even on the floor, clothes had been flung in disorder; a rich white silk dress, flowers, and ribbons. On a little table at the head of the bed there was the glitter of diamonds that had been taken off and thrown down. At the end of the bed there was a crumpled heap of lace and on the white lace the toes of a bare foot peeped out from under the sheet; it seemed as though it had been carved out of marble and was horridly still.

4. His silver skin laced with his
   golden blood,
   And his gashed stabs
   looked like a breach in
   nature
   For ruin's wasteful
   entrance.

5. Then they fired — single rounds, three or four, and he felt her shudder. Her thin arms slipped from his hands. . . .

    Shielding his eyes he looked down at the foot of the wall and at last he managed to see her, lying still. For a moment he hesitated, then quite slowly he climbed back down the same rungs, until he was standing beside her. She was dead; her face was turned away, her black hair drawn across her cheek as if to protect her from the rain.

6. (He) lay on his face, his arms out, his fingers dug into the ground, and his features convulsed with some strong emotion to

such an extent that I could hardly have sworn to the identity. There was certainly no physical injury of any kind. But one false statement was made by Barrymore at the inquest. He said that there were no traces upon the ground round the body. He did not observe any. But I did — some distance off, but fresh and clear. . . . They were the footprints of a gigantic hound.

7. The chauffeur — he was one of Wolfsheim's protégés — heard the shots — afterwards he could only say that he hadn't thought anything much about them. . . . With scarcely a word said, four of us, the chauffeur, butler, gardener, and I, hurried down to the pool. There was a faint, barely perceptible movement of the water as the fresh flow from one end urged its way toward the drain at the other. With little ripples that were hardly the shadows of waves, the laden mattress moved irregularly down the pool.

8. He bent over the body. Finally he straightened himself with a slight grimace.
    "It is not pretty," he said. "Someone must have stood there and stabbed him again and again. How many wounds are there exactly?"
    "I make it twelve. One or two are so slight as to be practically scratches. On the other hand, at least three would be capable of causing death."

9. *"But, gentlemen, I have a wife and children!"* he suddenly said in Dutch, in a surprised and gentle tone: then died, not so much of any mortal wound as a number of superficial gashes he had received.

10. "He'd been sawed up in pieces and buried in lime

or something so there wasn't much flesh left on him, according to the report I got, but his clothes had been stuck in with him rolled up in a bundle, and enough was left of the inside ones to tell us something. There was part of a cane, too, with a rubber tip. That's why we thought he might be lame, and we —" He broke off as Andy came in. "Well?" Andy shook his head gloomily. "Nobody sees him come, nobody sees him go. What was that joke about a guy being so thin he had to stand in the same place twice to throw a shadow?"

Earl Warren

Earl Warren stands in our nation's history as one of the monumental chief justices of the supreme court. Loved and hated for his decisions, he changed the country more than most of our presidents did.

The early years of his public life have not been as thoroughly studied as his years on the Supreme Court. Yet he was as remarkable a figure in Alameda County as he was later in Washington. In whatever direction he turned, storm winds began to blow, trees, houses, and people flew through the air, but he always seemed to be calm, disinterested, simple, and straightforward, there at the center of the hurricane, as though it were none of his doing.

Warren spent seven months in 1919 as an Oakland assistant city attorney. That was enough public service to whet his appetite for bigger things. In 1920 he went to work for Ezra Decoto, the district attorney of Alameda County.

Decoto was an honest and kind man whom Warren remembered affectionately and whose public style he took as a model for his own. For Decoto was a fighter without bombast, and in Alameda County, the early years of this century were a time of extravagant bluster. Decoto took on tough cases, and, win or lose, he left a lot of tooth marks.

When Decoto was appointed to the California State Railroad Commission in 1925 and Warren succeeded him as district attorney, his influence on Warren showed. Consistently low-key and mild in public, Warren was tough as nails on the job. Successful as a trial lawyer, he developed a manner more solid than flashy. His deputy and successor Frank Coakley said of him, "Before a jury and judge he was very fair but firm, and a vigorous cross-examiner. If a man was lying, it was too bad for him. His courtroom manner was able and workmanlike. He never missed any bets, but covered all the bags."[*]

There were, of course, many ways in which Warren was different from Decoto. As D.A., Decoto never backed away from a fight, but as Warren said in later years, he did not go out looking for business. Decoto took the office pretty much as he found it and left it that way. Warren, on the other hand, was a man of ambition and vision, an organizer, and something of an administrative genius. Though Warren's appointment as D.A. was only provisional, and he would have to stand for election the next year, he had strong ideas of what he wanted the D.A.'s office to become. They included independence from the pressures and petty graft of local politics. He lost no time in making a beginning. He persuaded the county

[*] Irving Stone, *Earl Warren*, p. 56.

board of supervisors to give him his own investigative staff.

One of the first problems Warren took on as D.A. was that of Oakland's bail bondsmen. It had come to his attention that in the police court (as the municipal court was then called), there was a nasty little racket flourishing that involved collusion among police officers, court officials, and bondsmen.

It worked this way. The bondsmen posted runners at the jail and at the courts. When an arrest was made or when an arrestee was brought in for arraignment, some-one — a police officer or court clerk — would give a bondsman's card to the arrestee and suggest that the bondsman could help him get out of jail. If the person wanted help, the runner was dispatched to the bondsman's office. Even if the person had enough cash with him to post bail, he was told he could not pay cash. He had to go through the bondsman. As you can see, the bondsman truly had a captive customer. After the arres-tee signed for a bond and was al-lowed to make bail, the bondsman paid a kickback to the officer or the court clerk. When the arrestee

Earl Warren and Ezra Decoto, his predeces-sor as district attorney of Alameda County, in 1925.

paid off the bond, the interest charge, always stiff, was stiffened more to cover the cost of the kickback. Small-time bootleggers, lottery operators, and other frequently arrested petty offenders all knew what was going on, but they were in no position to complain about this chiseling.

What moved Warren to act was the darker side of this murky business. In cases where serious offenses were involved and bail was high, the bondsmen and their henchmen frequently arranged a series of continuances and other delays to keep the meter running on the bond's interest. Thus, the bond quickly became a debt the average person could not pay off, even if ultimately set free. For such bonds, deeds were taken as collateral. Poor men and women lost their homes to this gouging; wives and children were put out in the street.

When the bondsman's debtor could not pay, collection was swift, but the opposite was true when it was the bondsman's turn to pay the court. If a defendant skipped town — which properly causes bail to be forfeited — continuances and delays were arranged to postpone the trials over and over again, sometimes keeping them in abeyance until the statute of limitations expired. In these cases, the bail bondsmen recovered their money. A number of them became extremely wealthy.

Warren tackled the problem by setting his staff to investigate Charles Meyers, the biggest of the bail bondsman. When Meyers's friends began telling Warren to lay off or suffer the political consequences, the D.A. dug in and worked even harder. He reviewed the records of all of Meyers's transactions, and he and his staff interviewed hundreds of Meyers's clients. Then he took what he found to the grand jury. One of his

principal witnesses was a woman whose home had been sold by Meyers to pay the interest on a bail bond that had not actually been defaulted on. She was a pretty young wife, and she came to court carrying her six-month-old boy, who was, Warren later said, as beautiful a child as he had ever seen. When the mother went to testify, one of the women on the jury offered to hold him. "The child was so attractive and so good natured that before the mother had completed her testimony," Warren remembered, "every grand juror had held him for a few moments."[*] The jurors decided they did not approve of Meyers's behavior and indicted him for grand larceny.

When Meyers was arrested, the other bondsmen promptly cleaned up their act. Even though Meyers beat the rap — he induced a woman in his office to take responsibility for the "clerical errors" that led to the illegal sale of the victim's home — there were no more bail bond scandals in Alameda County while Warren was D.A. Far from harming him politically, breaking Meyers probably won him the election.

This case displays three of Warren's best qualities. First, his habit of getting directly to the heart of the matter: he took on the biggest guy in the racket. Second was his courage: though he hadn't been elected yet, and the bondsmen and their allies threatened to use all of their influence to beat him at the polls, he scorned to play it safe. Third, he used his office to defend the underdogs, one of the constant, reverberating themes of his public life.[†]

[*] All quotes attributed to Earl Warren in this story are from *The Memoirs of Earl Warren*.

[†] The young mother whose testimony Warren used to put fear into Meyers was married to a convicted burglar. She and others like her were quite powerless against official abuses.

After he was elected district attorney, Warren continued to take on powerful people. He prosecuted members of the Alameda city council, a member of the Berkeley board of education, the sheriff of Alameda County, and several Oakland city council members. Of these, the cases involving the sheriff and the Oakland officials stand out.

Warren's relationship with the sheriffs of Alameda County was uneasy for many years. It began with Sheriff Frank Barnet, in a case where Warren came off not looking so good. Barnet was a high school graduate who had begun life as an apprentice paperhanger and interior decorator. Moving on to public service, he became successively a deputy tax collector, an assistant deputy clerk of the California Supreme Court, and a court reporter for the Alameda County Superior Court. In 1905 he was appointed sheriff. By the time Warren became D.A., Barnet was fifty-seven years old and had been sheriff for twenty years. Though Barnet's career was not without distinction, Warren did not think much of him. Barnet was, he said, "willing to handle cases of murder, robbery, and burglary, but had no stomach for such things as bootlegging, gambling, and prostitution."

Then came the Bessie Ferguson murder case. Bessie had been killed, on August 24, 1925, sliced up, and thrown into the bay. For weeks, investigators kept turning up bits and pieces of her along the shore of the East Bay, all the way from Richmond to Alameda, a distance of fifteen miles. Some of the best investigators in the area worked on the case, including E. O. Heinrich, who reassembled Bessie.

Others assembled the facts of

GIVING TESTIMONY

The final and hardest job of the police officer is to give testimony that will convict the criminal. It is not much good for an officer to preserve the crime scene, gather evidence, interview witnesses, make arrests, interrogate suspects, and write reports if, when he testifies in front of the jury, he makes a fool of himself and blows the case.

During the investigation the officer must make sure the evidence he collects is admissible. In court he must guard against having evidence thrown out because of errors in presentation. To do this, the officer must know the rules of evidence and make his presentation in a clear, complete, and authoritative manner. He must protect his information from being discounted by the jury because of misstatements, contradictions, and omissions. So he must prepare thoroughly, reviewing his connection with the case.

Because the prosecuting attorney is prohibited from asking leading questions, the officer should be able to anticipate how the former is developing his case and to present the evidence in a way that underscores important points. Likewise, he's got to have his wits about him to sidestep traps the defense may set for him. The officer must have the facts well in hand, having studied his notebook and reports.

Because stage fright, nervousness, and timidity can look like dishonesty and shiftiness, the officer on the witness stand must project his own candor and composed authority. Since sarcasm or displays of anger can prejudice the jury against the officer and the evidence he presents, he must learn self-control.

Finally, any indication that the officer has an emotional stake in convicting the defendant — that the officer is out to get him — will make the defendant appear to be the victim and the officer the aggressor. Therefore the officer must cultivate a fair-minded and disinterested attitude that puts truth before any other consideration.

**Alameda County
Sheriff Frank Barnet**

Alameda County Sheriff's Dept.

Oakland History Room, Oakland Public Library

Bessie Ferguson

Alameda County Sheriff Burton Becker

her life. Bessie was, they learned, an extortionist. As mystery writer Marjorie MacDonald put it, she was "a pretty girl, wide-eyed, with masses of blonde hair — a 'sweet' face, trusting, naïve, sincere, the perfect face to lend verisimilitude to the beseeching words: 'I trusted you — and I'm pregnant! Oh dear, what shall I do?' The portrait emerged of a girl well loved by sundry . . . professional gentlemen, carefully compartmentalized so that each thought he was the only one."

Her circle of lovers included a dentist, an accountant, and several doctors — one of them a surgeon.

According to her mother, it also included Sheriff Barnet. Mrs. Ferguson told investigators that the last time she saw her daughter Bessie, she said she was going out on a date with the Sheriff.

Barnet denied it.

The statement by Bessie's mother was the only evidence — if such it can be called — against Barnet. There were letters from all her (other) lovers, but none from the sheriff. A hotel clerk supposedly saw them together, but then he denied that Barnet was the man he had seen, identifying one of her other known lovers instead. As the bits and pieces of Bessie were pulled out of the bay, it was evident that her killer had the skill of a surgeon. Barnet was no surgeon.

The day after her murder was discovered, the investigators learned that the surgeon in Bessie's circle had moved to Florida. A background check showed that he had been convicted of murder in the third degree for malpractice. Inexplicably, no attempt was made by the D.A.'s office to extradite this obvious suspect, nor even to send an officer to question him.

The investigation bogged down, and, as time passed without progress, Warren began to take a lot of heat from the press. He was only thirty-five and still new on the job. In order to satisfy his critics that as much as possible was being done, he gave a briefing to all the local papers on where the investigation stood — strictly off the record. He mentioned Barnet as one of the primary suspects.

A year later, during the campaign of 1926, a newspaper that supported Warren's opponent revealed that Warren suspected Sheriff Barnet as Bessie's murderer. Warren, who won the election anyway, was furious and got the editor who violated his confidence fired. But Barnet's good name was ruined. He was defeated in the same election by Burton F. Becker, chief of police in the city of Piedmont, bringing to end a twenty-two-year career as sheriff.

Bessie's killer was never apprehended. Her case had already been put on the back burner, and there were never any further developments in it. She faded into history as an issue in an election that has long been forgotten.

Warren said this episode taught him not to give confidential briefings to newspapers. Rather pointedly, he never expressed any regret for the damage it did to the sheriff. Frank Barnet died, at sixty-seven years of age, on March 19, 1935. Because the Ferguson case was never solved, he was never able to redeem his reputation.

Barnet may have been a murderer or a deeply wronged man, but the new sheriff was definitely a bad hat. At thirty-nine, Becker was close to Warren's own age, much younger and more energetic than his predecessor. He was a leading member of the secret Alameda County Ku Klux Klan, and this supposedly gave him important connections. During his ten years as chief in Piedmont, he had learned all, or almost all, the angles. As far as he was concerned, Warren was just a new kid who didn't know the territory.

Before he was even sworn in, Becker met with the leading figures of the county's underworld and told them what they would have to pay if they wanted to stay in business. When Warren got a whiff of what Becker was doing, he decided it had to stop. He called Becker to his office to give him a warning. The sheriff was unimpressed. "You take care of your business, and I'll take care of mine," he told Warren.

Warren's duel with Becker stretched over several years. There was a lot of skirmishing. Becker collected money to protect businesses involved in racketeering, and Warren used the Berkeley Police Department to raid places Becker was protecting. (Chief Vollmer's officers could be relied on not to tip off *anybody*.) The duel heated up when Warren got a complaint against Becker's bagman, Fred Smith, an automobile salesman who specialized in fraudulent sales contracts. Smith fled to Los Angeles and hid there for a year. But Warren's investigators found him and arrested him. They gave Smith the choice of going to trial or snitching on Becker. Afraid of landing in the county jail, Smith turned state's evidence.

Smith sang to the grand jury. Warren backed up Smith's testimony with that of the people — "vicemongers," he called them — who handed over the protection money for delivery to Becker.

Now, as it happened, five members of the grand jury were also in the Ku Klux Klan. Becker counted on them to refuse to vote an indictment, as a matter of Klan loyalty and trust. Warren was worried that they might do just that. But he counted on the fact that Klansmen, though they broke laws in their fanaticism, generally considered themselves upright, honest men. They disapproved of criminality. He called the sheriff for questioning under oath. Rather than perjure or incriminate himself, Becker took the Fifth Amendment. This upset the Klansmen, and they all voted for the indictment, making it unanimous. Becker resigned.

During the period between the indictment and the trial, Becker threatened to murder Warren and kill himself. Becker's wife spread the word in women's circles that something bad might happen to Warren's children. This made Warren angry and implacable. He took care to keep Klansmen off the trial jury, presented his evidence remorselessly, and had Becker convicted. Afterward, to underline his contempt for Becker, he acted blasé in public, saying it was not a particularly difficult trial.

While all this was going on, Warren's office was also investigating the activities of one of Becker's friends, William H. Parker, Oakland's commissioner of streets. An elaborate conspiracy for milking kickbacks out of Oakland paving contracts was going on, and Parker and two other com-missioners were at the center of it. The companies Parker favored became members of the "Greater Oakland Construction Company." Freezing out nonmembers by using a variety of underhanded stratagems, they divided all the contracts among themselves.

As if this were not enough, the paving companies cheated the city on the cost of materials, and, as Warren wrote, "they also cheated on the actual construction work by diluting the concrete mix, poorly preparing the foundations and otherwise cutting corners."

Warren's investigation of the paving scandal was an elaborate, convoluted masterpiece. It is worthy of study by anyone interested in governmental corruption. When it was over, Comissioner Parker and the biggest street paving contractor were convicted of bribery and sent to prison, the other two Oakland commissioners resigned, and various members of the paving companies were convicted of lesser crimes.

For the city government, the results of Warren's prosecution were just short of revolutionary. Almost from its founding, Oakland had been governed by a commission system; that is, the members of the city council were commissioners of the various departments — streets, police and fire, health, and so on. Because the commissioners took an active role in the management of their departments, patronage became deeply entrenched and the civil service relatively weak. Scandals there had been in the past, but until Warren the system always survived them. Warren's investigation of the paving contracts discredited it completely. In the next election, Oakland voters approved a major reform, voting in the city manager form of municipal government, under which the city still functions.

Once Sheriff Becker and the paving contractors had been disposed of, things settled down in Alameda County, and with a few exceptions the district attorney's work became relatively routine. Warren now devoted time to improving the quality of his staff and its working conditions. He overhauled the administration of the district attorney's office. He arranged to have his lawyers paid full-time salaries, putting an end to their need to maintain private practices. He also expanded his investigative staff, which completely freed him from depending on the sheriff or the municipal police departments for assistance.

Within a few years he began to feel restless. Underneath his placid surface, Warren was a hunter, and he liked a lot of action. It wasn't enough for him to have straightened out the county and to have made his office a model for others. He began to look for new problems to solve. In 1938 he ran for and won the office of attorney general of California.

"Incompetent, Irrelevant, and Immaterial!"

When D.A. Hamilton Berger rises in objection to Perry Mason's interrogation of a witness, those are the words he uses. What is he talking about?

He is talking about the rules of evidence. These rules govern the admission of information before the court in criminal and civil suits, and they apply to the prosecution and the defense.

Information that does not bear directly on the case confuses the issue. The purpose of the rules of evidence is to screen out this confusing information. For instance, in a trial to determine whether Helen Quincy Blot was guilty of cruelty to animals, it would be irrelevant that her husband was recently convicted on a misdemeanor larceny charge. That information might prejudice or confuse the jury when it weighed the evidence of her alleged cruelty.

There are lots of rules governing evidence, and they are constantly being redefined. Those of materiality, relevance, and competence are most often lumped together. One good reason is that the meanings of the three are — or have been — so close as to boggle the mind. By the time Hamilton Berger had stopped to untangle which of the three was best suited to the moment, the witness would have answered Perry Mason's question and let the cat out of the bag.

To understand what these three terms mean, you first have to understand that all evidence is presented in order to try to prove something.

To be *material* evidence, the point that the lawyer — prosecution or defense — is trying to prove with it has to be part of the case. If the evidence is meant to prove that there were three pygmy goats in the bedroom, but goats are not part of the case, then the evidence is immaterial.

To be *relevant*, the evidence must go some way toward really proving what the lawyer is trying to prove with it. If the question before the court is part of the case, but the evidence doesn't have anything to do with guilt or innocence, then the evidence is irrelevant. For instance, if the D.A. was trying to prove that Mrs. Blot starved her seventeen dogs, a neighbor's testimony about the noise and smell would be judged irrelevant.

Again. To be material, the point being proved has to be part of the case. To be relevant, it has to be part of the proof of that point. Do you have that clear? You still want to go to law school?

To be *competent*, the witness must be eligible to testify as to the evidence. Insanity, senility, or babyhood, of course, makes one incompetent. A witness would also be incompetent to testify if the court decided he didn't have enough experience, knowledge, or understanding of what he was talking about. The question of whether Mrs. Blot left town for a week, leaving her dogs uncared for, might be material. The testimony of old Mrs. Matthews about the empty water and food dishes in the back yard and the dogs crying might be relevant. But the competence of old Mrs. Matthews to testify that the dogs were starving — she not being a veterinarian — would certainly be attacked by the defense.

But there has grown to be a wider use of the term. Referring originally only to a witness, incompetence now covers any evidence that is inadmissible for any reason — whether the fault is in the witness, the document to be presented, or in the physical evidence itself.

Bill Fallon

William J. Fallon was a famous New York criminal attorney in the 1920s. He was the archetype of the shady defense lawyer who helped hoodlums beat the rap. His friend — such men do have friends — Gene Fowler wrote his biography and gave it the title by which he was known to the underworld, *The Great Mouthpiece*.

Fallon was tall, redheaded, personable, charming, and agile-minded. His fees, according to Fowler, "were the first tremendous ones paid by captains of modern crime syndicates for legal advice. He became, in fact, a corporation counsel for the underworld." He was certainly as well paid as any good corporate attorney. During the years when he was at his peak, Fallon earned and spent over a million and a half dollars. Even today, that's a lot of money.

Was he worth it? His clients thought so.

Bill Fallon graduated from Fordham Law School in 1912. After two years in private practice, he became an assistant district attorney in Westchester County, just north of New York City. The best-known case he handled in his two years as a prosecutor was that in which Thomas Osborne, the warden of Sing Sing Prison, was accused of abusing his authority. The allegations included forcing prisoners to commit homosexual acts.

The charges against Osborne may have been politically motivated. He was a reformer and introduced some decent, humane changes at Sing Sing, including a requirement that food contractors deliver edible meat and vegetables to the prison comissary. Because Sing Sing contracts were an important gift of patronage, there might have been some connection between that and the governor's opinion that Osborne was soft on the prisoners.

A rough and tumble affair, the Osborne case made Fallon a star. Like the trials in which he later spoke for the defense, it was a three-ring circus. It featured wiretapping, missing documents, and masses of inflammatory press releases — and Fallon exuberantly in the middle of the action. In addition to a willingness to outrage the proprieties of the court, Fallon demonstrated his intense competitiveness, a desire to win at almost any cost.

Osborne was not convicted, but the trial ruined his good name. Many observers thought he was innocent, but Fallon always claimed the warden was guilty as charged.

After the Osborne trial, Fallon returned to private practice. In January 1918 he moved to New York City, the scene of his triumphs and disasters. Within a year he became the attorney for one of the major gangsters of the 1920s, Arnold Rothstein, and began using his talents to protect him and his hirelings ("serfs," Fowler called them) from the law. More than one newspaperman described Rothstein as a good companion, a cultivated man who happened to be in a tough line of business. Actually, Rothstein was a very sinister figure. F. Scott Fitzgerald caught something of his evil aura in *The Great Gatsby*, sketching him as Wolfsheim, "a very smart man."

Rothstein was dapper, well spoken, and crooked to his fingertips. He was primarily a gambler and a loan shark, but he was also involved in illegal whiskey, stolen securities, drugs, labor union rackets, and sports bribery. He controlled a number of New York City judges, having them under obligation to him for loans. He is thought by some to have railroaded Charles Becker, a strong-armed, grafting New York cop, into the electric chair. Rothstein, the acknowledged top dog in New York's underworld, was known there as "Mr. Big" and "the Big Bankroll," until the day in 1928 when somebody shot and killed him.

Rothstein was a man who lived in the shadows and stayed behind the scenes. He acted through intermediaries who kept their own identities secret. Fallon described him as "a man who waits in doorways . . . a mouse, waiting in the doorway for his cheese." The crooked World Series of 1919 was

a typical Rothstein operation. His role remained unclear until 1963, when it was reconstructed by Eliot Asinof in his brilliant book *Eight Men Out*. The mystery surrounding the scandal was due to Fallon's legal and illegal maneuvers at the time and to what Asinof described as a "residue of fear" among the White Sox players that "sprang from a deeply imbedded awareness of the vindictive power of the 1920s gambling-gangster world."

The fix began among the players, who felt they were not being paid what they were worth by Charles Comiskey, the owner of the White Sox. They approached several small-time gamblers and offered to throw the Series for $80,000. Later they upped their price to $100,000. These gamblers did not have that kind of money and were not able to raise it. So the gamblers contacted Rothstein, the Big Bankroll, the only man in the underworld who could meet the players' demands. By this time, of course, rumors were flying among those in the know and those not quite in the know.

When first approached, Rothstein refused to back the fix. But a pal of his named Abe Attell couldn't resist the opportunity, so he put up $10,000 of his own money, saying it came from Rothstein. The players took it, thinking it was a first installment, but it was Attell's limit. Soon the players began demanding more money, even threatening to back out of the deal. Acting through an intermediary who used the alias Brown, Rothstein secretly chipped in $80,000 to keep the players from going sour. So, although Rothstein did not initiate the crooked World Series, he became the principal gambler behind it.

Fallon's first important job for Rothstein was to keep him from

Arnold Rothstein, "the Big Bankroll"

When the grand jury's attention turned to Attell, Rothstein kept him in line by providing him with money and a good attorney — Bill Fallon. From New York, Fallon announced that the Abe Attell who was wanted in Chicago was not the same Abe Attell who was his client. When the Chicago authorities sent one of their witnesses to New York to make an identification, Fallon met him at the train, got him drunk, suggested that fingering Attell might be dangerous, and bribed him with enough money to cover his $3,000 in losses on the Series. The next day, when asked to identify Attell, the witness said, "I never saw this man before."

Eventually, the prosecution of the gamblers fizzled out. The only people punished for corrupting the World Series were the ball players.

Another Rothstein associate and Fallon client was the gambler and confidence man Nicky Arnstein (a.k.a. Jules Arnstein, Jules W. Arndstein, John Wilson Adair, James Wilford Adair, and J. W. Arnold). Nicky is best known today as Fanny Brice's' first husband, as portrayed in *Funny Girl*. Arnstein was suspected of masterminding robberies on Wall Street, in which $5 million in securities were stolen.

Nicky went on the lam for a year, and when he came back to New York to face the music, the authorities festooned him with charges. Nicky filed for bankruptcy, and when prosecutors questioned him about his sources of income, Fallon directed him to invoke the Fifth Amendment. No one had ever done this in a bankruptcy hearing before. Arnstein was promptly slapped into the clink for contempt of court. Fallon applied for a writ of habeas corpus. It was denied. "I'll take it to

being arrested and sent to jail when the players confessed in 1920. Fallon coached him in a plausible story that would persuade the Chicago grand jury not to indict him. Rothstein, who had bet at least $370,000 on the Series, blandly told the jurors, "Abe Attell did the fixing. I'm here to vindicate myself. . . . The world knows I was asked in on the deal and my friends know how I turned it down flat. I don't doubt that Attell used my name to put it over. That's been done by smarter men than Abe. But I wasn't in on it, wouldn't have gone into it under any circumstances, and didn't bet a cent on the Series after I found out what was under way." The grand jury bought it. Fallon and Rothstein returned triumphantly to New York.

the Supreme Court," said Fallon, and he did. The U.S. Supreme Court directed issuance of the writ and affirmed the new use of the Fifth Amendment. (The case was *Jules W. Arndstein, appellant, v. Thomas D. McCarthy, U.S. Marshal, etc.*, Nov. 8, 1920. Many years later, Chief Justice Earl Warren cited it as one of the precedents for his decision in *Miranda*.)

Arnstein faced federal and state charges for his role in the bond thefts. Since the penalty under New York law was up to twenty-five years in prison, as against two years on the federal charges, it was much in Nicky's interest to be tried in federal court. Fallon managed to achieve this too.

In December 1920 Nicky went on trial in Washington, D.C. He was charged with transporting the Wall Street securities stolen in New York to Washington and depositing them with a stockbroker. Through the stockbroker they were, as the U.S. attorney phrased it, "exchanged for loans of large proportions at local banks." Today it would be said that Nicky

Peggy Hopkins Joyce — a Broadway doll and one of Fallon's clients.

was laundering the bonds. While much about this case is murky, it is clear that Nicky was acting as an agent for Rothstein.

Fallon picked his jury carefully, kept Nicky off the stand (so that his testimony could not be used in New York if he was tried there later), and attacked the government's witnesses. One witness against Nicky was a black man, a Pullman car waiter who had served Nicky's meals while the train traveled between New York and Washington. Among the jurors Fallon chose were two white Southerners he knew had Klan sympathies. He got a hung jury. The government announced that it would seek a new trial.

Fallon was a high-living man who liked to spend lavishly. He squired expensive showgirls like Peggy Hopkins Joyce and Lillian Loraine — the "dolls" in Damon Runyon's phrase "guys and dolls" — up and down Broadway, dressed well, and indulged himself prodigiously. When Fallon fell for a chorus girl named Gertrude Vanderbilt, Arnstein objected. He wanted a lawyer with his mind on business. Fallon and Arnstein quarreled, and Fallon withdrew from the case. When Nicky was retried in 1924 without Fallon as counsel, he was convicted and sent to Leavenworth for two years.

Fallon was a hard drinker, and alcohol did him in. As it hardened his liver, it led him into personal and professional irresponsibilities. In 1922 Edward J. Donegan paid Fallon $125,000 to defend him against federal charges of bootlegging. According to Gene Fowler, Fallon spent the fee in one wild night of partying. Despite the tales that treat Prohibition laws as a joke, a federal indictment was a serious matter. Fallon did not prepare a defense for his client. Donegan was convicted, sentenced to

ten years in prison, fined $65,000, and tapped by the IRS for $1,653,797 in back taxes.

Many of the Broadway gangsters, including Rothstein and Arnstein, were attracted by the smell of easy money on Wall Street when speculative fever swept the country in the early twenties. Where they went, Fallon followed. The monetary aroma was particularly strong around what were known as bucket shops, crooked brokerage houses that took real money for phony stocks and bonds. There was no Securities and Exchange commission to regulate the stock exchange. Investigative reporters for a Hearst newspaper, the *New York American*, uncovered eighty-one bucket shops that had sold some $5 billion worth of nonexistent securities.

Fallon represented twenty-four of them. In 1922 he defended twenty-three members of the Durrell-Gregory house on charges of mail fraud and won acquittals. His clients at E. M. Fuller and Company, a bucket shop that failed for $4 million on the Consolidated Exchange, were tried three times in 1923 for misappropriation of funds and got off scot-free.

Durrell-Gregory came back to haunt Fallon. Hearst reporters discovered a juror in that case, Charles W. Rendigs, who said he had been bribed to hold out for a not-guilty verdict. He alleged that through intermediaries (the Rothstein touch!) Fallon had offered him $5,000 for his vote, but had paid him only $2,500. After coming clean with the reporters, Rendigs confessed to federal attorneys.

Fallon was indicted for jury tampering and went on trial in 1924. He denied bribing Rendigs. He claimed that he was being persecuted by William Randolph Hearst. The publisher wanted to

get him, Fallon announced, because he had birth certificates "here in this room" for Hearst's illegitimate children by Marion Davies, a movie star and Hearst's long-time mistress.

This caused a sensation that is hard to understand today. It succeeded in distracting the jury from whether Rendigs was telling the truth. In 1924 very few people knew of Hearst's affair with Marion Davies, and those who did generally respected their privacy. Though it was the sort of scandal the Hearst papers gladly exposed, it was not mentioned in his competitors' newspapers until Fallon made it a public issue. Hearst was hoisted on his own petard.

Of course, Fallon was bluffing when he said that he had the birth certificates. There were none because Marion Davies had never had children. But he got away with it because nobody asked to see them.

Fallon argued his conspiracy hoax so passionately at every possible opportunity during the trial that he convinced at least some of the jurors that it had an important connection with his guilt or innocence on the charge of jury tampering. He was acquitted. Like the White Sox players, Rendigs was not so fortunate. He pleaded guilty to accepting a bribe and was given a suspended sentence.

Beating the bribery rap was Fallon's last hurrah. Though he avoided prison and disbarment, his career went downhill from 1924 until his death in 1927. Clients stopped coming to his of-

William Powell as a character loosely based on Rothstein in *Street of Chance*. In this unlikely story, the gambler sacrifices himself to keep his brother (played by Regis Toomey) honest.

fice, and Rothstein cut him loose. The gangster was too discreet and cautious to risk having his affairs handled by a drunk.

In a *New Yorker* article published in the early 1930s, Alva Johnston described Fallon as "the cult hero of the criminal bar." But with the passage of time, his reputation faded. A more recent student of criminal justice, Thomas Reppetto, dismissed him as "an actor who was able to put on dramatic shows before Tammany judges."

Like many defense attorneys,

GAMES LAWYERS PLAY

Magazine writer Avery Hale described a case of Bill Fallon's that "rotated around a sucker identifying a bucketeer on the witness stand. Fallon simply had his client completely alter his appearance. He put the man on a severe diet and reduced him from two hundred pounds to 140. He changed the color of the defendant's hair from brown to black, mixed with gray. He had the man shave off a naturally imposing moustache and wear needless eyeglasses so thick they looked like magnifying glasses. To top off everything, he sent the defendant to a dramatic coach and vested him with a Southern accent.

"After the sucker had testified for the government, Fallon cross-examined him at length about the appearance of the villain who had bilked him out of his life's savings. The sucker described the villain as a moustached, brown-haired man weighing about two hundred pounds who talked like a typical New Yorker. 'And did he wear eyeglasses?' asked Fallon. 'No.' 'You're sure about that?' 'Positively.'

"When Fallon put the defendant on the stand, the man got up from the counsel table and began to walk toward the witness chair. He walked into the counsel table and fell over it. 'Why,' said Fallon, 'you're so nervous you forgot to put on your glasses. There's nothing to be nervous about. The complainant in this case certainly wasn't talking about you.'

"So the villain put on the thick-lensed glasses and took the stand, and made a categorical denial of the charges against him in moss-and-honeysuckle tones. Then Fallon asked the sucker to stand up. 'Is this the man you say took your money?' he asked the sucker, pointing to the defendant. 'No,' said the sucker."

The charges were dismissed.

Fallon did not invent this stunt, though he used it with élan. Today, however, it is a risky maneuver and can backfire when prosecutors are alert and know their work. Recently in San Diego, a young gardener kidnapped and molested a seven-year-old girl, fled, and was captured a mile from the Mexican border. On Monday, his attorney demanded a lineup for what was really a superfluous identification. The lineup was scheduled for Wednesday, and the preliminary hearing was to be on the following Friday. On Tuesday, the attorney had the suspect's head shaved. When the prosecutor, Thomas McArdle, discovered what had been done, he obtained a judicial order that vacated the lineup — that is, canceled it.

The courts require lineups to be fair and will reject one that is not. In this instance, anticipating a conviction, the defense attorney played for an unfair lineup so that he could build a constitutional issue into the case that would lie dormant until he used it in the appeals court. There are not many bald five-foot-five twenty-year-olds in San Diego, and it was not likely that the prosecutors could have found one by Wednesday to make the lineup look fair in the written record, which is all an appeals court looks at.

Another example from the same prosecutor is a drug case. When arrested, the suspect had a huge red beard and a long red ponytail, and he usually wore blue jeans and a vest sporting biker colors. His lawyer had the beard and ponytail cut off, had him comb his hair, and put him in slacks, tie, and sport coat for what may have been the first time in his adult life.

But the prosecutor was prepared. He deliberately put an officer on the stand who did not recognize the suspect in this metamorphosis. Then he used the officer's failure to identify as the grounds for entering the booking photographs of the suspect as people's exhibit A. He passed them to the jury for examination. Then he brought other officers to the stand who had, of course, no problem identifying the defendant. In due course, the defendant was convicted.

When the defense tries to alter a suspect's appearance excessively — that is, beyond making him neat and clean — and the changes are brought to the jury's attention, it never fails to remember the attempted deception.

Nicky Arnstein and Fanny Brice

Fallon was extremely competitive and viewed winning as everything. He did not take seriously the idea that, as an officer of the court, he had an obligation to see that the proceedings led to truth, so that justice might be done. He did the kind of "lawyering" — to use current lawyers' jargon — that turned the courtroom into a circus.

Fallon treasured a piece of advice from his first law partner, David Hunt, who said, "Most lawyers break their necks trying to get a jury to be favorable to a client. The thing to do is to make them favorable to you, yourself. After they are won to you, the rest is easy. It's like shooting fish in a barrel."

Fallon cultivated jurors. He became expert at reading them and their susceptibilities. Once he had a sense of what they felt and thought, he would pitch his summations in weak cases — and he handled many weak cases — to the one juror he believed he could convince. The typical Fallon victory was a hung jury. Eleven to one was his trademark. Some saw this as little short of miraculous, but others were not so impressed. A tough-minded crime reporter named Emanuel H. Lavine wrote that Fallon "didn't take any chances. Whenever there was a case at all in doubt he kept an ace in the hole. Of course, he fought tooth and nail in the courtroom — employed all his eloquence, all his charm. That made it easier for the juror he had bribed to hold out for a disagreement or, if the chances were better, to win over the other jurors to acquit the prisoner."

Fallon was an expert in the use of insinuation. He applied this skill particularly to make honest witnesses seem to be liars or incompetent. He cultivated a sure, confident manner, and he relied on the inability of ordinary people to remember details with precision. As his questioning took them over and over each episode and little changes in detail were drawn

Omar Sharif and Barbra Streisand as Mr. and Mrs. Arnstein in *Funny Girl*.

Joseph Goodwin

forth and imbued with ominous meanings, he destroyed their credibility.

He was a quick study. In a defense attorney, this often means acquiring enough superficial knowledge of a subject to be able to ask, in a seemingly knowledgeable way, a wide range of technical questions that are intended to confuse witnesses and undermine their testimony. Nowadays, this is one of the main refuges of public defenders in drug cases: "What do you mean, Mr. Hype's pupils were pinpointed? 'Pinpointed' is a term with no medical validity."

Fallon did not build his cases on consistency. He was ready to improvise, to bluff, and to make sensational statements for their momentary effect, hanging on to them if they worked, dropping them if they misfired. He was always on the lookout for a good diversion, as when he conferred motherhood on Marion Davies.

And then, of course, there was the slide of his advocacy into criminality. In addition to tampering with jurors, he appears to have employed agents to steal documents from a prosecutor's office on more than one occasion, and, in many other cases, to have destroyed documents to prevent them from being entered as evidence.

Bill Fallon was a rogue attorney. Perhaps his vices were due to the times, and today he might have adhered to a higher set of standards — as a practical matter, if not out of conviction. Maybe, maybe not. Fallon's career, like Aaron Burr's, was scandalous, mythic in its proportions, and remains one of the country's bad memories.

LIBRARY
San Quentin
PRISON

USE THIS BOOKMARK TO KEEP YOUR BOOK CLEAN AND TO AVOID BENDING PAGES

☆
Compliments of Vocational Print Shop

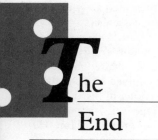

The End

Finally the chase is over. The case is wrapped up. The perpetrators begin to exit the scene, often in handcuffs. The stage is left to the detective and his cronies.

With his adversary vanquished, with evil defeated, it is time for the re-emergence of the good. It is time for the detective to celebrate. Or is it?

Here, to begin with, Lord Peter Wimsey has solved the puzzle. The murderer has been arrested, tried, and convicted. Condemned, unrepentant, he is to hang in the morning. Lord Peter and his Lady Harriet wait together for it to be over:

The light grew stronger as they waited.

Quite suddenly, he said, "Oh, damn!" and began to cry — in an awkward, unpractised way at first, and then more easily. So she held him, crouched at her knees, against her breast, huddling his head in her arms that he might not hear eight o'clock strike.

— Peter Wimsey, in *Busman's Honeymoon* by Dorothy L. Sayers

"You reasoned it out beautifully," [Watson] exclaimed, in unfeigned admiration. "It is so long a chain, and yet every link rings true."

"It saved me from ennui," [Holmes] answered, yawning. "Alas! I already feel it closing in upon me."

— Sherlock Holmes, in "The Red-Headed League" by Sir Arthur Conan Doyle

"No." said Mr. Queen gladly, "putting it all together, I'm satisfied that Mr. Big Bill Tree, in trying to murder his wife, very neatly murdered himself instead."

"That's all very well for *you*," said the Inspector disconsolately. "but *I* need proof."

"I've told you how it happened," said his son airily, making for the door. "Can any man do more?"

— Ellery Queen with Inspector Queen, in "Man Bites Dog" by Ellery Queen

"And, between ourselves," said Thorndyke, when we were discussing the case some time after, "he deserved to escape. It was clearly a case of blackmail, and to kill a blackmailer — when you have no other defense against him — is hardly murder."

— Dr. John Thorndyke, in "A Case of Premeditation" by R. Austin Freeman

"It was unpremeditated, but in my opinion he hit to kill."

"Will he get off?" Dr. Otterly asked.

"How the bloody hell should I know!" Alleyn said with some violence. "Sorry, Dame Alice."

"Have some punch," said Dame Alice. She looked up at him out of her watery old eyes. "You're an odd sort of feller," she remarked. "Anybody'd think you were squeamish."

— Inspector Roderick Alleyn, in *Death of a Fool* by Ngaio Marsh

Even Thatcher was slightly exhilarated. He had closed the proceedings with a promise of increased financing. The Parents' League had cheered. On his way out, total strangers had pounded him on the back and congratulated him. Even his old neighbor, Harry of the folded arms, had wrung his hand warmly.

— John Thatcher, in *Ashes to Ashes* by Emma Lathen

"Heavens! man, consider what it could mean to me — one of your own class."

"What shall we do, Carrados? We never like to prosecute."

"I know you don't," replied the blind man. "I've already drawn up his confession. Read this and then sign it." . . .

"What are you going to do with it?" asked the unfortunate wretch.

"Keep it as a guarantee of future good behavior, and to vindicate these others if the necessity occurs."

— Max Carrados, in "The Vanished Crown" by Ernest Bramah

Smiley presented an odd figure to his fellow passengers — a little, fat man, rather gloomy, suddenly smiling, ordering a drink. The young, fair-haired man beside him examined him closely out of the corner of his eye. He knew the type well — the tired executive out for a bit of fun. He found it rather disgusting.

— George Smiley, in *Call for the Dead* by John le Carré

Mendoza said, "I need a drink. The damned thankless job — why I stay on at it, the dirt at the bottom — "

— Lieutenant Luis Mendoza, in *No Holiday for Crime* by Dell Shannon

"Do you think she will confess?"

"There will come a time, tonight, in ten days' time, or in a month, when she will crack; and I would rather not be present . . ."

— Chief Inspector Maigret, in *Maigret Hesitates* by Georges Simenon

The fantastical was for adolescents; for adults there were adult joys.

And no joy of his "green" years had ever filled his breast with a more tingling anticipation than the thought of Superintendent Bryce's face when he made his report this morning.

It was a glorious and utterly satisfying prospect.

He could hardly wait.

— Detective-Inspector Grant, in *To Love and Be Wise* by Josephine Tey

BIBLIOGRAPHY

BOOKS

Allen, Hervey. *Israfel: The Life and Times of Edgar Allan Poe.* New York: Rinehart and Company, 1949.

Asinof, Eliot. *Eight Men Out: The Black Sox and the 1919 World Series.* New York: Holt, Rinehart & Winston, 1963.

Barzun, Jacques, ed. *The Delights of Detection.* New York: Criterion Books, 1961.

Belin, Jean. *Secrets of the Sûreté: The Memoirs of Commissioner Jean Belin.* New York: G. P. Putnam's Sons, 1950.

Bell, Josephine *Crime in Our Time.* London: Abelard-Schuman, 1962.

Benet, Stephen Vincent. *Selected Works of Stephen Vincent Benet,* vol. 2. New York: Farrar and Rinehart, 1942.

Bertillon, Alphonse. *Signaletic Instructions — Including the Theory and Practice of Anthropometrical Identification: The Bertillon System of Identification.* Chicago: The Werner Company, 1896.

Biggers, Earl Derr. *The Chinese Parrot.* New York: Grosset and Dunlap, 1926.

Block, Eugene B. *Famous Detectives.* New York: Doubleday, 1967.

Block, Eugene B. *Fingerprinting.* New York: David McKay, 1969.

Block, Eugene B. *The Wizard of Berkeley.* New York: Coward-McCann, 1958.

Bokun, Branko. *Spy in the Vatican: 1941–45* New York: Praeger, 1973.

Browne, Douglas G., and Alan Brock. *Fingerprints.* London: Garrap and Company, 1953.

Browne, Douglas G. *The Rise of Scotland Yard.* New York: G. P. Putnam's Sons, 1957.

Browne, Douglas G., and E. V. Tullett. *The Scalpel of Scotland Yard.* New York: E. P. Dutton, 1952.

Caesar, Gene. *Incredible Detective: The Biography of William J. Burns.* New York: Prentice-Hall, 1968.

Carr, John Dickson. *The Life of Sir Arthur Conan Doyle.* Garden City, N.Y.: Doubleday, 1949.

Carte, Gene and Elaine. *Police Reform in the United States.* Berkeley: University of California Press, 1975.

Chappel, Charles E. *Fingerprinting: A Manual of Identification.* New York: Coward-McCann, 1941.

Christie, Agatha. *Murder on the Calais Coach.* New York: Pocket Books, 1960.

Christie, Agatha. *Ten Little Indians.* New York: Pocket Books, 1965.

Considine, Shaun. *Barbra Streisand.* New York: Delacorte Press, 1985.

Cooke, Alistaire. *Masterpieces.* New York: Knopf, 1981.

Cornelius, A. L. *Cross-Examination.* Indianapolis: Bobbs-Merrill, 1929.

Corrigan, Robert W., ed. *Laurel British Drama: The Nineteenth Century*. New York: Dell, 1967.

Crouse, Russell. *Murder Won't Out*. New York: Doubleday, 1932.

Cunningham, E. V. *The Case of the Poisoned Eclairs*. New York: Rinehart, 1979.

Davidson, Bill. *Indict and Convict: The Inside Story of a Prosecutor's Staff in Action*. New York: Harper & Row, 1971.

Dickson, Carter. *Scotland Yard: The Department of Queer Complaints*. New York: Dell, 1940.

Doyle, Arthur Conan. *The Complete Sherlock Holmes*. New York: Doubleday, 1930.

Fowler, Gene. *The Great Mouthpiece*. New York: Bantam, 1962.

Freeman, R. Austin. *The Eye of Osiris*. New York: Dodd, Mead, 1911.

Freeman, R. Austin. *The Red Thumb Mark*. London: Hodder and Stoughton, 1911.

Gloag, Julian. *Blood for Blood*. New York: Holt, Rinehart, and Winston, 1987.

Gordon, Dr. Richard. *Great Medical Disasters*. New York: Stein and Day, 1983.

Guinn, James M. *History of the State of California and Biographical Record of Oakland and Environs*. Los Angeles: Historic Record Company, 1907.

Herschel, Sir Wiliam J., Bart. *The Origin of Fingerprinting*. London: Oxford University Press, 1916.

Jackson, Joseph Henry. *Bad Company*. New York: Harcourt, Brace and Company, 1949.

Johnson, Diane. *Dashiell Hammett*. New York: Random House, 1983.

Johnson, Dorothy M. *Western Badmen*. New York: Dodd, Mead, 1970.

Katcher, Leo. *The Big Bankroll: The Life and Times of Arnold Rothstein*. New York: Harper and Row, 1958.

Katkov, Norman. *The Fabulous Fanny: The Story of Fanny Brice*. New York: Knopf, 1953.

Kennedy, Ludovic. *The Airman and the Carpenter*. New York: Viking, 1985.

Klein, Alexander, ed. *The Magnificent Scoundrels*. New York: Ballantine, 1960.

Lathen, Emma. *Ashes to Ashes*. New York: Pocket Books, 1972.

Le Carré, John. *Call for the Dead*. New York: Bantam, 1981.

Lewin, Michael. *Night Cover*. New York: Knopf, 1976.

Marsh, Ngaio. *Death of a Fool*. New York: Berkeley, 1963.

Montagu, Ewen. *The Man Who Never Was*. Reprint. New York: Scholastic Book Services, 1967.

Mosley, Leonard. *Lindbergh*. New York: Doubleday, 1976.

Nash, Jay Robert. *Almanac of World Crime*. Garden City, N.Y.: Anchor/Doubleday, 1981.

Osborne, Charles. *The Life and Crimes of Agatha Christie*. New York: Holt, Rinehart and Winston, 1982.

Parker, Alfred E. *Crime Fighter: August Vollmer*. New York: Macmillan, 1961.

Porter, Katherine Anne. *The Never-Ending Wrong*. Boston: Little, Brown, 1977.

Pronzini, Bill and Martin H. Greenberg, eds. *The Ethnic Detectives: Masterpieces of Mystery Fiction*. New York: Dodd, Mead, 1985.

Queen, Ellery, ed. *The Great Sports Detective Stories*. New York: Blue Ribbon Books, 1946.

Queen, Ellery. *The Perfect Crime*. New York: Pyramid, 1968.

Reit, Seymour V. *The Day They Stole the Mona Lisa*. New York: Summit, 1981.

Rhodes, Henry T. F. *Alphonse

Bertillon: Father of Scientific Detection. New York: Abelard-Schuman, 1956.

Rohmer, Sax. *The Return of Dr. Fu Manchu.* New York: McKinlay, Stone and Mackenzie, 1916.

Ross, Walter S. *The Last Hero.* New York: Harper and Row, 1964.

Rubinstein, Jonathan. *City Police.* New York: Ballantine, 1973.

St. Johns, Adela Rogers. *Final Verdict.* New York: Bantam, 1964.

Sayers, Dorothy L. *Busman's Honeymoon.* New York: Avon, 1968.

Sayers, Dorothy L. *Unnatural Death.* New York: Harper and Row, 1927.

Schlossberg, Harvey, and Lucy Freeman. *Psychologist with a Gun.* New York: Coward, McCann and Geoghegan, 1974.

Schwartz, Bernard. *The Law in America.* New York: American Heritage, 1974.

Severn, Bill. *Mr. Chief Justice: Earl Warren.* New York: David McKay, 1968.

Shannon, Dell. *Shannon Strikes Again.* New York: Doubleday, 1973.

Simenon, Georges. *Maigret and the Mad Killers.* New York: Doubleday, 1980.

Smith, Sir Sydney. *Mostly Murder.* New York: David McKay, 1959.

Stone, Irving. *Earl Warren: A Great American Story.* New York: Prentice-Hall, 1948.

Swanberg, W. A. *Citizen Hearst.* New York: Charles Scribner's Sons, 1961.

Thorwald, Jurgen. *The Century of the Detective.* New York: Harcourt, 1965.

Twain, Mark. *The Adventures of Tom Sawyer.* New York: Grosset and Dunlap, 1946.

Twain, Mark. *Pudd'nhead Wilson.* New York: Bantam, 1984.

Tey, Josephine. *To Love and Be Wise.* New York: Berkeley, 1975.

Van Dine, S. S. *The "Canary" Murder Case.* New York: Charles Scribner's Sons, 1927.

Vollmer, August. *The Police and Modern Society.* Berkeley: University of California Press, 1936.

Vollmer, August. *Crime, Crooks and Cops.* New York: Funk and Wagnalls, 1937.

Wallace, Irving. *The Fabulous Originals.* New York: Knopf, 1955.

Waller, George. *Kidnap: The Story of the Lindbergh Case.* New York: Dial, 1961.

Wambaugh, Joseph. *The New Centurions.* New York: Dell, 1970.

Warren, Chief Justice Earl. *The Memoirs of Earl Warren.* Garden City, N.Y.: Doubleday, 1977.

Wilson, Colin, and Pat Pitman. *Encyclopaedia of Murder.* London: Pan Books, 1964.

Wishman, Seymour. *Confessions of a Defense Lawyer.* New York: Times Books, 1981.

Woollcott, Alexander. *Long, Long Ago.* New York: Viking, 1943

ARTICLES AND
MONOGRAPHS

Alameda County Sheriff's Department. *Liaison.* Volume VIII, numbers 1, 2, and 3 (January and February 1970).

Bittner, Egon. "The Functions of the Police in Modern Society." Report of the Center for Studies of Crime and Delinquency, National Institute of Mental Health, Rockville, Md., no date.

Faulds, Henry. "On the Skin-furrows of the Hand." *Nature,* October 28, 1880, p. 605.

Gordon, Officer Walter. "Job Analysis: Beat #20." Berkeley Police Department report, 1929.

Haag, Lucien, and Andrew H. Principe. *"The Lindbergh Kidnapping — 50 Years Later." Police Chief*, March 1984.

Hale, Avery. "The Redheaded Mouthpiece of Broadway." *True*, 1953.

Henshall, John A. "Tales of the Early California Bandits: Black Bart." *Overland Monthly*, volume 6, number 53, June 1909.

Heinrich. E. O. "The Challenge of the Clue." *California Monthly*, February 1929, pp. 12ff.

Johnson, Alva. "Samuel Leibowitz." *The New Yorker*, June 4, 1932.

Johnson, Capt. Thomas W. "Observations of the British Police System." Berkeley Police Department, 1971.

Kropotkin, Princess Alexandra. "To the Ladies." From *Liberty* magazine (reprinted in *Reader's Digest*, November 1938).

MacDonald, Marjorie. "The Bits and Pieces of Bessie Ferguson." In *The Quality of Murder*, edited by Anthony Boucher. New York: E. P. Dutton, 1962.

"The Man of Promise." *Saturday Review of Literature*, November 2, 1935.

Mast, Dexter H. "Six Gold Stars: On the Beat with Dexter H. Mast, OPD." *The Express*, August 22, 1980.

Muir, William Ker. "The Development of Policemen." Paper presented at the sixty-sixth annual meeting of the American Political Science Association, 1970.

Reiss, Albert J., Jr. "Policing a City's Central District: The Oakland Story." Report of the National Institute of Justice, U.S. Department of Justice, 1985.

"The Man of Promise." *Saturday Review of Literature*, November 2, 1935.

Simon, Donald R. "How Effective Are Firearms Against Automobiles?" FBI Law Enforcement Bulletin, October 1963.

Stewart, James K. "Effective Criminal Investigation." *Police Chief*, August 1980, pp. 71–76.

"Willard Huntington Wright: S. S. Van Dine." *New York Times*, April 13, 1939.